Effective UI

Jonathan Anderson, John McRee, Robb Wilson,
and the EffectiveUI Team

Beijing · Cambridge · Farnham · Köln · Sebastopol · Taipei · Tokyo

Effective UI

by Jonathan Anderson, John McRee, Robb Wilson, and the EffectiveUI Team

Published by O'Reilly Media, Inc., 1005 Gravenstein Highway North, Sebastopol, CA 95472.

O'Reilly books may be purchased for educational, business, or sales promotional use. Online editions are also available for most titles (*http://my.safaribooksonline.com*). For more information, contact our corporate/institutional sales department: (800) 998-9938 or *corporate@oreilly.com*.

Editor: Steve Weiss

Development Editor: Jeff Riley

Production Editor: Rachel Monaghan

Copyeditor: Genevieve d'Entremont

Proofreader: Nancy Kotary

Indexer: Julie Hawks

Cover Designer: Karen Montgomery

Illustration and Interior Design:
The EffectiveUI Team

Printing History:

February 2010: First Edition.

ISBN: 978-0-596-15478-3

[F]

Contents

Preface

When the Internet first came online in 1969, it linked computer systems the size of two-car garages that had only a tiny fraction of the power of a modern smartphone. They were programmed and maintained by researchers and scientists, and performed functions that would be ludicrously rudimentary by today's standards. The complexity and size of these systems ensured that computers and software were pretty remote from the everyday lives and experiences of people. But as the power and sophistication of computing systems and software have grown, their proximity to our lives has increased to the point where software is integral to the daily home and work life experiences of most people.

The sophistication of software has grown tremendously while at the same time software is reaching a much less technical audience. This creates a nexus of tension around the user interface (UI); for sophisticated products to be fully useful, they must be easy to operate. At its heart, software is like any other tool; its purpose is to make people's lives and work easier, and to give people access to capabilities previously beyond their reach. This demands, of course, that the software itself not be beyond their reach.

It's taken a while for the standards of UI design and user experience (UX) quality to catch up with the advances in software capabilities and ubiquity. But the time for better UX has, at long last, finally come. When we began writing this book in early 2009, there was a noticeable increase in the attention to and awareness of the importance of UX in software. At the same time, though, there was a generally poor understanding of how to build UX-focused software products. Many large companies were struggling to build a UX competency from within and finding that UX requires far more than just graphic design and IT. Prestigious digital, interactive, and ad agencies were trying to get a foothold in the field but were failing with remarkable regularity. The promise of better UX and the benefits it confers was, and still is, harder to achieve than many companies expect.

This is why our publisher, O'Reilly Media, asked us to write this book. They noted the disparity between the growing expectations and demands for better UX and the poor success rate of companies trying to meet that demand. And so it's for the companies and people who recognize the importance of gaining competency in building better UX in software that we have written this book.

This is for product managers who need a risk-reducing roadmap, for technologists and designers who need guidance and advocacy, and for businesspeople who need to understand and manage UX-focused initiatives.

O'Reilly is perhaps the best known and most respected provider of knowledge resources created by and made for technology innovators. We've been presenting at their Web 2.0 conferences for years, and our employees' bookshelves are filled with O'Reilly books. We're thrilled to add a book to their prestigious animal series. If you're wondering what the rainbow lorikeet on the cover has to do with effective UIs, it's simple:

> *What does the dog say? Woof, woof! What does the cow say? Moo, moo!*
> *What does the rainbow lorikeet say? Ui, ui!*

It's a privilege to be participating in the present fast-growing trend of building better UX in software. EffectiveUI has been riding the UX trend as it has grown from a small surge into a tidal wave. At a time when other companies were focusing either on design or on engineering, we built our company around the marriage of the two.

This is the most basic ingredient for good UX—the cooperation of design and engineering that results in design-minded engineers and technically savvy UX designers. We've also regarded UX as a new, highly advanced specialty, very seriously and have endeavored to hire the best, most creative people available in the industry. It's thanks to these people and an early focus on UX that we've been able to help a long list of clients succeed in their product initiatives. They've also helped us stay ahead of the curve with the exciting new things that are happening in the mobile, multitouch, and other emerging domains of software.

Everything we know about building software and delivering great UX has come from the contributions of the people working here and the lessons they've learned in approaching a lot of hard challenges over the past five years. The subjects covered in this book span the dozens of professional domains within EffectiveUI. The ideas we share in these pages are an aggregation of the thoughts, experiences, and contributions of over a hundred members of our staff. The process of writing this book was very much like a very long journalistic assignment. We conducted countless hours of interviews, had numerous group and one-on-one discussions, and performed a lot of research—all for the purpose of discovering what we as a company, and as a group of individuals, collectively knew.

This book gives a snapshot of the best advice we found in investigating our own approach over the period of about a year in 2009. But we work in a fast-changing, cutting-edge field, so even as we were putting the final touches on this book, many new ideas and concepts were being conceived and applied in our work. Because this book covers a very broad subject, we provide only a high-level overview of some very complex domains. You may want to learn more about these domains, and to find resources on how to develop your own expertise in those fields. So, to provide updates and link you to useful resources, we've created a page on our website to complement this book:

http://effectiveui.com/book-resources/

We'll also be posting updates on Twitter. Please follow us: **@uitweet**.

Two of us, Jonathan and Robb, also work as managing editors for *UX Magazine* (*http://uxmag.com*). The magazine is a good source of current ideas and information about the UX strategy, technology, and design.

Thanks and Acknowledgments

As we've said, this book represents the thoughts and contributions of over a hundred people. We're very grateful to have these people as our friends, coworkers, teachers, and supporters. We're also deeply grateful to O'Reilly Media for giving us this opportunity and for toiling long and hard to help us pull this off.

Thank You to Our Virtual Coauthor

The role of a project manager is a tough one—you're responsible for the results of a project, and at the same time you're entirely dependent on other people doing the majority of the work. Eileen Wilcox may not have written any of the words that went into this book, but without Eileen none of the words in this book would have been written. Eileen also conducted much of the early research and interviews that went into this book, and her thoughtful questions and follow ups ensured that the information captured was useful.

Just like software engineers and UX designers, writers need a balanced measure of stern pressure and reassuring supportiveness. And since this book arose from the ideas of so many people inside our company, the amount of coordination the writing effort required was enormous. Eileen provided that pressure, support, and coordination masterfully.

Eileen's ideas and contributions are everywhere in this book, so we consider her a virtual coauthor.

Thank You to Our Friends at O'Reilly Media

Thanks first to Steve Weiss for coming up with the idea for this book, and for his confidence in us. Steve's enthusiasm and patient stewardship are the reasons this book exist. Thanks also to Marlowe Shaeffer for her vote of confidence, patience, and support.

Thank you to our development editor, Jeff Riley. Thank you, Jeff, for suffering to read some atrocious first drafts so our poor readers didn't have to. Thank you for making us much better writers, especially since we thought we were pretty good to begin with. Thank you also to Genevieve d'Entremont, Rachel Monaghan, and all of the other people who were just beginning to work with us even as this thank-you section was written.

Thank You to Everyone at EffectiveUI

Everyone at EffectiveUI contributed to this book in some way. Some gave us a lot of information that's found all throughout these pages, and others gave us just one or two ideas that proved foundational. It's impossible to rank the degree to which people contributed, so we thank everyone in equal measures.

There were a number of people who spent a lot of their time—much of it after-hours and on weekends—helping with the content, graphics, and production of the book:

Chris Aron
Jeremy Balzer
Eddie Breidenbach
Jason Bowers
Greg Casey
Lance Christmann
Anthony Franco
Jeremy Graston
Catherine Horning
Bobby Jamison
Beth Koloski
Joy Sykes
Tony Walt

Since our people are our company, the best way to know the face of EffectiveUI is to know the faces of our staff. For this reason, we've included a portrait section at the back of this book to pay homage to our people. It's done in the style of a yearbook class page as a further tribute to Herff Jones, the yearbook company that let us use their product as an example in this book.

Additional Thank-Yous

The following people outside of EffectiveUI helped us a great deal:

Catherine Anderson
Truman Anderson
Constantinos Demetriadis
Tony Hillerson
Gregg Peterson
Alexandre Schleifer

Thanks to Our Partners

Thank you to our friends at Herff Jones and *National Geographic* for generously allowing us to use their projects as examples in this book.

Safari Books Online®

Safari Books Online is an on-demand digital library that lets you easily search over 7,500 technology and creative reference books and videos to find the answers you need quickly.

With a subscription, you can read any page and watch any video from our library online. Read books on your cell phone and mobile devices. Access new titles before they are available for print, and get exclusive access to manuscripts in development and post feedback for the authors. Copy and paste code samples, organize your favorites, download chapters, bookmark key sections, create notes, print out pages, and benefit from tons of other time-saving features.

O'Reilly Media has uploaded this book to the Safari Books Online service. To have full digital access to this book and others on similar topics from O'Reilly and other publishers, sign up for free at *http://my.safaribooksonline.com*.

Chapter 1
Building an Effective UI

Just as a finished software product never looks anything like the original plans and expectations for it, writing this book carried us in a surprising but interestingly different direction than we'd originally assumed. When you imagine what it might take to succeed at building an effective user interface (UI) built with a modern standard of user experience (UX) quality, you might think of high-end design, innovation and inspiration, and technical best practices. These are certainly all important components, but our experience helping other businesses build great products has shown us that a team's ability to deliver on the promise of good UX is only partially dependent on its creativity and technical competency. The rest depends on creating the right climate for the team and within the company that allows the team to be effective and helps success come more reliably and easily.

Too many people have endured the pain of participating in the building of a software product in a bad climate—so many, in fact, that most are resigned to the belief that building software is an inherently difficult and disappointing undertaking. Whether you're a business leader who's frustrated at the frequency with which software projects disappoint or fail, or you're a software professional who feels like execs just don't "get it," or that your stakeholders are their own worst enemies, then you already know what we're talking about. Everyone is feeling a frustration that has the same root cause, but each is experiencing it from a different perspective and consequently reaching a different conclusion. The way companies have historically handled software development projects is extremely flawed, and everyone knows it without having any idea of what to do differently. And the ways IT and software engineering teams have coped with business constraints and responded to the need for better UX have also been weak and are undermined by entrenched problems and flawed approaches. These issues combine to cripple the ability of project teams—no matter how talented they may be—to produce great results. Succeeding in building a product with a superior UX quality is a particularly significant challenge that requires an intensity of design and engineering productivity, and anything that interferes with that diminishes the quality of the result.

And so as we asked ourselves how could we best assist people in succeeding at building products with great UX, we arrived at an unexpected answer: focus less on training people in how great design is done; focus more on how to create a setting where great product design can occur and succeed. If you are opening a restaurant, just having a great chef isn't enough; the chef's talent will be meaningless if the restaurant is in a bad location, the wait staff is poorly trained, the kitchen doesn't have a supply of fresh food and isn't well equipped, and the restaurant isn't marketed effectively. The artistry of exceptional cooking can't easily be taught in book form, but the business of being a restaurateur can. Likewise, the skills of great UX architects, visual designers, and software engineers are gained through individual professional experience rather than through books, so the most valuable information we can offer in helping people succeed in building UX-driven products is information on how to enable the success of those professionals.

If you're one of those professionals and want to help your organization or clients become better at building software, or if you're a businessperson trying to make a UX-driven initiative successful, we've written this book to be of help and reassurance to you. The best of intentions, the most cogent of business strategies, and the most talented professionals are routinely thwarted by having to operate in settings that are inherently disabled in ways that no one can quite identify or solve. So a principal goal of this book is to give you an understanding of what the most fertile and hospitable environment for UX-driven software development looks like, and to provide some tips on how to move an organization in that direction. We consistently find that success in building high-quality software products requires major changes in thinking and process across an organization. It takes much more than just one person to create the right climate for building better software, and so much of the work of creating that climate requires understanding, teaching, and advocating for the principles we'll discuss in this book.

Building a product with a focus on UX also involves people and practices that might be new and unfamiliar to you and your company, so another principal goal in this book is to give you a general orientation and clear roadmap of what it will take to get from a concept to a successful completion. Unless you're specialized in one of these domains, you won't find yourself writing code, designing interfaces, or conducting user research, but understanding what to expect, what to avoid, and how all of the professional domains contribute to the forward momentum of a project will help you ensure its success.

Understanding UX

Good and bad UX is typically easy to identify but difficult to define in generalities since the medium of UX is individual, subjective human experience. But in order to understand whether your company's products or internal systems have successful UX design and to convince skeptical executives of the value of UX, it helps to have a clear explanation of UX design and what makes its contribution valuable.

User experience is, as the name suggests, the experience a user has when interacting with software. Just as is the case with music, a software product's UX falls somewhere along a range between subjectively good and subjectively bad. This is obvious enough, but in that simple analogy are a number of truths that are often misunderstood or overlooked in software development. The process of creating good music involves a combination of the underlying mathematical principles of music that govern how we interpret sound, the technical skill required to write and play the music, and the artistic sense required to know how to make it all come together pleasingly in the subjective consciousness of the intended audience. Take away any of those elements, and you make it impossible to bring new music into being. Also, the quality of music is not an objective one, but is specific to the subjective experience of the individual listener. A group of people might love techno and hate country, but that doesn't mean that techno is objectively good and country is objectively bad; it just means that if you're making music for that group, you need to bear their subjective needs in mind.

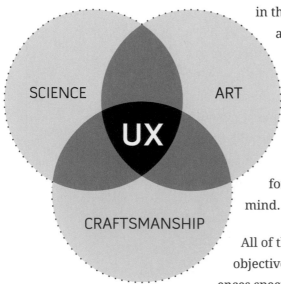

All of that is also the case in software UX. There's no such thing as objectively bad or good UX, only subjectively bad or good experiences specific to the user. The process of creating great UX involves some combination of quasi-scientific disciplines such as human factors engineering, usability, and information architecture; the technical skills to produce not only great UX and user interface design but also the working software itself; and the artistic sense required to intuit and design for how the different subjective perspectives of different users will experience any given aspect of the software. Briefly, building great UX requires the combination of science, skilled craftsmanship, and art to address a subjective need.

In the way your company has approached the development or improvement of its software products, has it demonstrated an understanding of these concepts? Evidence of failure is easy to perceive in hindsight. If you've neglected the scientific aspects of building software, you've built products that are confusing, hard to use, cumbersome, poorly organized, and frustrating. Undervaluing the technical need on the engineering side usually means you've produced gorgeous UI designs but a disappointing, hacked, utterly compromised final product that performs poorly. The technical need on the UX design side—and yes, design for software is highly technical and not just subjective artistry—is also often overlooked or misunderstood. This leads to product UIs designed in ways that are graphically interesting but that cause undue difficulty in how the software will actually work and be developed. And finally, if you haven't recognized the subjective nature of UX, it's likely that, despite all the best of intentions and efforts, you've built products that users hate or reject. It also means you've worked with team members who narrowly focused on their own disciplines and deliverables without being constructively mindful of how their work assembles into a larger whole.

This entire book is dedicated to ways you can avoid those bad outcomes, but it's important at the outset to point out explicitly that delivering on the promise of great UX requires that you and your company's view of and approach to software development is sensible and correct. Just having some talented team members won't lead to success if your general approach to the endeavor is wrongheaded. And it's not enough to have just one person on the team who understands how things need to be done; this is knowledge that needs to be shared and needs to become part of a broader organizational competency. And so you'll find that most of the insight you'll gain in this book isn't specific to innovation, design, technique, or artistry; it's about how you can clear the way for innovation, design, technique, and artistry to come together successfully.

What Good UX Accomplishes

Having a strong UX in your software product is a good goal to have, but high-quality UX isn't in and of itself the real goal. It's the means to another, more important end that, though it's easy to appreciate firsthand, is incredibly hard to describe. Good UX enhances *user engagement*, and UX design is the art of creating and maintaining user engagement in software. Whereas UX is an abstract concept and UX design is a professional discipline, user engagement is the all-important subjective experience.

This naturally begs the question, what is engagement? This is best explained through analogies.

Engagement as immersion

The easiest, most intuitively obvious example of engagement in software is the experience of playing a great video game. Video games—particularly those of the first-person variety—aim to create a high degree of immersion for players.

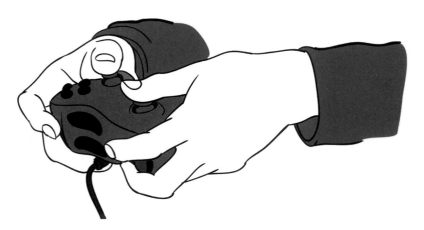

Deep immersion occurs when the player becomes less and less aware of his surroundings, and his perception of the space separating him and the screen starts to fade. His experience of the game becomes one of being the character rather than just being a guy in a chair manipulating the controller. If you've ever seen someone leaning his body to one side to try to steer a car in a game or dodge an incoming missile, you've seen someone who's heavily immersed in the game. Robbie Cooper produced a wonderful video for the *New York Times Magazine* showing just how immersed kids get in the game play experience: *http://video.nytimes.com/video/2008/11/21/magazine/1194833565213/ immersion.html*.

Creating that deep immersion is an art form, and many things must be controlled lest they diminish or entirely break the immersive experience. A player can be snapped out of immersion and the game play experience can be destroyed by simple problems like controllers that are difficult to operate, jarring inconsistencies in the game's physics or rules, badly delivered lines by voiceover actors, or any jumping and skipping in the video or audio.

The example of immersion in gaming may seem quite remote from what you're trying to accomplish. If you're building a new Customer Relationship Management (CRM) tool for internal use at your company, for example, your goal in focusing on the UX of the product isn't to make your sales team so enthralled by the experience of managing their customer interactions that they forget where they are, mentally merge with the application, and stay up until 4 a.m. trying to reach the next level of enterprise marketing automation efficiency. Well, maybe that wouldn't be so bad. But certainly most software products are meant to be useful—not entertaining.

Deep immersion is, however, just an extreme example of user engagement. In the case of games, the goal is to bring the player's focus away from manipulating the controls or comprehending the game dynamics, and even away from being aware of playing a game, and to put it squarely and deeply on goals internal to the game: winning the race, killing the aliens, solving the puzzle, and so on.

Engagement as the fourth wall

The *fourth wall* is a term from theater that is often used in filmmaking. The action on the stage is bounded by three walls, one in the back and two at the sides, but there is no fourth wall between the action and the audience. The audience members watching an engaging play infer and build that fourth wall in their minds, ignoring its absence. Just as the gamer loses awareness of the space between the screen and himself, and of the screen itself, the audience members become so engrossed in the action that the theater around them fades away. If an actor flubs a line, or a baby starts crying in the back of the theater, that fourth wall is "broken," detracting from the experiential quality of the play. Rather than being engrossed in the plot and action, the audience members are suddenly reminded that they're in a theater and have been sitting in their chairs for an uncomfortably long time.

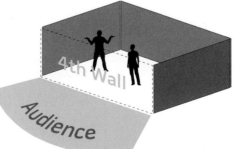

Most filmmakers pay a tremendous amount of attention to the fourth wall. They attempt to keep the audience in a constant state of high engagement through the art of good filmmaking. The art of filmmaking helps them build and maintain engagement, and ensures that they avoid the simple little problems that break the fourth wall and remind the audience they're in a theater watching a film—like when the boom mic briefly appears at the top of the frame, or when actors or extras look straight at the camera, or when the special effects are noticeably fake or overdone. The filmmaker wants to keep the audience immersed in what's going on in the movie, and not on anything else outside it.

Engagement as frictionless accomplishment of goals

We're beginning to arrive at the heart of what engagement is: an undistracted, unencumbered focus on the ultimate goal of the activity a person's engaged in. In movies, as in video games, that goal is to be engrossed and entertained, to be carried away by a story and an experience. The point of software isn't necessarily to engross your users in the experience of using the software, it is to keep them focused on the ultimate goals they're trying to accomplish in using the software, rather than on the actual use of the software itself. Software is, after all, just a tool people use to accomplish certain goals. To be truly and unobtrusively useful, software must clear the straightest, most frictionless path to the accomplishment of the user's goals.

One of the most common instances of frictionless user experience that people encounter comes while driving a familiar route, such as from work to home at the end of each weekday. Almost everyone has had the experience of arriving in their garage or driveway with no memory whatsoever of the drive. In this case, rather than the product being software, it's the car, and instead of a keyboard and a mouse, the user is operating pedals and a steering wheel. The high degree of familiarity people have with the operation of the car allows for such a frictionless experience that their awareness of all the little tasks involved in driving slips away. On leaving work, the driver decides on the goal of returning home; the more familiar the route and the more skilled the driver, the less attention is required to accomplish the goal.

It's easy to imagine ways in which friction could be increased and attention drawn to the tasks involved in driving. Swapping the positions of the accelerator and brake pedals, for example, would shatter the driver's acquired easy familiarity with driving and would force her to pay very careful attention to working the pedals for the entire drive home. By changing the goal from going home to going to a restaurant in an unfamiliar part of town, the driver must focus her attention on navigation. And if something important in the car is malfunctioning—say, one of the tires is running flat—the driver will need to focus on controlling the steering wheel. Each of these will make for a more memorable experience of driving because the driver's attention will be on managing the little tasks involved in driving.

Engagement in software

The goal of UX design in building engagement in software is to help people be more focused on and effective at the accomplishment of their goals. This involves expert combination of the science, technique, craft, and art of UX design to create user experiences that effectively engage their target users. It also involves avoiding or smoothing over things that tend to create friction and diminish or break engagement. Breaking engagement, like breaking the fourth wall, is crossing the line where the user must focus on operating the software instead of achieving her goals. Broken engagement both causes and indicates difficulty for the user, which in turn causes displeasure. Strong engagement, on the other hand, both causes and indicates ease for the user, which in turn brings about pleasure.

The aim of UX design, with its principal goal of creating and maintaining engagement, is therefore to bring software past the point of frustration, difficulty, and displeasure, to first create engagement and then to deepen it according to the needs of the user and the aims of the product. UX design tries to reduce the friction that diminishes from engagement and that interferes with a user's ability to focus on accomplishing his goals. UX design works to apply a certain artistry that helps elevate simple engagement to higher levels of ease and pleasure, which are what make exceptional software.

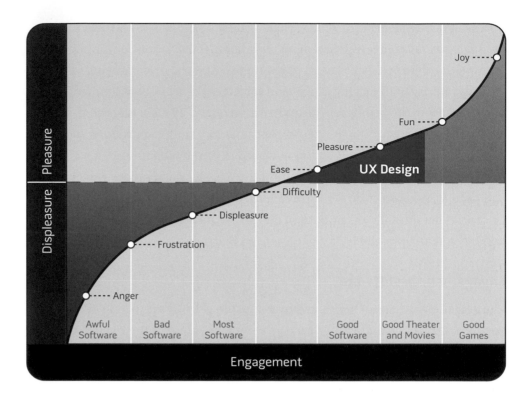

Why Engagement and Good UX Matter

If you understand that positive engagement leads to greater pleasure and effectiveness for the user, and negative engagement leads to difficulty, displeasure, and wasted time, it's easy to imagine why engagement and good UX are important in customer-facing products and internal information systems. To ask whether good UX should be a priority for an organization is essentially to ask whether assisting and pleasing customers and helping employees to be happy and effective are important goals in business. If a software product has been well conceived such that helping users accomplish their goals is directly connected to an important business goal, then reducing the friction experienced in achieving the users' goals should be the same as reducing resistance against the accomplishment of business goals.

With the growth of the customer experience (CX) trend, there's been an increased recognition in business that every aspect of a company's interaction with its customers ("touch points") is an effective, rewarding experience. There's also an increased understanding of the importance of experience quality over just service delivery. Simply having a well-stocked, conveniently located grocery store is not enough; the store must be visually appealing and clean, the checkout process must be quick and easy, and the store must have ample and accessible parking. The corollary to this in software is that it isn't sufficient to simply provide the user with a complete range of features; a good experience in using those features to accomplish one's goals is also required. The grocer doesn't want to waste his customers' time by not having enough checkout stands, or to trouble and confuse them by not organizing and labeling the shelves properly, or to deter potential customers by being hard to access or appearing unprofessional and untrustworthy. Likewise, companies with customer-facing products should avoid wasting their customers' time, confusing them or insulting their intelligence, or pushing them away. The linkage between acquiring and satisfying customers and business success is uncontroversial, but the direct relationship between UX quality and those goals is underappreciated.

The value of good UX and engagement extends to internal information systems and isn't limited to customer-facing applications. The goals change, but the means of accomplishing them remain the same. In the case of internal applications, exceptional UX has the ability to increase productivity, improve the timeliness and relevance of business data flowing to decision makers, increases adoption of the product and therefore the reach of its benefits, improves employee satisfaction, and generally reduces cost and increases opportunity.

The Elements of Engaging UX

EffectiveUI has spent a long time trying to define, in concrete and measurable terms, the substance of engaging UX. Since good UX is something that's measured subjectively and is dependent on the individual needs of the specific users of a given product, there's no 100-point checklist of good UX design; nevertheless, it's important to have a structure and lexicon for expressing problems and opportunities related to UX that otherwise can be recognized only at a gut level. There are a number of concepts that are focal points of good UX design, or can be fault points for bad UX. This list of elements of engaging UX can serve as an evaluation tool for assessing the UX quality of your company's current applications, understanding where past efforts have missed the mark, and identifying where investments are needed.

Familiarity

All else being equal, it's easier to operate a tool you're entirely familiar with than one you've never used before or one that is unfamiliar in some aspects. In the example of engagement in driving from work to home, swapping the positions of the brake and accelerator pedal destroys engagement and plunges the user into difficulty, even though the change is very minor in the context of the complexity of the rest of the car. The need for familiarity appeared in an interesting way when EffectiveUI was building a desktop version of the eBay application. Because the application wasn't delivered through a web browser but rather was deployed as desktop software that had no discrete page states like websites do, we initially didn't think to include a "Back" button such as those found in web browsers. Though the new application broke free of the page-based constraints of the browser and offered improved, more fluid means of browsing content, users who were accustomed to the original eBay experience frequently had the experience of feeling trapped in some corner of the application without knowing how to go back. And so even though a "Back" button made little logical sense in the context of the eBay Desktop application (as it wouldn't in a product such as Microsoft Excel), we were compelled by deference to the user's needs to add a "Back" button to ensure that a comfortable degree of familiarity was preserved.

There are plenty of other examples of things that aren't the most elegant, efficient, or sensible solution but are nevertheless the right solution for the moment because of their strong familiarity. The QWERTY keyboard layout, for example, came about because the layout helped reduce the frequency of typebar clashes in old typewriters, and not because it's the most efficient from an ergonomic perspective. But at this point the layout has become so familiar and people have become so expert in using it that making any changes would cause nothing but frustration. One exception to this is stenotype machines, used by stenographers, which employ a radically different approach to typing because the need to type quickly (225+ words per minute) necessarily overrides taking a familiar approach.

Responsiveness and feedback

Responsiveness in software is also often referred to as providing feedback to users. This responsiveness, or feedback, is what confirms and reassures the user that the action he has taken has been effective.

Elevators provide a simple, real-world example of the importance of feedback in user interfaces. Imagine that you'd like to take an elevator from the 18th floor of a skyscraper to reach a meeting on the 32nd floor, but with this elevator all of the button lights and up/down arrow lights are burned out. When you press the "up" button on the 18th floor, though the order is successfully sent to the elevator's controller, you receive no confirmation that an elevator has in fact been summoned to go up. The absence of this feedback suddenly diverts your attention from the goal of reaching the meeting on the 32nd floor and puts it onto the task of summoning the elevator. You mash the button a dozen times, and still receiving no response, you decide to hold the button down until the elevator arrives. Your anxiety begins to build, as your uncertainty about whether you'll be able to accomplish your goal has increased.

When the elevator finally arrives, no "up" arrow illuminates to let you know that this elevator is in fact going up. If it's going down, you could be in for a long ride, so your anxiety ratchets up another level. Upon boarding the elevator and pressing the "32" button, you receive no confirmation that the selection has been accepted, so you do some more button mashing and hold your breath as the doors close, waiting to see whether you go up.

At this point, you're in such a state of uncertainty that as the elevator begins moving upward, you briefly think it's actually going downward, and feel another small surge of panic. Still holding down the "32" button, you don't know that everything is OK until the elevator finally arrives at the 32nd floor and you quickly jump out, irrationally worrying the doors will snap closed and whisk you away from your goal before you reach solid ground.

In this scenario, the elevator itself was, from a functional perspective, operating perfectly. It provided the necessary input mechanisms and responded correctly to its variable directives, and conveyed its user from one floor to another without incident. For you as the user, however, the experience of using the elevator has been bizarrely nerve-racking. The simple failure to provide valuable feedback pulled your focus away from your goal and forced you to focus intently on the microtasks required to accomplish the goals that, in a properly maintained elevator, you would have performed without thinking.

When we released an early version of the eBay Desktop application, several users said they had trouble determining whether the information on their screens about the status of an auction item was up-to-date. This was surprising feedback because we'd built the application to always display the most current information. With the original eBay web-based application, users needed to click the browser's "Refresh" button to see the most current information; with the eBay Desktop application, however, the most current information was automatically displayed. But it turned out that the ability to click "Refresh" and see the page reload in the original eBay application gave users confidence that they were seeing the latest information. What was missing in the eBay Desktop application wasn't a "Refresh" button, though; it was a feedback mechanism that gave users confidence that the information was fresh. So we added a timer to the auction pages that counted down the seconds until the auction closed. When users looked at the auction page, they saw a clear, visual, second-by-second indication that the information was current. We didn't have to change anything else to address the data freshness concern; we needed only to provide the right kind of feedback.

Engagement in e-commerce is very important, because it correlates strongly with the user's willingness to buy, her ability to complete transactions, and her experience of the brand. Any friction along the way leads to uncertainty, distrust, and confusion, which decrease the likelihood of the user completing the transaction or developing an affinity for the brand that would lead to repeat business. There's another straightforward example of poor feedback that occurs frequently in e-commerce sites even to this day, though simple solutions have been found and really ought to be universally implemented. After having added the desired items to her shopping cart, and after having filled out all of the billing and shipping information, including her credit card information, the user is finally asked to press a button that submits the purchase. A lot of implied assurances should be associated with the pressing of that button: she should be able to know that her purchase has been accepted, her credit card has been charged, and that it's no longer necessary to worry about preserving the shopping cart or to take additional steps to complete the purchase. She's essentially made a commitment of money, time, and trust, and requires the reassurance that it has led to success.

But an inexplicably large number of e-commerce sites betray that need by failing to provide the necessary feedback. Certainly you've encountered sites where under the "Purchase" button there's a note saying, "Please push this button only once; otherwise, your card may be charged twice." This is a band-aid solution for a failure to be responsive. It takes at least a couple of seconds after you press the button to validate the order and authorize the charge with your credit card, and if during that time nothing has happened to acknowledge that you successfully submitted the purchase, your uncertainty and worry increase. If you're not particularly tech-savvy and don't notice that the browser has submitted something and is waiting for a response, you'll spend a few nervous seconds wondering whether you actually pressed the button, you missed clicking on it, or your Internet connection is down, and you might decide to click it again for good measure. If the "Purchase" button had simply changed its visual state to acknowledge the click and then deactivated, you'd have some of the reassurance you need and your focus would remain on the goal of acquiring products rather than on the microtasks of submitting the purchase request. And if this experience of uncertainty leads the user to wonder whether her card has been charged twice, she'll pick up the phone and call customer support, destroying the efficiency and cost savings sought by having an e-commerce site.

Responsiveness is important at all levels of an application, and for all features big and small. Good feedback is the UX equivalent of the polite nod or "uh-huh" that a listener provides to a speaker to reassure her that he's still listening and understanding. Consistent, valuable responsiveness builds a sense of confidence in the user and thereby improves engagement, allowing him to focus on achieving his goals rather than fretting over whether each of his actions taken toward that end have been effective.

Performance

An application's performance—that is, how well it handles the strains of processing, display, data traffic, and other technical considerations—can strongly affect the experience of using it. Performance issues can cause the application to stall and lag, and for certain operations to take a disruptively long time to complete. Some performance issues are inevitable as the application performs complex operations or interacts with data over the Internet, and many can be mitigated at the UX design level by extending the simple courtesy of providing good feedback through progress bars or handling heavy processes in a way where the loading and processing are more evenly distributed and less apparent to the user.

Whereas minor performance issues are irritating and diminish the UX quality and the productivity of using the product, major ones can go beyond breaking down engagement and cause the user to get upset with and distrust the product. Being forced to endure long or frequent waits, especially in settings where efficiency is important or the application is supporting repetitive tasks, can ratchet up the user's irritation level to the point of anger. This is somewhat akin to the experience of trying to watch a scratched DVD, when your immersion in the film is constantly being broken by lagging or pixelation that pulls your attention out of the story and puts it back into your living room and onto the DVD player. Most people have also had the unfortunate experience of working in an office with a very expensive copy machine that jams every 50th copy, making it a source of disproportionate frustration and anger instead of the office efficiency miracle it was sold as.

And if the product performs poorly—if the interface lags or hangs during heavy processing, certain things happen inexplicably slowly, the user is subjected to frequent progress bars that move slowly and at inconsistent rates—besides the irritation that results from having to pay attention to the delays instead of staying goal-focused, the user's trust of the product also begins to break down. Performance issues indicate a poorly engineered product or some sort of technical malfunction occurring behind the scenes, which leave the user to wonder about the reliability of the product and the safety of the data he's entrusting to it. This, once again, injures the user's ability to benefit from the product as a tool for accomplishing goals, when those goals seem to be in jeopardy because of uncertainty about the product's reliability.

It's also worth noting that performance quality is based on a constantly changing, subjective impression. Things that used to be considered fast in the computing world in 1999 would be agonizingly slow by modern standards—96 baud modems compared to high-speed cable Internet, 2-page-per-minute dot-matrix printing compared to 100-page-per-minute laser printers, and so on. We were also far more willing to accept a bit of technical crudeness in the products we used regularly 10 years ago because the state of the art was far from advanced. But as computer capabilities and the sophistication and quality of software have increased rapidly, our patience for poor performance has decreased enormously. Thus a product that delighted customers or employees three years ago may very easily be irritating them today.

Consistency in performance is also important. If you're a regular patron of a fast food restaurant and every time you go in, it takes five minutes to get your meal, then five minutes becomes an acceptable waiting period. If occasionally it takes 10 minutes, those occasions cause frustration. If one day you get your meal in two minutes, then five minutes is no longer acceptable. With software, a user should be able to count on the same task taking roughly the same amount of time for each use, so the delays are familiar and are therefore less likely to break engagement.

Intuitiveness and efficiency

Intuitiveness is the degree to which the process of accomplishing a goal or performing a task within a product is obvious to the user, without explanation or confusion. It relates strongly to familiarity, because a great deal of a UI's intuitive ease comes from functions being handled in familiar ways, buttons being in familiar places, and things having familiar names. With the goal of allowing the user to remain focused on the goal instead of having to pay attention to the microtasks of operating the product, intuitiveness allows the user to more easily slip into engagement and retain undistracted focus and productivity. Intuitiveness and the efficiency the product makes possible for the user are also strongly related, as intuitiveness allows a user to remain focused on accomplishing her goals without having to expend time figuring out or focusing on the microtasks needed to accomplish those goals.

If they're misunderstood and misapplied, though, intuitiveness and efficiency can wind up being competing ideals. Many people view intuitiveness as the ease with which a person can figure out how to operate a product in his first few uses of it. But what may be the easiest approach to figure out on first use is likely not the most efficient long-term approach, and the most efficient application UX may be less intuitive to new users. These two ideals are both coupled and also in some degree of tension with each other, and the right balance must be struck according to the requirements of the product. Consumer products generally tend to favor intuitiveness over efficiency wherever there's tension, because it's important not to drive new users away by confusing them at the outset or providing them with overly complicated "Getting Started" guides. But products that are made for daily intensive use—an internal call center support application or a customer-facing CRM tool—should generally err on the side of efficiency, since the first couple of weeks using the tool are less important than the subsequent two years, and users of such applications are willing to undergo a bit of training. Some products address the tension between ease of learning and ease of long-term use by letting users switch between basic and advanced interface modes.

But despite the occasional conflict between intuitiveness and efficiency, in much of UX design, a focus on intuitiveness also yields an improved quality of efficiency, as well as lower long-term costs to training and support.

Herff Jones eDesign: Intuitiveness Versus Efficiency

Intuitiveness

Presenting the yearbook in a way that closely resembles a physical yearbook has clear intuitive appeal. Users apply their knowledge of how to use physical books to how to use this screen. As a result, no training or instruction is necessary to help people use this yearbook preview screen, and it also provides students with the most accurate view of what their yearbook will be like. But this view is also very limited, and is not ideal when a student is doing complex work on the yearbook or trying to manage the whole book.

Efficiency

This screen doesn't have the clear intuitiveness of the yearbook preview screen, but is nevertheless much more useful. It allows many aspects of the yearbook creation process—the management of colors, templates, sections, student assignments, progress, and so on—to be viewed and managed for hundreds of pages. Having all of this capability on one screen is an efficient approach, but isn't immediately intuitive. That is more than made up for in how the efficient approach of the screen makes the student's work easier and more effective.

Helpfulness in accomplishing real goals

Since software is a utility meant to help people and businesses accomplish their goals, the requirement that a product actually help accomplish those goals should be so obvious that we shouldn't have to point it out. But a surprising number of products fail to help the business and the user accomplish their real goals. If a product is to succeed, both the user's and business' real goals need to be accounted for. If the user's goals aren't addressed, the product will cause frustration or won't be used and thus won't help the business; if the business's goals aren't met, the product's development will have been a waste of money.

Companies will sometimes build a product with the hope of helping the company itself accomplish some of its goals, but don't bother finding out whether or how those goals were aligned with actual user goals. This comes about as a result of companies undervaluing the role of user research in software design. They assume that they understand the user well enough or that their interests are the same as their users' interests, or they underestimate the significance of the role the product plays in their customers' relationship with the company. If this causes them to produce a product that fails to help users accomplish their real goals and causes them frustration, whatever business goal the product was intended to satisfy will also not be accomplished. Helping users accomplish their real goals is thus a stepping stone to the accomplishment of business goals.

A solid business goal that may be the basis for funding a new software initiative might be, for example, to reduce the cost to call center support operations by reducing the support volume and diverting requests to lower-cost channels. This is a perfectly legitimate starting place and basis for a new product initiative. It is, however, certainly not the explicit goal of the company's customers to help the company save money on call centers and providing support. To be successful in meeting the business goal, a means of aligning it with a real customer goal must be found and pursued.

There are plenty of instances of big companies taking on just this sort of initiative and getting it terribly wrong. Solely focused on reducing call center costs, the companies simply make it very difficult to reach an actual phone agent. In order to obtain support, they make the user go through a long series of self-help, web-based procedures or browse through incomplete and poorly organized "knowledge bases." If the user tries all of those things and still fails to find a solution, he's finally provided with a "Contact Us" support form where he's required to type a detailed request for support. Sometime within the next week, he gets a two-sentence email response from an overseas support operator who, as it turns out, is reading from the same support information the user already went through online and through the knowledge base. For users of a software product, this kind of experience is like being given the middle finger by the company. It's clear the company's primary interest was in reducing the cost of supporting its customers. But the company took no steps to actually address the user's goals.

The reality is, no user wants to contact customer support. Users would much rather have an application that operates as they expect it to. When the application doesn't operate in this way, users expect to easily find answers to their questions through sources that are instantaneous and readily intelligible. The business's goal of reducing support costs can be achieved through helping the users accomplish their real goals, which are to have a product that is effective in helping them accomplish their goals (without the need of support) and of having answers readily at hand for common problems and questions. Rather than investing in the infrastructure necessary to divert customers and force them through tedious self-support systems—which, in effect, simply makes the customers work harder to get the support they wish they didn't need— the business should invest in improving the overall UX quality of the product to reduce the need for support altogether. This winds up being more broadly positive, because it not only reduces the cost to support operations, but also improves the user's experience of using the application, which in turn translates into benefits such as improved brand affinity for consumer applications or increased productivity and job satisfaction for internal applications.

That's a pretty egregious example of how companies can myopically focus on business goals without attending to user goals, but most failures to attend to real user goals are more subtle than this and descend from the best of intentions. Businesses tend to make a lot of false assumptions about what's important to their users and set out priorities that, while they deliver some value to the user and business, fall short as a result of failing to keep a strong focus on the user's actual goals. Supporting a user in achieving his actual goals is always the first step to achieving related business goals.

On a recent project, EffectiveUI interviewed a large number of call center support staff and found that over half of their calls are for password resets. Evidently our client, concerned about security—or their customers' perception of security—required users to change their passwords every 45 days. We reviewed the online password change process and found that ambiguous labels and poorly written copy were contributing to customer confusion. By interviewing users, we discovered most were irritated by the 45-day password change rule, and that most already operated under company policies that required periodic password changes on schedules that didn't align with the product's 45-day rule. Allowing users to set the date and frequency of their password changes solved most of the problems and reduced call center volume dramatically.

Delivery of relevant, valuable content

There are some products—Wikipedia and Craigslist, for example—where the entire purpose of the product is to deliver useful content. The quality of the experience of using those products is therefore most strongly determined by the quality, accessibility, and relevance of the content they provide. Other types of products are much more focused on capabilities rather than content and information—Adobe Photoshop and Microsoft Excel, for example. In the middle are content and capability applications, such as online investment trading tools like E*TRADE or sales force management and CRM tools.

Wherever it may fall along the spectrum of content-focus, the UX quality of a product is strongly dependent on its effectiveness in delivering appropriate, relevant content at the right times and places. This is fairly obvious in the case of the content-intensive products such as Wikipedia and Craigslist, where the role of the application is to assist the user in getting from a question to a useful answer as rapidly and easily as possible while ensuring that content is available and valuable. But even in far less content-intensive products such as Microsoft Excel, the product's ability to deliver useful content to the user at appropriate times is very important in enhancing the experience of using the application. The necessary consequence of Excel's breadth and depth of capabilities is that it is a rather complicated product, and taking full advantage of its capabilities requires the ability to perform some complex tasks, such as writing intricate formulas for ranges of cells in a spreadsheet. Rather than simply providing the user with a thick manual to use in trying to figure out how to write formulas, Excel provides that information directly within the application as part of the workflow. So instead of requiring the user to become an expert prior to using the product, or forcing users to constantly refer to help content, Excel delivers the information the user needs at the moment he needs it (while performing a complex task). This type of intelligent assistance can also take the form of context-specific help. Rather than requiring users to access a separate help application to find their answers, buttons and tool tips can be placed where users are likely to need assistance, giving them the exact information they'll require at the exact spot they'll require it.

In online trading tools, there's a pretty balanced emphasis on both the capabilities of trading and managing investments, and the content. The content—stock prices, news, market analyses, and so on—helps users understand the market, learn about specific industries and companies, and make educated decisions about their portfolios. An investment tool in which streams of accurate, timely information are presented alongside the ability to act on that information, and key content is automatically made available at junctures where it's important to the user's activity, is of far greater value than a product that keeps that content separate from its capabilities. Products that successfully anticipate what information and content a user will need at any given point and make it readily available will build a far greater sense of confidence and engagement in their users, helping them to remain focused on their goals rather than managing all the small details that must be assembled in the accomplishment of those goals. A simple and very useful example of this is when an application pops up a calendar when the user clicks into a date selection field, saving the user from having to break engagement and look to another resource to figure out the correct date or to have to format the date entry according to the needs of the system.

Arrival:

October 16, 2009

Departure:

A travel site that provides calendar-related content when the user needs it

◀ OCTOBER | 2009 ▶

S	M	T	W	T	F	S
				1	2	3
4	5	6	7	8	9	10
11	12	13	14	15	16	17
18	19	20	21	**22**	23	24
25	26	27	28	29	30	31

There are even opportunities within this domain to delight users and radically enhance the UX quality of the product by providing them with information that's important to meeting their goals but that they didn't realize was available or relevant, without their having to actively seek it out.

Internal consistency

Internal consistency requires that the application handle similar tasks in similar ways. In a CRM tool, for example, the process for adding a new customer record should be as similar as possible to the process of adding a new job record. Although the information being input is different, the essential task is still the same: inputting information to create a new record. Internal consistency can be a simple as ensuring that buttons are in the same places and have the same labels ("OK" versus "Save" versus "Submit"), and that screens are generally organized and presented in similar ways so the user knows where to look and what to expect. But it can also extend to much more complex interactions and tasks; in fact, the more complex the interaction or task is, the more important it is that it be as internally consistent with other similar interactions or tasks as possible. This will make it so the user needs to learn how to operate that type of capability of the product only once, and that knowledge can be intuitively generalized to allow him to use other, similar capabilities with ever-increasing ease.

A product should be internally consistent from a visual design perspective, too, to ensure that the user has the impression of it being a unified, well-organized, professional product. Internal consistency is often lost in large product initiatives where multiple teams are working on different aspects of the product and aren't well coordinated, resulting in badly integrated Frankenstein products that look like the forced combination of several different products, and that require the user to master multiple approaches to accomplishing similar tasks.

A Frankenstein look-and-feel can also come about as part of the design concept process. Every professional designer has had the experience of presenting several different concepts to a stakeholder and being asked to take the best from each concept and mash them all together. Occasionally this can be lead to positive progress, but most times it leads to incoherence in the resulting design. Most people understand the problem of mixed metaphors ("I'll bite the bullet and step up to the plate to nip it in the bud!"), and UX and visual designs for software are akin to metaphors in how they simplify complexity through appealing abstraction, and different approaches don't mix together very well.

The internal consistency of a product should disguise a lack of consistency in the functions it's handling. If the product is interacting with a dozen different "backend" systems, the user shouldn't have any clue that's the case— everything should all feel like the same experience. The same is true of products that span multiple departments or divisions of a single company. Users should be left to think about their goals without having to understand the nuances of how a company is divided and structured. For example, with a travel site, buying a plane ticket should be the same experience as reserving a hotel room. And an employee using a workplace information system to sign up for benefits shouldn't have to perform separate, redundant tasks just because benefits enrollment involves three different departments within the company.

External consistency

External consistency in functionality is very similar to the ideal of familiarity; the more similarly the product operates compared to other products the user is already familiar with, the less of a learning curve there will be in its use, and the less jarring it will be for the user to switch between the different products he uses in any given day. Obviously, external consistenty with other products that have bad UX design shouldn't be overemphasized beyond the limits of respecting familiarity. External consistency is actually much more of a concern when it comes to the visual design of a product, which conveys to the user on both a conscious and subconscious level a message about who and what the product is for. Software, like literature or architecture, has a recognizable set of genres. In architecture, if you see a building made out of white stone with Greek- and Roman-style columns and ornamental sculptures on the facade, you're likely to assume that it's a government building of some sort.

Herff Jones eDesign: Integrated Experience

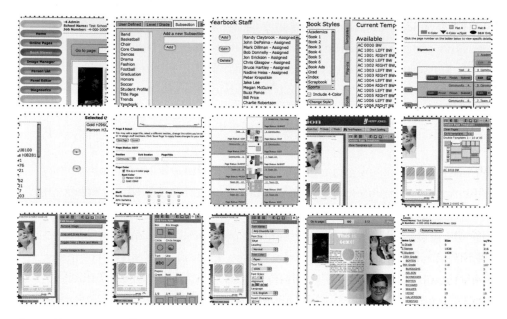

Many disparate applications in the legacy software...

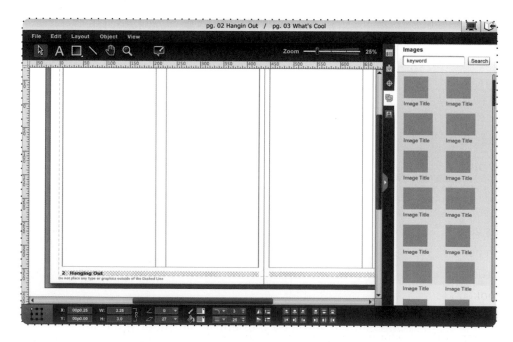

...become a single unified experience after the redesign.

If you're browsing the shelves of a bookstore and see a book with a cover that has a painting of a muscular, shirtless man with long, flowing hair riding a horse with a flushed, swooning lady in his arms, you'd be safe in assuming you're standing in the fiction section looking at a torrid pulp romance novel.

Likewise, the visual appearance of a software product should indicate its purpose and audience. The benefits this confers to the UX are very diffuse and hard to explain, but they have something to do with giving users the impression and confidence that the product is the right tool for their needs. When you walk into a lawyer's office, for example, you expect to be surrounded by mahogany paneling, expensive burgundy leather chairs ornamented with brass studs, and wall-to-wall bookshelves filled with ancient-looking law books. Even though the office design has nothing at all to do with the competence of the lawyers in it, it conveys a sense of confidence in the strength and professionalism of the firm. When you walk into the offices of a creative ad and marketing design agency, you instead expect bright, cheery colors, informally dressed staff members, desks littered with art and toys, foosball tables, and bizarre modern furniture. This gives you the confidence that you're dealing with hip, modern designers. But put the designers in the lawyers' offices and the lawyers in the designers' office, and you're likely to lose all confidence in both. The visual design of software has the same general effect of first convincing the user that he's in the right place, and then giving him confidence that the product is well suited for and effective at meeting his goals.

It's also important to note that within the various genres of software and in the field of software UI design generally, trends and tastes are constantly evolving. Whereas in the design of law offices, there's an emphasis on conservatism, age, and experience, it's pretty much always the case that in software, the application should appear new and modern within the bounds of its genre. Old software is generally understood to be inferior software, and so users are looking for the visual hallmarks of modernity in the UI of the product. Because of the constantly evolving trends and tastes, a product that looked modern six months ago often is beginning to look middle-aged today. Even if the functionality has been updated and is best-in-class, if the visual design belies the modern capabilities of the product, users will tend to trust it less and have a more fretful experience using it.

This external consistency in visual design also applies to conformity with brand standards. A product built by a recognizable brand should have a design feel that's clearly consistent with that brand. Beside the fact that the visual standards for established brands are generally very well thought out and are themselves externally consistent with the how the company wants to be seen within the broader market, consistency with brand standards also enhances the user's trust of the product. The customer's affinity to the brand is inherited by a visually consistent product, and the customer's trust of the brand extends to trust in the security and value of the product. Conversely, a product that fails to match the brand's visual standards will give the impression of being less professional, potentially less trustworthy, or may be seen as a repackaged third-party tool.

National Geographic brings its strong brand consistency to its software products.

Appropriateness to context

Software products exist within, and are thus beholden to, multiple layers of context that must be respected in UX design. Software operates on a variety of different devices and platforms, and is used in a wide range of settings and by a great diversity of people. The appropriateness of a software's UX to a given group of users is a huge subject unto itself and is covered in depth throughout the rest of this book, but we note it here as a reminder that the constraints and needs of the people using the product must govern how it works.

Until recent years, when individuals talked about software, they were always talking about systems running on enterprise-scale servers and computer equipment or running on a personal computer. But the growth in the capabilities of web-based, mobile platform, embedded systems, and device technology have meant that software can be found on the Web, on screens embedded in refrigerators, on cell phones, in the control bridge of yachts, and strapped to the hips of FedEx delivery drivers. It may seem obvious that software UX design should be cognizant of the device, physical, and task setting that it will be used in, but quite frequently it's not. A recent example of this has come with the massive popularity of Apple's iPhone in the U.S., as many companies have scrambled to make an iPhone version of their product or web application available. The screen size, performance constraints, and capabilities of the iPhone are much different than other platforms, and a product built for the iPhone must embrace those differences. For example, interacting with an application using your fingers instead of a keyboard and mouse imposes new constraints, but it also opens up new opportunities. It's important to account for the new constraints and take advantage of the new capabilities.

The context in which the software is operating also has to do with the physical place it's being used and what's happening in that environment while it's being used. Not all software is meant to be used from the relative serenity of the office or home. An extreme example is a product made for soldiers on the battlefield, such as portable systems that connect soldiers directly to surveillance, weather, and situational intelligence data. The need for the software to be usable under stress, under fire, and while wearing bulky clothing in limited visibility conditions is going to put some very specific demands on the UX design of the product. In a less extreme example, point-of-sale systems for restaurants and retail stores must be designed with a keen awareness that the user will be multitasking, standing, and engaging with the customer, and will need to work very quickly. This would suggest that highly controlled and streamlined processes with large buttons (among many other specialized refinements) will lead to a better experience.

Trustworthiness

Underlying most of these elements of good UX has been the need to gain and maintain the trust of the user—trust that the product is up to snuff, that it's secure, provides good information, is safeguarding data, is of high quality, is the best option for the user, and so on. Failing to achieve trust can deter users, and failing to maintain it can cause the user to be preoccupied with whether or not to trust the product and wondering whether his actions are having the desired effect, rather than simply being focused on his goals while assuming (trusting) that everything is working as it should.

The very same issues that break engagement also have a tendency to injure the trustworthiness of the product, so a focus on UX quality leads to greater trust in the product, which in turn reinforces the UX quality. Trust is won and lost at an emotional level that's determined by the accumulation of all the various aspects of the UX while using the software. Design issues tend to weigh disproportionately on the user's impression of the trustworthiness of the product, though. A study was performed where two kiosks that offered driving directions around the town were placed at opposite ends of a commercial center. Both kiosks used the same data and underlying "backend" systems, but one had a modern UI design, and the other had a design that suggested the product was older. When the users of the kiosks were asked whether they trusted the directions provided by a given kiosk, the one with the modern design got dramatically higher marks, despite the fact that its output was no different than the other kiosk.

Summing up

To fully explore all the elements of engagement and UX design would require its own book, so we've simplified a lot of concepts here for the sake of providing a quick, high-level understanding. This list should be useful in getting a sense of whether your company's existing products and internal systems are passing muster and whether the right people in the company are aware of what it takes to create a strong UX in a software product. There's a tendency for companies to relegate responsibility for UX design either to engineering teams or to web or ad design teams without understanding the full breadth of what goes into great experiences in software. If you look back over the elements of good UX in this section, you'll note that each draws on different skills and domains of experience and study in the software world, and that they aren't neatly compartmentalized. UX design is something that is best performed by generalists who have the wide-ranging training and experience necessary to handle the gamut of issues we've described. And as we'll discuss in the next section, UX design isn't an activity that's exclusive to visual designers, nor even to what we call UX architects; software engineers and product managers also play a vital role in UX design and in producing products that people love.

Reviewing the elements we've covered in this section, it's clear that the work of and responsibility for good UX design falls not to a single UX design team, but rather to the entire collection of professionals involved in the project. The performance element, for example, requires a strong contribution from every member of the product team. Each participates in many capacities at different points along the project.

Stakeholders and product managers

- *Facilitate infrastructure decisions and connections to existing or third-party systems that support good performance*

- *Work with the team to make tough choices when unavoidable performance issues force changes in approach*

UX architects and designers

- *Settle on information architecture plans, interaction designs, workflows, and feedback mechanisms that avoid, diminish, or conceal from the user the negative effects of performance issues*

- *Respond to performance issues discovered by the engineers through new UX architecture and design plans that account for the issues*

- *Develop friendly approaches to progress bars or component state changes that help diminish the disruption caused by performance issues*

Technical architects

- *Design efficient approaches to managing the processing, data transit, and external resource connections that can make or break performance*

- *Continuously audit the product architecture to look for performance bottlenecks and issues*

Software engineers

- *Write code and design approaches that are efficient and actively mitigate performance issues*

- *Execute faithfully on the UX and visual designs in ways that don't impair the performance or compromise the UX quality*

- *Actively work with stakeholders, project managers, technical architects, and UX architects to identify unforeseen risks and issues related to performance, and to figure out how to address them*

Quality assurance (QA) and user acceptance testing (UAT)

- *Work with actual users to identify where performance-related pain points arise*

- *Stress-test the application to identify hidden performance issues and bring them to the attention of the rest of the team*

A similar list can be made for each of the elements of good UX. Good UX in software arises not from simply hiring a couple of UX professionals and having them put forth perfect designs, but rather from the collective experience, skills, attention, talent, and enthusiasm of an entire team that's working toward the single, joint ideal of producing an exceptional UX. Forrester Research has wisely said in a number of articles and whitepapers that the responsibility for good customer experience—a goal that's very similar to that of UX, and in a sense, UX is the technological subset of CX—cannot be held by one single CX officer or an isolated CX team, but rather needs to be an organization-wide competency for it to succeed. UX design is not an isolated professional discipline; it's a general orientation of an entire product team, and good UX is a responsibility of the entire team.

Redefining Two Fundamental Terms

We will be using two key terms in a way that differs from their normal connotations in software. Those two terms are *design* and *development*. Since these concepts are so fundamental to software and to how we recommend approaching the building of software, taking a close look at our differing understanding of the two terms gives an early glimpse into and foundation for the rest of this book. As we said in the previous section, responsibility for good UX isn't exclusive to people with "UX" in their titles, but is rather a broader team orientation and competency. Similarly, but more broadly, it's also the case that product design isn't the sole domain of visual designers, nor is the development of the product strictly the domain of software engineers.

Design

When people talk about design, they usually mean visual design, and in software they usually mean graphic and UI design. Because businesspeople deal in meetings and paperwork and software engineers deal in code, there's a tendency to assume that because they're not producing visual works, what they're doing isn't design. On the other hand, people readily acknowledge that the researchers at Intel and AMD are busy working on new *designs* for microprocessors, or that city planners *design* traffic control patterns to manage congestion, even though neither of those are visual design fields. This arises from an ambiguity in the ordinary connotation of the word "design," and confusion about this is at the heart about some very serious misapprehensions about what goes into building software.

It's necessary to abandon the assumption that design is just concerned with visual media. Design, very broadly, is the application of creativity and intelligence against solving a problem. Often the problem is a visual one, but the means of solving it is nevertheless an intellectual and creative process. In order to create a visually appealing logo that does a good job of representing a company's brand and goals, a graphic designer embarks on an intensive effort of thought, creativity, experimentation, and trial and error. This is no different at a fundamental level than what a software engineer does to build a component for an application. It's only the form of the output and the experience and training required that differ. Businesspeople and product managers planning and guiding a project are also undergoing a process of design. They've identified a business problem and are applying their experience, intellect, and creativity against forming an initiative to respond to it, and continue to participate in design as they contemplate challenges and make decisions in shepherding the project along the way.

Holding this broader understanding of design keenly in mind is important for two very different reasons. First, it helps you appreciate what the people with "designer" in their titles, or the people whose design output is in visual form, actually do. Their area of concern is not some fuzzy, entirely subjective, artsy thing. To arrive at the visual deliverables they produce, they have applied their deep professional experience, intellect, and creativity toward solving a problem. The undervaluing of what designers do in software projects is in part the fault of fading trends in the web design world, where flashiness and high-concept design were held as greater ideals than effective problem solving in design. But if you have the good fortune to work with a talented team of visual designers, it's important to understand that their work is carefully thought over, and is best judged according to how adeptly it solves the problem and not simply how it registers subjectively to a nondesigner.

The second reason this understanding of design is important is in better understanding what software engineers do. For some reason, people outside the software field tend to think of software engineers as being workers on an assembly line mindlessly producing units of progress at a linear rate, or as low-level construction workers who build things that other people design without applying much thought of their own. This view is terribly, terribly wrong and is one of the principal roots of why projects fail or disappoint with such great frequency. Software development is an extremely design-intensive process—that is, every increment of progress that's made comes from an intensive effort of thought, creativity, experimentation, and trial and error. Software engineers may be working from designs passed on from other members of the team, but those designs come nowhere close to solving the problem of the actual code implementation. How to translate designs and specifications into working, stable software is a challenging task that relies on a high degree of creativity and intelligence. Software engineers are tasked with solving a mountain of problems ranging from the simple and routine to the hyper-complex and unforeseeable, and the process they go through to solve them is fundamentally a process of design.

Design does not lend itself toward linear thinking or management. Eight designers or engineers don't produce results eight times faster than one designer or developer does; in fact, in many cases throwing more bodies at a problem only makes things worse. As we'll discuss in depth in Chapter 3, progress in design work is very difficult to plan and predict, since so much of it relies on experimentation and discovery. Trying to force those who perform design-intensive roles to also produce with the consistency and predictability of assembly line workers ignores the true nature of the work being done and does nothing to gain any greater measure of certainty.

Development

Development in software projects usually means the phase when the software engineers are coding, and it's normal to hear software engineers referred to as developers. Generally speaking, there's nothing wrong with this, but we've found it necessary to break with this convention to give greater clarity to the approaches we advocate.

With the ordinary connotation of both design and development in software projects, design is typically a big phase that happens and finishes before development begins. This approach is a bad one, and you'll learn more about this in Chapters 3 and 8. By understanding design in broader terms, we've acknowledged that visual designers design, UX architects design, and software engineers design. At this fundamental level, the work these different professionals do on a software project is the same, though the experience required and the nature of their specific contributions differ. The ideal setting for producing exceptional UX in software is one where everyone involved in the design of the product—the businesspeople, the product managers, the visual designers, the UX architects, the software engineers, and (in ideal circumstances) the target users—are working closely in tandem and collaborating to solve the myriad problems the project presents as part of a unified effort. Every feature that goes into a product has an underlying business goal, a visual design, a workflow and interaction design, a technical implementation, and a connection to user goals. It's the complementary combination of those elements that results in great UX, and each requires the contribution of a different type of professional.

Segregating the contributions of the different participants on the product by separating their efforts into serial, distinct phases, is a setup for difficulty, increased risk, and poor results. Again, this will be discussed in great depth in the coming chapters, but it's necessary to bring it up now because we need to settle on a word that describes the stage where the businesspeople, product managers, visual designers, UX architects, and software engineers are working together to build the product—and that word is "development." Development, in the sense that we will use it through the rest of this book, is the stage of the project in which the product gets built, and is not, as the normal connotation holds, a time when only software engineers are working. Thus the "development" of the product is not exclusive of the contributions of everyone else on the project team.

Chapter 2
Building the Case for Better UX

Since you're reading this book, odds are that you already have an intuitive sense of some of the ways improved attention to UX can drive value for your company, your product, your company's employees, or your customers. After all, we are each consumers of technology, though we may also be producers of it. Savvy consumers of technology are witnessing with great pain the growing distance in quality between what's available to them as consumers and what exists in their workplace, or what is being offered to their own clients and customers.

EffectiveUI frequently encounters people who have a gut sense that software can be, and ought to be, much better than what we're sadly accustomed to. These people may be software designers and engineers who know that their professional lives and the lives of their users—their true judges and audience—could be better. They may be marketers in companies where marketing is the only department truly tuned into the customers' needs, and is therefore the closest thing the company has to user advocates. Or they may be product managers or leaders of business units who know deep down in their souls that their company could be doing better by its customers and employees if only they could figure out how and convince their bosses to feel the same.

We call these people "champions of change" and are excited to find any opportunity to work for and with them. One of the primary challenges in convincing potential clients of their need for our services is to educate them about the value of and opportunities available through investments in UX. It's a joy to find clients who already intuitively understand the first part, because we can lend them our experience in translating that gut sense into words and arguments that can sway the support of others. Since most companies are just following each others' leads in pursuing innovations, the world needs people who are willing to be the first and lead their companies and industries.

One of the greatest challenges you're likely to face in trying to bring a UX-centric project to life is convincing other people to support and pay for it. Many people whose fingers are on the purse strings or who control resources are still influenced by management climates, priorities, and incentives that are incompatible with good UX:

- *First to market instead of best to market*
- *Saving money instead of investing it effectively*
- *Using Six Sigma techniques to manage innovation*
- *Trying to keep parity with competitors' feature lists instead of differentiating on experience quality*
- *Taking the view that design is all about subjective aesthetics and belongs strictly to marketing and advertising*

And so on.[1]

Even companies with established customer experience (CX) initiatives and executive-level CX advocates often struggle to connect the business of CX to the technology of UX. Executives are also rightly skeptical of requests for investments in software since so many initiatives fall short of expectations or fail outright, and the moment they're done spending a million dollars on a product, it ends up requiring another million to keep pace.

So, to be an effective champion of UX in your organization and to get your project funded, you need to know how to parlay your intuitions into a fluency of words and a preponderance of evidence, to explain how UX aligns with business goals in a real and measurable way, and to successfully understand and appeal to the interests and concerns of your colleagues. To get there, it helps to gain perspective on the trends and changes that underlie the current impetus toward better UX.

1 *Fortune*'s Betsy Morris gives an interesting overview of changing management strategies that, though addressed at business generally, bears very directly on the changing strategies for software. See her July 11, 2006, series "Tearing up the Jack Welch playbook," found at *http://money.cnn.com/2006/07/10/magazines/fortune/rules.fortune/index.htm*.

Why Now Is the Moment for UX

There's something undeniably special about this moment in history with respect to UX. Things are truly happening, progress is actually being made, and it all seems to have begun with such a suddenness that one wonders who fired the starting gun before most people realized there was even a race. But this moment we find ourselves in is no singular event; rather, it is the culmination and point of convergence of a number of significant, long-running trends in business and technology.

To answer the questions "Why UX?" and "Why now?", it's useful—if a bit perverse—to borrow a concept from criminal law and examine the motive, means, and opportunity that bear on the current climate:

- *Motive, to understand what would make a person or company desire and perceive the need for better UX.*
- *Means, to understand what is now available to make better UX possible.*
- *And* **opportunity**, *to understand how means and motive combine to kick off actual projects and initiatives.*

Motive

Pressure is mounting on businesses to provide better UX in their customer-facing applications and internal information systems. That pressure, by and large, isn't coming from top-down mandates from executives demanding better UX, but rather from a grassroots groundswell from the users of software in the market and in the workplace.

People are beginning to expect more from the software systems they interact with. They're becoming more intolerant of the pain and aggravation bad UX causes, and are getting savvier about the capabilities available through software systems. Not only are they getting more experienced with software due to its increased ubiquity in their lives, but the broader demography is also changing. GenY, or "Millenials," a generation that's not only grown up with but is largely defined by its relationship to technology, has entered adulthood and is flooding into the workplace and consumer markets. Older workers who suffered through the software nightmares of the 1980s, the 1990s, and the bursting of the dot-com bubble are either retiring or have been promoted to supervise a retinue of younger workers who are accustomed to a more modern age of software.

And we shouldn't suggest that pressure for better UX in software is coming only from young people; they're the most intensive consumers of technologies, but certainly not the only ones. For GenY-ers and retirees alike, software systems have become so ubiquitous that it's impossible to avoid interacting with them, whether at home, at work, at a grocery store self-checkout stand, at a bank ATM, checking in for a flight, and so on. People who have grown up with technology tend to have a natural facility for it that allows them to use a system despite major UX challenges. With older users, people with certain types of disabilities, and less tech-savvy users, better UX might be what determines whether they can use the systems at all. For these people, UX serves the very basic purpose of providing accessibility into software systems.

There are powerful trends in the software technology space that are adding fuel to the UX fire. These trends are bringing better and more usable software to people, which in turn is continuing to raise expectations for what software can do, and how pleasant it can be to use.

UX leaders and innovators are raising the bar

Let's just get this out of the way: Apple, Apple, Apple, iPod, iPod, iPod, iPhone, iPhone, iPhone.[2]

It has become unbearably trite in our industry to bring up Apple, the iPod, and the iPhone when talking about UX, but it's also pretty much unavoidable,[3] so it's best to address it straight on. Under Steve Jobs's leadership, Apple has rebuilt itself as a company with UX as the soul and primary driver of its product strategy and design, and that approach is manifest in the iPod, iPhone, and other Apple products. Other companies and products are also leading the way in embracing superior UX as a core value, and EffectiveUI has had the good fortune to help many of them along that journey.

If you're looking at the iPod or any other positive examples of UX and asking why the experience of using your product isn't nearly as good, you can bet your users are thinking the same thing. Great UX in the consumer space has given people a glimpse of what's possible, dispelling at long last their resigned belief that software systems, like VCRs, are inherently and incurably painful to use.

2 Steve Jobs, Steve Jobs, Steve Jobs.
3 So says Adaptive Path: "As a discussion of product design grows longer, the probability of using the iPod as an exemplar approaches one." Peter Merholz et al., *Subject to Change* (O'Reilly Media Inc., 2008), 78.

For customer-facing applications, merely having a software offering has quickly gone from being positive and differentiating to potentially damaging if the UX doesn't hold up to customers' heightening expectations and decreasing patience. Even workplace information systems are subject to this pressure, as employees begin to realize their jobs could be easier and less frustrating, which in turn increases their frustration and injures their job satisfaction and productivity as nothing improves.

Web technology is pushing the envelope

The trend toward better UX has a number of concomitant web technology trends that feed both off of and into it. Better UX has made some remarkable capabilities accessible to web users, and exposure to those capabilities is driving people to demand more from the other software systems they use, whether web-based or otherwise.

Web 2.0

The Web 2.0 trend has been very interesting to watch and participate in, though the concept seems to have caused more hype and anxiety in the business world than has been due. The exact definition of the term "Web 2.0" is hard to get a fix on, in part because, being more of a trend or a genre than a discrete thing, it has very fuzzy edges and is an abstract concept that exists nowhere concretely, but only diffusely in the minds of those concerned with it, none of whom seem to agree with one another. There's also been some reasonable pooh-poohing of the trend, and much warning that Web 2.0 is another "bubble."[4]

It's hard to deny Web 2.0's impermanence when even its own name makes it sound ephemeral. How much longer until Web 2.98 gives way to Web 3.0? Is Web 3.0 already in beta somewhere? The whole thing is a little silly, as if anything as amorphous as the evolution of technology could be neatly parceled into ordinal numbers.

Stealing from the Wikipedia definition (a very Web 2.0 thing to do), "Web 2.0" has been said to mean:

4 See Michael Hirschorn's "The Web 2.0 Bubble" (*The Atlantic,* April 2007).

A perceived second generation of Web-based services—such as social networking sites, wikis, communication tools, and folksonomies—that emphasize online collaboration and sharing among users.

This definition has its flaws. Social networking capabilities—blogging, community building, sharing, chatting, etc.—are nothing new. Those existed 'round about Web 0.85 with personal web pages, Geocities, Java IRC widgets, and so on. The definition is also a bit narrower than the interpretation of Web 2.0 that our clients and the general public seem to have. Most perceive Web 2.0 as a trend of general improvement in the capabilities and usefulness of the Web, which are manifest in some of the new new things. In many people's minds, Web 2.0 is the name of today's advanced generation of web capabilities and features.

The force behind the Web 2.0 phenomenon is a deep, abiding trend that isn't about the social networking capabilities, but is rather about their fast-rising popularity. That popularity has grown because of the new usefulness and dramatically improved usability of Web 2.0 applications, which is a result of the recent advances in technology and UX design. What we're seeing in Web 2.0 is not foremost a collection of innovations in the features of the Web, but rather evidence of the major trend of improving UX. The social capabilities inherent to the Web that were previously accessible only to the ultra-geek are now accessible to a broader public, thanks to radical improvements in UX, and to an overall increase in geekiness—that is, tech savviness—in people generally.

Rich Internet applications

This discussion overlaps significantly with that of Web 2.0, because the general public doesn't usually distinguish between rich Internet applications (RIAs) and Web 2.0 applications. RIAs are, in a nutshell, software made to work over the Internet through a web browser but that behaves and performs in a way more typically associated with desktop-based software.[5]

Traditional web-based software relies heavily on the remote application server to do the processing and presents every aspect of the application to the user as a discrete page. RIAs, on the other hand, shift much of the processing to the user's machine and allow for a completely fluid, non-page-based presentation.

5 Adobe and Microsoft also have runtime "shells" for RIAs that allow them to be installed on the desktop and run outside of a browser.

These differences allow RIAs to have much more desktop application–like behaviors and capabilities, which allows for animation, video, and other rich media to be easily distributed through the Web. A comparison of simple examples should help make the definition and value of RIAs clearer.

A good example of a very simple, *traditional web application* is an online questionnaire used by your bank to help you open a checking account online. After clicking "Open an account" from the bank's main site, the next page you'd encounter might ask you to select the account type. Based on that selection, the site might send you to another page that lists the accounts terms and fees. After clicking a button to agree to the terms, the next page might be the place where you enter your personal information. If you make a mistake on this form (such as omitting a response for a required field or entering an invalid email address), you're alerted to this omission only after you've clicked the "Submit" button, the page has been sent to the server for validation, and the page has then been spat back with the errors reported.

One advantage of RIAs over traditional web apps is that they avoid full-page refreshes, making the experience of using them feel faster and more seamless.

Even this simple example requires four pages to be loaded in serial progression. This is a result of how traditional web applications put the burden of processing on the server. For example, to check whether you entered your zip code, your input must be sent to the server, checked for completeness, and a page showing errors must then be returned to you. Processing power is also what's required to display video, animations, and more visually and intuitively compelling interaction design, so traditional web applications are very limited in those regards. Though most people have grown accustomed to the page-based, heavily server-dependent nature of traditional web applications, their UX is undeniably poor in comparison with what's possible in desktop applications and RIAs.

Desktop applications do all of the processing on the user's machine, enabling much broader capabilities in the UX and behavior of the application. And since desktop applications aren't dependent on the call-and-response relationship with data and processing, they don't need to organize and present everything as discrete pages like a traditional web application does. If you think of standard office software such as Microsoft Office Excel or Word, although there may be documents, there are certainly no pages, and no discrete states. The user can do pretty much anything at any time, work with multiple documents simultaneously, build complex calculations and charts, and perform other fluid tasks and interactions out of reach from traditional web applications. On the other hand, desktop applications tend to be disconnected to the valuable resources of data and infrastructure available on the Internet.

RIAs put capabilities like those of desktop applications in the context of the Web. Google, ever the innovator, has launched an impressive RIA called Google Docs (*http://docs.google.com*), which is essentially a web-based version of standard office software for word processing, spreadsheets, presentations, and dynamic form creation. Google Docs can be used to work with spreadsheets, for example, with an ease that is roughly equal to Microsoft Excel. If it weren't for the fact that Google Docs runs in a web browser, it would be easy to forget that it is a web application. The way it presents things isn't restricted to the page-based structure, it isn't continuously forcing page loads and refreshes, and it elegantly enables the complex, fluid interactions necessary for editing spreadsheets.

Simply replicating the features of Microsoft Office, Word, and PowerPoint on the Web, though an impressive accomplishment, would be pointless on its own. But by virtue of being web-deployed, Google Docs has access to capabilities not available to desktop applications. For example, Google Docs:

- *Can be used on any computer with a web browser with an Internet connection, whereas desktop applications must be installed on the machine they're to be used on.*

- *Can save documents in the "cloud," meaning they're available anywhere to any computer, rather than being stuck on one machine, and are automatically backed up by Google.*

- *Can allow multiple users to collaborate over the same document without creating tons of disparate versions of the same document. The standard way of collaborating over a document with others is to email versions of the document back and forth amongst each other, leading to a clutter of emails, overlapping versions of the document, wasted storage space, and inefficient collaboration. Putting the document editing and collaboration capabilities on the Web means that everyone can work on the same, single instance of the document at the same time without the need for transiting versions through email.*

Another compelling example of an RIA comes from EffectiveUI's portfolio. A major yearbook manufacturer, Herff Jones (mentioned in Chapter 1), found that its customers had problems with the technological process behind creating yearbooks and getting them to press. Building a yearbook requires professional print layout software such as Adobe InDesign or QuarkXPress, which are desktop applications. This approach posed a number of problems for schools:

- *Licenses for print layout software can be pretty expensive, especially for school budgets.*

- *Schools tend to have aging computers that aren't fit to run the software, and they have onerous IT policies that make it difficult to procure and install software.*

- *Schools usually have only one or two computers for a dozen or more yearbook staffers, making parallel progress and collaboration difficult.*

- *Photos came from many disparate sources and were stored on multiple computers. Even when these computers were networked, photo management was cumbersome and created confusion among the teachers and students. It also led to a greater frequency of errors in photo resolution, placement, and cropping.*

- *Layout files were often passed to Herff Jones at the last minute and through email or postal mail, making it difficult for Herff Jones to actively review the designs and collaborate with the schools. This made it harder to provide support to the schools, and concentrated Herff Jones's support workload in one narrow timeframe near the end of the school year.*

So Herff Jones came to EffectiveUI to rebuild most of the capabilities of InDesign and QuarkXPress in an RIA. As an RIA, the Herff Jones layout software (eDesign) solved all of the critical problems:

- *Herff Jones was able to provide eDesign to schools for free, radically improving the company's ability to compete against and differentiate itself from other yearbook manufacturers.*

- *eDesign works on any computer with a web browser and Internet connection, so the number of school computers that could be used for yearbook creation was dramatically increased, and it also became possible for students to work on the yearbook from their homes.*

- *Photos and other graphics became available as digital assets through a single resource in the application itself, making the management, cropping, and placement of the photos dramatically simpler, and making it much easier to make changes and fix errors.*

- *Since all of the layout files were online, Herff Jones was able to proactively look at the schools' files and collaborate with them using built-in communication tools to make improvements and corrections so the layouts could be correct and ready for press much more quickly.*

Layout editing is a very complicated, processor-intensive task that would be utterly impossible with traditional web development techniques, but is now possible thanks to RIA technologies.

RIAs also have a strong technological advantage in enabling better UX. RIA development frameworks such as Adobe Flex, Microsoft Silverlight, and Sun's JavaFX were built around a core goal of enabling richer, more engaging UI and UX design. There has also been tremendous innovation in using HTML, CSS, and JavaScript techniques (for example, AJAX and DHTML) to build richer, more application-like experiences on the Web without requiring browser plug-ins. Compared to more traditional development technologies, these frameworks and techniques are uniquely well suited for making exceptional UX and innovative application UIs.

More RIAs are coming online every day, and every day people are being exposed to the richer capabilities and UX available through RIAs. This exposure is having the effect of dramatically increasing users' expectations for the other software systems they interact with in their personal and work lives. It's increasingly likely that a new software initiative will wind up being an RIA, even if previous incarnations of the product were desktop or traditional web applications, because the intersection of desktop capabilities with the benefits of data from the Internet and distribution over the Web are extremely compelling. Additionally, the skills necessary to build an RIA are quite similar to those required to build iPhone and Android (Google's mobile platform) applications, so companies pursuing cross-platform and cross-device product strategies are increasingly looking to RIAs and RIA professionals as a model for building new products.

Means

Software engineers are occasionally maligned as being inconsiderate of the needs of "normal" people—arrogantly, thoughtlessly, and geekily building user interfaces that make sense only to the engineers themselves, not to anyone who actually uses the software. But this is generally unfair. Software engineers have, in fact, often been the ones who best recognized the need for better UX. The professional fields of UX and interaction design are relatively new.

Before these fields existed, it fell to the engineers to carry the UI design mantle, and they suffered mightily at the sight of their own interfaces. But their problem was threefold:

- *UI design is not a typical competency of software engineers, so one wouldn't reasonably expect them to do it well.*
- *The tools, priorities, and constraints they were working with didn't allow for good UX.*
- *Because UX design wasn't assumed to be part of their role, they weren't given the time and budget necessary to do it well while also delivering on their core responsibilities.*

Put simply, they didn't lack the desire to deliver better UX, but rather the means with which to accomplish it. Part of what makes this a special time for UX is that the means for building better UX is now more readily available.

The tools for better UX

Software engineers rely on development frameworks and libraries to build both the guts of software and the UI. The frameworks and libraries available for UIs have, until recently, been ill-suited for building good UX. From the advent of Microsoft Windows until recently, most software UIs have been built using the library of UI components available through Windows, which are notoriously ugly and difficult to ply into passable UX. Sun's Java UI libraries have also been weak in enabling highly customized, innovative UI and UX design. As well, web application UX was constrained by the very limited capabilities of traditional web development technologies and application architectures.

The tools available have grown considerably.

But things are finally changing. RIA development technologies, which have been built primarily around the goal of enabling better UX, have given engineers a much more powerful toolkit to work with. Other, more traditional technologies such as Java, Cocoa, C, and C++ are also beginning to offer much more advanced UI development libraries that in turn enable the development of more powerful, innovative UX. Greater broadband availability and the rapid increase in the power of personal computers have also made it possible to solve certain performance-dependent UX challenges. And new types of devices and user input methods (the iPhone and multitouch, for example) are giving UX professionals more ways of creating highly intuitive and usable interaction designs to address new user behaviors and environments.

The money and time for better UX

The most significant challenge of building an application has historically been in building its "guts"—the internal, invisible workings of the application—rather than its UI. Especially in times when the business requirements for an application centered entirely on features and not at all on UX quality, the development of the application's UI was often the last stage in the project that got whatever remaining slivers of time and budget remained after everything else was done.

But now many of the more difficult engineering challenges of the guts of the application have been solved or are at least substantially in place. This frees up time and money to focus on the UI and to give UX quality a higher priority. Coupled with an increased recognition that products also should compete on quality and not features alone, this has meant more resources and time are being allocated to the design and development of the application UI, and for user research and professional UX design.

The professional support for better UX

There's an increased recognition that UI and UX design go beyond colors, graphics, and logos, and that it's a recipe for failure to ask engineers to play the role of UX and visual designers. There's also an improving understanding that UX design is a specialized subset of the design field—that print, advertising, or even web designers are not necessarily qualified to do UX design simply by virtue of being designers. This all adds up to a greater likelihood that professional, specialized, and qualified UX design resources will be available for a project, which naturally leads to better UX outcomes.

Opportunity

Now that better UX is both desired and possible, all that's needed is the match strike of opportunity. Opportunities present themselves as companies identify needs that can be met with investments in UX and as companies and technologies shift to make openings for UX innovations.

The CX trend

The CX trend can be instrumental in pushing companies to invest in UX. Good CX requires that a company ensures that each of its touchpoints with customers is a positive experience. With the increasing ubiquity of software systems as products and services, and as interfaces between companies and their customers, an attention to CX demands an attention to UX. The understanding and adoption of CX principles is wider and stronger than that of UX, so CX provides much of the impetus for UX investment opportunities.

Successful CX doesn't come from an individual job role, nor is it the sole purview of one department or one CX Officer; rather, it is an organizational competency where all areas of the organization are pursuing CX excellence and ensuring their efforts are well orchestrated. This requires a radical change in structure for many companies whose efforts, staffs, budgets, and customer touchpoints are siloed in departments with little or no coordination amongst them. Companies that are undergoing this change in structure are also moving toward a structure in which better UX is easier to achieve. Good UX is achieved only when everyone working on a project is focused on the user's needs and is effectively collaborating, and it cannot be achieved in companies where business, design, engineering, and customer advocacy are siloed and disconnected from one another.

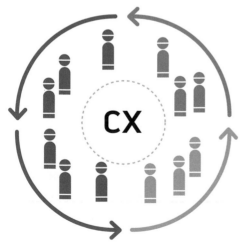

CX is a responsibility of the whole company...

...and not something that can be handled by siloed departments.

The rise of the information workplace

While the CX trend is driving opportunities for better UX for customer-facing applications, the increasing information-centricity of business is driving organizations to invest in better UX for the modern information workplace. Making relevant, timely, and valuable information available to employees and decision makers, simplifying and streamlining complex tasks, and increasing the scope of what an individual person can manage have long been recognized goals. But most custom information systems that have been built to date, lacking the means to deliver UX quality, have fallen short on the promise of the information workplace and have suffered from poor adoption, longevity, and relevance. Now that the means to make workplace information systems usable and effective exists, the increasing need for such systems can spur a lot of opportunities to build better UX into the information workplace.

Standing on the shoulders of giant IT expenditures

Companies that have already made sizeable investments in IT and software systems that so far have had terrible UIs may now find themselves in a position of having excellent opportunities to make investments in UX. Many companies have made significant investments to transition their major IT systems to a service-oriented architecture (SOA), which is a strong jumping-off point for UX-focused "client" UI initiatives. If many of the difficult engineering challenges involved in building a software system, excepting those of the UI, have been largely solved, it may be possible to simply build a better UI on top of the existing monster. EffectiveUI frequently works on projects where this is the case; we've even built a UI on top of a backend that was running, in part, on vacuum tubes. Assuming the monster behaves properly, these projects have been some of the most cost-effective opportunities to improve the product's UX quality. With the "backend" challenges largely solved, the product team can focus its attention and energy entirely on the "frontend" UX, rather than being mired by invisible technical challenges. A new UX initiative built on an existing backend can be an opportunity to entirely reinvigorate the product without having to start over with the messy parts.

Winning Support for Better UX

Unless you're one of the few fortunate people who manages her own budget with complete autonomy, who works for an organization where the mandate for investments in UX comes down from the top, or who is an independently wealthy investor in his own project, you're going to need to drum up support for your project and generate buy-in across your organization. Buy-in is as much an emotional state as it is an intellectual one. No matter how rational the justification for your project may be, the final leap of commitment—of buy-in—is made on an emotional level. The stronger a person's emotional engagement with the idea, the greater her receptivity to rational arguments in favor of the project will be.

The first challenge in convincing people to support an investment in UX is to educate them about its value and the opportunities it can create for a business. This challenge is accompanied by the need to do the research for building an objectively compelling case for the investment. The second principal challenge is to materialize the idea in some form to make an effective subjective case for it. How you accomplish these challenges will differ greatly depending on the nature and politics of your company, but our experience working with a broad range of companies on widely varied products has given us some insight into how best to make the case.

Stakeholders

Stakeholders either can be a tremendous asset or can represent your single greatest hindrance. They can bring products into being with a nod of their heads and they can cause them to fail with the slightest touch. Your success may very well be measured not by the objective quality of your accomplishments, but rather by the difference between what you've done and what your stakeholders expected you to do. Projects might be terminated not because of any serious issues with the schedule, cost, or technical challenges, but simply because they lost the support of key stakeholders.

A project that is terminated, undermined, or shelved because of its stakeholders' interference or lost support is just as much a failed project as one that runs aground for any other reason. Though stakeholders may at times inadvertently be the project's worst enemy, anticipating and mitigating this is a key responsibility of the project's leader. And since your stakeholders are also accountable to their own superiors and stakeholders, stakeholder management is a key responsibility of every person who wants the project to succeed. Since this book is about helping you successfully build your product, we'll give a significant amount of attention to how to work with stakeholders to get the best benefit of their contributions.

We define "stakeholder" as any individual who has significant influence or authority over the project, or who has control or influence over the money and resources needed by the project. Who your stakeholders are varies based on the project, the organization, and the stage of the project. For client services organizations, the stakeholders are typically appointed representatives of the client, who in turn have their own stakeholders within their company. For internal product teams, stakeholders are typically budget managers, executives, department heads, or product managers. There can also be hidden stakeholders who must be identified and managed, lest they unexpectedly appear and derail your efforts.

It's important to remember that stakeholders are individual people, not departments, business entities, or groups. Finance doesn't buy in to a project so much as some leader from that department does. This is an important distinction to remember; keep your efforts to bring stakeholders on board focused on a manageable group of individuals rather than entire sections of your organization.

Early on, your stakeholders will be representatives of three key needs: mandate, money, and resources. In making your initial appeal, make sure you not only clearly identify the stakeholders who represents these needs, but also those who have authority and influence to such an extent that their buy-in will ensure the buy-in of others.

Understanding the stakeholder perspective

Just as understanding the users' perspective is essential to crafting a product that meets their needs, building an effective case for an investment in UX requires an understanding of and sympathy for the perspective of stakeholders and executives. Entire books are written on this subject; we can just scrape the surface here. But there are simple misunderstandings that exist in the minds of many nonexecs, particularly people in technology jobs, that we can address.

Though it may seem that the main challenge of an executive or budget owner is finding good ways of investing their resources, their problem is actually more one of exclusion than inclusion. There's typically no shortage of ongoing costs and opportunities for investment, and so the challenge becomes to decide which of opportunities to forgo given the scarcity of resources. In the late 1970s, Xerox executives notoriously forwent the opportunity to invest in the then-innovative graphical user interface that their PARC team had developed, handing it over to the fledgling Apple Computer Company. Clearly this was not the best choice, but the Xerox executives at the time weren't stupid people; they were simply making hard decisions about how to apply their resources without the benefit of the information that we all now have about the value and potential of the innovation.

The nature of being an executive is that you're required to oversee large areas of a company, including some complicated domains where you may have limited or no specific experience. This is particularly the case in the management of technical domains, because technology fields change and evolve so quickly, and because the complexity associated with them multiplies rapidly. Risk is one of the key considerations that goes into the triaging of priorities, and from the perspective of an overwhelmed executive, something is risky if she doesn't understand it. This is why education is the first and most important priority in building the case for investments in UX. Most UX initiatives will appear to be high-risk proposals to someone who has too little information.

In reality, however, these initiatives should be opportunities to mitigate risk. There's also a tendency for people disconnected from technology trends to think, "We got this far without it, so why start now?" It's the responsibility of those who have the time and specialization to perceive the opportunities to make them plainly comprehensible to those with the ultimate accountability for their outcomes. Remember that there's a dismal track record for software initiatives in most companies. A tremendous number of software initiatives fail, and they fail because of factors that this book will help you avoid. Organizations typically don't reward risk taking, so your job is to reduce the perception of risk and increase the perception of opportunity.

Software products also are very expensive undertakings that never stop requiring large amounts of money, even after they're supposedly complete. Building a new office is always expensive, aggravating, and over budget, but once the ribbon is cut, the costs taper dramatically, and that particular problem is solved for a decade or so. If the project was somewhat unsuccessful, then there will be unexpectedly large costs to maintenance, but even those will diminish to a low burn after a while. In a software project, on the other hand, by the time you've finished building the product, it's already out of date and its development has exposed whole new realms of problems and opportunities. Thus, when the ribbon is cut on the software and the executive is hoping to put that challenge behind her, someone is waiting at her door asking for yet more money to resolve a problem or improve an area she thought was already solved.

If the project was in any way a failure, then she'll be forced to make the tough decision to undertake yet more risk and spend yet more money to salvage it and validate the original investment. If the project was generally a success—and here's the bitter irony—she'll find herself confronted with rapidly escalating costs to maintain and support the product. She will be too quickly thrust into a position of needing to decide whether to commit the organization to make a second version of the product. Getting started is costly, failing is costly, and succeeding is costly.

Fortunately, this is all a bit of an exaggeration and relies on the misperception that money spent on software is an expense rather than an investment. Though it may be stressful and fatiguing to never seem to reach the light at the end of the tunnel, each new expenditure should be in response to an opportunity to drive return on investment (ROI) and reduce risk.

One problem that makes it difficult to get legitimate software initiatives supported has been caused by the push for companies to chase after hype and trends. Executives are getting fad fatigue, having chased after half-baked corporate blogging and Web 2.0 initiatives for no perceptible business reason other than everyone else was doing it. Technology is a means to an end for both the business and the users, never the end unto itself, and a lot of the skepticism that exists today about new tech initiatives is fairly deserved. An important part of educating executives on the value of a proposal is putting it in the context of its value to the business. While it's true that the primary orientation of the project once it's started will be in solving the needs of the user and providing the user value, that goal is just a means of accomplishing some governing business goal.

Many software projects proposals are either ill conceived, poorly researched, or do a bad job of making the business value clear, so with just a bit of diligence and a respect for the executive perspective, you have an opportunity to stand out. If done right, you'll find yourself being asked, "How much do you need, and how soon can we have this?" rather than "How much would this set us back?"

Education

Much of the information that's helpful in educating stakeholders on the value of UX was addressed in Chapter 1 and in our explanation of what's driving the current opportunities in, and attention to, UX. Things that are obvious in in-store or in-office experiences somehow become less obvious when it comes to software. All the reasons why a company wouldn't want to aggravate, deter, or insult customers at stores and why it doesn't want to slow down, frustrate, and overburden employees are the same reasons why good UX is important in customer-facing and internal products. A focus on UX in customer-facing products is the same as a focus on customer service and quality CX, and in internal products it's the same as a focus on productivity, business intelligence, and job satisfaction. Better UX helps make the company money. The goal in educating stakeholders is to draw that connection in clear terms.

Because UX is lumped in with "design" in the ordinary, fuzzy connotation, there's a tendency for people to think that doing a UX rehab on a product is something like slapping a fresh coat of paint on an aging building. This dramatically underestimates the value and

It's just not that easy.

complexity of creating good UX in software, and creates the false assumption that UX outcomes can only be measured subjectively.

And so a focus on first helping stakeholders develop a true understanding of the function and value of UX design is critical. Design, generally, is a set of disciplines with concrete outcomes that enhance the value and viability of whatever it's concerned with. Organizations that have a strong design competency are edging out those that treat it as a strictly aesthetic, fluffy, marketing function. Progress is being made in establishing the concrete business value of investments in UX. Although there's no magical Excel spreadsheet we can offer to help you establish an irrefutable ROI case for your project, there are a number concepts that are very useful in educating stakeholders so they can draw the connection to the business value.

Finding a means of making the investment value of UX clear to stakeholders has benefits beyond simply getting initial support for the project. If your project can be sold as an investment, it's more likely to be treated as an investment once it's underway. In business there's a general recognition that you have to spend money to make money, and that spending too little money may result in making too little money. But if executives relate to UX as a fuzzy art thing, their impulse will be to manage it as a cost where success is measured by how little you spend, rather than as an investment where success is measured by the earnings or savings realized relative to the expenditure. By providing a means of seeing how investments in, not simple costs of, UX can yield compelling results, you may induce stakeholders to relate to UX more intelligently. This, in turn, will help ensure the stability of their support as money begins to be spent. Measuring how an investment can and is delivering ROI from the beginning of the project to its end will prevent people from thinking about the project as a cost center and instead will help them see it as an opportunity.

The UX Fund

At the end of 2006, the UX design consultancy firm Teehan+Lax devised a novel experiment to demonstrate the value of UX in economic terms. They created the UX Fund, a one-year mutual fund–like investment of $50,000 in the public securities of companies they considered to be UX leaders, chosen according to the following criteria:

- *The companies demonstrated care in the design of their products and website.*
- *They have a history of innovation.*
- *They inspired loyalty in their customer base.*
- *Doing business with them was a positive experience.*

During the fund's year of existence (11/1/2006 to 10/31/2007), its value increased 39.37%, outperforming the NASDAQ by 118% and the S+P by 316% (which grew 18.09% and 9.47%, respectively, during the same period). These results are striking, particularly when you consider that the results were significantly weakened by a number of factors in the portfolio that have nothing to do with UX. Much more information on the UX Fund is available on the Teehan+Lax blog at *http://www.teehanlax.com/blog/?p=293*.

Although the example of the UX Fund doesn't help in getting to concrete figures for any specific UX initiative, it does provide compelling evidence that attention to UX is a successful strategy in today's markets.

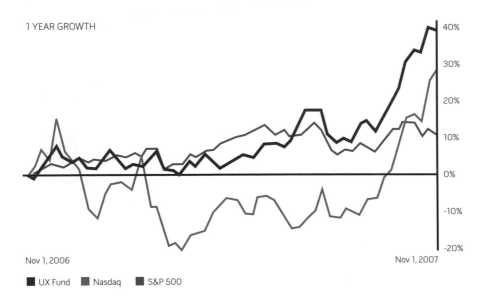

The UX Fund outperforms NASDAQ and the S&P.

Connecting user goals to business goals

Satisfying user needs and helping users meet their goals are necessary stepping stones to achieving business goals in software product design. Good UX design is principally about making an application effectively and easily serve the needs and goals of its users, goals such as, "I want to feel confident my money is invested properly." Some user goals may at first appear disconnected from or unrelated to the business's financial goals, but their linkage to the success of the business isn't usually hard to uncover.

Consider the example just given: *"I want to feel confident my money is invested properly."* For individual, nonprofessional investors, there's tremendous potential for anxiety about how their money is invested. Investment is as much a dark art as it is a science for them, and they pursue investments because they know they ought to, but are perpetually nervous they've done too little research, placed too risky of bets, and generally made the wrong decisions.

> *Confidence is as much based on emotion as it is on intellect. The emotional component of confidence is why people buy name brands.*

It's standard and expected of investment brokerages that they offer customers online access to their accounts. But many of these online systems were built in earlier times when it was a differentiating feature to simply have online access, and these systems have been hacked over the years to add on features to keep parity with competitors, with the quality of their UX suffering as a result. Imagine, then, that a customer of the brokerage who's generally nervous about her investments and who has the goal of gaining confidence in the wisdom of her decisions goes to the online portal and has difficulty with the following tasks:

- *Enrolling and getting immediate access to her accounts*
- *Finding information about and interpreting the performance of her investments*
- *Taking action on her investments and immediately seeing the effects of those actions*
- *Finding useful support and information to help guide her decision making*

If the portal's design is also unattractive (giving the sense of lack of polish and professionalism), and if it behaves strangely or performs poorly (giving the sense of lack of quality, trustworthiness, and reliability), it all adds up to more anxiety.

Though the UX and capabilities of the portal have absolutely no connection to whether or not the customer's money is invested wisely, they bear heavily on the customer's confidence in and perception of the firm. An investment brokerage's portal should reinforce a sense of security, professionalism, abundance of support and expert advice, strong and instantaneous insight and control, and other qualities that are likely to also be key goals of the company's branding.

And so it becomes easy to see how the user goal of wanting "to feel confident my money is invested properly" directly bears on the success of the business. Links to quantifiable business concerns arising out of this user need might be:

- *Reinforcement of branding goals and investments.*

- *Customer retention. Higher confidence decreases the likelihood the customer will switch to another firm.*

- *Increase in customer lifetime value (CLV). A customer who's confident in her investments with a particular firm will tend to place more into it over time.*

- *Decrease in call center and in-store customer support. An anxious customer will be much more likely to pick up the phone or visit a broker if she can't get quick, reassuring, and intelligible information or can't take immediate and instantly apparent action on her investments.*

It's very likely that this company will have already developed models for calculating how investments in branding, customer retention, CLV, and support cost reduction affect the company's bottom line. So the person championing an investment in improving the UX of the brokerage's online portal just needs to develop credible estimates of how a certain investment in UX affects those four business considerations, and then the company's existing models can take it from there.

So, it's useful to discover what your company's key objectives and brand promises are and to find ways of demonstrating how your initiative can lend support to these goals. Your company's finance department should be adept at figuring out things like this. Seeking the advice and support of finance executives early on can be useful in making the case for better UX because they can help navigate some of the more mind-boggling financial justifications. And involving them early in the process of developing a credible ROI model for UX can easily turn them into allies rather than skeptical stakeholders.

Finally, make sure to explore the full range of opportunities for improvement that your project can bring to every marketing channel and every department in the organization, as there can be many subtle ancillary benefits to improved UX. The broader the positive effects of your project, the more support and resources may be available to you. Be warned that breadth of effect cuts both ways, though; more affected departments may mean more stakeholders who aren't necessarily happy about invasions into their turf.

Connecting business goals to user behaviors

The same idea works in reverse. The linkages between existing business goals and user behaviors can offer some of the most compelling and obvious justifications for investing in UX. The advantage of this approach is that there's usually no lack of recognition on the part of stakeholders of the existence of a certain problem or opportunity; they just haven't yet seen how UX can be its solution. We'll use an internal enterprise application as an example this time.

Call center information systems

For companies that run sizeable call center operations, the high cost of operating those call centers and the difficulty in maintaining consistent quality of service are usually identified as major concerns for the business. Investments in improving the UX of the call center's information system can create tremendous opportunities for savings and improved cost effectiveness. This benefit can come in a number of ways:

- *Improving productivity. If the application UI streamlines and simplifies the support process, and if it improves the accuracy, timeliness, and quality of the support provided to the customer, this in turn reduces individual call times, reducing the overall load on the call center and reducing the staffing requirements.*

- *Reducing training costs. The easier a system is to use and the more intuitively and effectively it responds to the operator's needs, the less training time will be required to bring on a new operator. This can be especially significant in high-turnover jobs such as call center operators, and can also reduce the cost to ongoing training, as well as technical and managerial coaching and oversight.*

- *Improved employee retention. This is harder to quantify, but if an investment in the UX of the call center information system can reduce aggravation, stress, and confusion for the operators, turnover and its accompanying costs should decline.*

- ***Improved consistency of service quality.*** *Improvements that ease the process of providing support, provide the right information at the right time, allow for more detailed tracking of operator performance, reduce the need for training, and improve the job satisfaction of operators also cause a general improvement in the quality and consistency of the service the operators provide.*

These benefits are clearly easy to link to the success of the business. The challenge is in estimating how a given investment in UX will affect any of these considerations, especially when counterbalanced against switching costs. However, a thorough investigation of the problems and opportunities should give you a good sense of the potential effects of the investment, at which point it's time again to seek out the support of someone from the finance department in building credible models. Getting to the point of having a financial model and a clear recognition of how an investment in UX can affect certain costs in the organization puts you on very solid ground. At this point, the debate can be over the accuracy of the estimates in the model, but no one is likely to doubt the validity of UX as an investment.

Using the examples of others

Now it's your turn to trot out the iPod example and see if it sways anyone's opinion. It probably won't; those who don't "get" UX will have trouble seeing how the example of a consumer electronics product relates to a software product, though a software initiative is just as much a product development effort as is developing a new consumer electronics product. Apple has also been put up on such a high pedestal that to emulate their success simply seems out of reach. What the Founding Fathers are to politics and law, Apple now is to technology and UX. Fortunately, there are other examples.

Online tax preparation software

The example of online tax preparation software such as TurboTax is a wonderful one because you don't need to have actually used the software to understand the example. In understanding the full range of the value created by TurboTax, it helps to think of it simply as a product rather than a company, and it helps to think of the IRS as being the company and the taxpayer being the customer.

It gives some useful perspective to realize that the iPhone, while wildly popular in the U.S., isn't popular in Japan. Consumer electronics in Japan are always a year or two more advanced than those in the U.S. and in that context the iPhone looks less innovative, and it also fails to support some of the activities Japanese users demand. This is a great example of how even UX that's exceptional to one set of users can be deficient to another, underscoring the importance of the understanding the perspective of actual users in UX design.

The process of completing a personal income tax return has long been noto-riously complex and anxiety inducing. But online tax preparation tools have completely changed that. Early versions of software-based tax preparation tools made very little difference in the experience of filing a return, because all they essentially did was allow the user to type directly into the 1040 form. But attention to UX eventually led to improvements that abstracted the com-plexity of the form into a very friendly, simple questionnaire model. The product walks the user through a simple progression of clearly explained questions presented in a very simple, pleasant, straightforward way. Meanwhile, the product works behind the scenes to assemble the answers to those questions into the final tax return. The result: less anxiety on the part of taxpayers, earlier and more accurate tax filings, increased electronic transmittal of returns (improving the IRS's efficiency), and a slightly less antagonistic relationship between the taxpayer and the federal bureaucracy.

Mint and Yodlee

Mint (a service you've probably heard of) is a web-based personal finance management system that lets users aggregate and track their spending and income on multiple accounts at nearly any bank. Yodlee, a company you've probably never heard of, did the very hard work of figuring out how to pull financial data from more than 11,000 sources to create back-end infrastruc-ture to support services like Mint. By licensing Yodlee's services, Mint was able to focus its attention on UX and marketing, and thus produced a service that became enormously popular. In September 2009, Mint was acquired by Intuit for $170M and disconnected itself from Yodlee's services, moving to an infra-structure created by Intuit.

The Mint and Yodlee story has been a very interesting case study in the value potential of UX. The technical, business, and logistical challenges sur-mounted by Yodlee were far greater than those of Mint. It would have been much, much more difficult to replicate Yodlee's technology than it would have been to replicate Mint's. Until their acquisition, Mint was, in essence, just a thin layer of UX and marketing atop Yodlee's much more compli-cated service. You might think that this means there's more inherent value in Yodlee than in Mint, but it hasn't played out that way. Yodlee has been around for more than 10 years and has consumed more than $100M in capi-tal. Mint has been around for just a couple of years and managed to parlay $32M in venture capital into a $170M acquisition.

Regardless of how sophisticated the backend infrastructure might be, users must have some interface into it for that infrastructure to be meaningful. The appeal and usefulness of the capabilities available to users through that backend infrastructure is entirely mediated by the UX quality of the UI. Despite its relatively limited standalone technological value, Mint's role in connecting to users was essential in making the Yodlee services meaningful to the users. Yodlee had other licensees and offers its own online interfaces into its services, but Mint won the day through superior UX quality. What allowed Mint to build value in itself was its ability to earn relationships directly with customers through attention to UX. Mint's opportunity was created in large part by the poor UX quality of online services offered by banks. And Mint's value ultimately wasn't dependent on Yodlee; they were able to sever themselves from Yodlee's services and move to Intuit's services following the acquisition. TechCrunch wrote a concise, interesting article about Yodlee and Mint, and how it relates to YouTube's similar, fantastically lucrative leveraging of Adobe's backend services; see *http://www.techcrunch. com/2009/09/18/mint-is-yodlees-youtube/*.

This sort of opportunity is often lingering unrecognized inside of companies. Many companies have spent a great deal of money on building or licensing a sophisticated set of backend capabilities, but they haven't seen it through to a UX-focused frontend. This means there's unrealized potential waiting to be seized. No matter how powerful the backend systems are, their value, success, and usefulness will always be mediated by the quality of the UI. By reinvigorating the UI layer with an attention to UX, companies have a tremendous opportunity to validate the investment in the backend and build new value.

Expose stakeholders to user feedback

Negative user experiences are hard to ignore or argue with. The trouble is, many companies aren't listening or watching for them, or they're being observed in the wrong ways by the wrong people. For example, some companies may perfunctorily order a usability study on a product sometime after it's launched, and though that study may be professionally performed and incorporate actual user feedback, it fails to provide motivation for improving the UX of the product. This happens for several reasons:

- *To the extent the study reflects users' experiences, those experiences have been aggregated and translated into data, charts, or textual excerpts that make an effective scientific case but fail to appeal to the intuition or empathy that helps to generate emotional buy-in to the need for improving UX.*

- *Usability studies often fall under the sole purview of IT and therefore are delivered only to IT. IT usually isn't focused on or driven by concern for UX on a deployed product, but is instead busy maintaining and supporting it. The studies may never be seen by anyone who drives budget or product strategies and who might see the information outside the context of maintaining an existing system.*

- *Usability studies tend to be oriented at suggesting small, incremental improvements to existing UIs, and this approach may fail to recognize the need for a product to be built around better UX instead of being hacked toward it.*

But when user feedback is sought and presented in the right way, it can be extremely useful in generating support. Since exposing stakeholders to the experiences of users is intended to play to their empathy and intuition as much as to their logical perspective, it's important that the way the information is presented have inherent visceral appeal. A major goal in presenting the user feedback must be to build empathy for users in the minds of your stakeholders, and that's easier when the feedback feels more "real" to them.

The easiest way to accomplish this is to simply bring stakeholders along on user interviews. Few things could be more jarring than to watch a user struggling to accomplish a key task in an application that was presumed to be simple, or failing to understand how to use the application to achieve the goal it was built for. And the negative feedback and thoughts the users provide will lodge directly and unfiltered in the minds of your stakeholders, helping them to develop real empathy for user needs and creating a sense of urgency to respond to the problems and opportunities discovered during interviews.

Second best to having stakeholders at the actual interviews is to show them video. Again, if the goal is to generate empathy and an intuitive understanding of the problems and opportunities, seeing and hearing users is a lot more effective than reading about them. Audio recordings can also be useful, even if the interviews involve observing the user working with the software, because the interviewer can ask the user questions about what she's trying to accomplish, why she may be struggling as she works with the software, and how her experiences are affecting her attitude toward the product and the company.

User research is covered in considerable detail in Chapter 6, so we won't go any further into the subject here, other than to suggest that it may be useful in making your case to do some of the user research up front, rather than bundling it all into the process of the project itself.

Quantifying the Business Value

Education alone may not be enough to make the magnitude of the opportunity clear. Executives trying to balance and triage opportunities need common measuring sticks by which to judge which opportunity offers the strongest value. Again, the goal is to convert the perception of a UX-driven initiative from it being a cost center to it being a tremendous opportunity, and that case requires hard numbers and facts.

What sorts of numbers and facts will be compelling is so specific to a given organization and opportunity that it's difficult to go into much depth here. But the processes of having connected the user's goals to the business's goals and vice versa should have exposed some clear points where the business value can be quantified. When you make conservative projections about the effects of a UX initiative on sales, customer retention, and brand equity, or on organizational efficiency, training costs, and employee retention, and connect those projections with existing models for estimating ROI, the strength of the opportunity is usually very obvious. It also can be useful to look to other organizations pursuing similar initiatives to get a sense of how they've benefited. If this information isn't readily available, analysts from research firms such as Forrester and Gartner can be helpful, and they frequently produce articles and whitepapers that are very valuable in building a quantified business case.

Materializing and Proving the Concept

When you're trying to generate buy-in for improved UX, written documentation or low-fidelity prototypes don't tend to do your ideas justice, nor make a compelling case on an intellectual and emotional level for stakeholders. Ideally, you'll want to generate the same sense of engagement and enthusiasm in your stakeholders as you propose to generate in your users when pitching your project. We sometimes call the process of materializing the concept for stakeholders the "puppy dog sale." Ask anyone whether he wants a dog, his answer is likely to be, "No, thanks." But if you just put an adorable, fuzzy puppy in his arms, you'll find it very hard to get him to give the puppy back. The value of good UX can at times be hard to explain, but once stakeholders have had a direct experience of it, they often just get it.

The other benefit of materializing the concept is it helps ensure that everyone involved has the same image of the project in their minds. If descriptions of the project's goals and anticipated outcomes are left in strictly verbal and written media, everyone is free to form their own preconceptions and mental images about what will ultimately be delivered, setting the project up for trouble with unifying those views and managing stakeholder expectations.

There are several ways to accomplish the goal of materializing the concept, depending on how much money you have available at the outset. EffectiveUI has seen a rapidly increasing number of clients willing to spend a bit of money up front to have their ideas brought to visible life and to help demonstrate a concept and generate buy-in.

Wireframes and graphic comps

As was the case with user research discussed earlier, it can be extremely useful to do some of the work of the actual project up front. The UX architects and designers produce two key documents during the course of planning and developing the product that can be very useful in generating buy-in: wireframes and graphic comps.

Wireframes are representations of an application's screens, workflows, and key interactions. Similar to blueprints, they are intended to clearly represent the structure and elements of an application, but the visual styling and look-and-feel are omitted. Leaving style out of wireframes makes it easier to focus on form and function without being distracted by aesthetic details that have no bearing on how the application will function. These are useful in generating buy-in because they're significantly more concrete than any written or verbal representation of an idea can be, and in being visual media they will tend to generate a much stronger emotional reaction on the part of stakeholders.

Professionally prepared wireframes also look very sophisticated and polished, which is useful in enhancing your credibility when seeking support. Though wireframes are often used as detailed specifications for a UI, wireframes for this purpose needn't be complete or comprehensive, only representative and compelling.

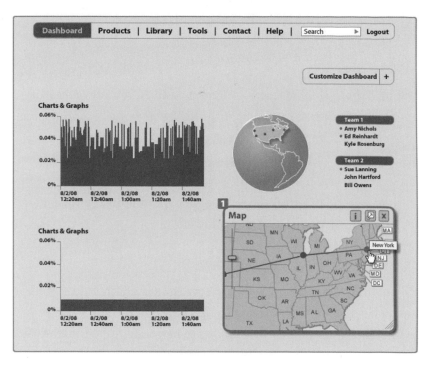

Example wireframe of an application dashboard

Graphic comps are images of screens from the application with the graphical look-and-feel applied. We frequently find that even the marginal level of abstractedness of wireframes is too much of a barrier to comprehension for certain stakeholders, making a higher-fidelity, more concrete representation of the application necessary. Though wireframes give a clear view of the function of the product, graphic comps appeal most directly to the subjective interests of stakeholders, and people generally perceive them to be more fully baked and professional than less graphically rich concepts. Preparing graphic comps can be risky, though, because you may find that some stakeholders can't see past objections to colors, graphics, or brand inconsistency to understand the assertions about UX you're trying to make.

Storyboards

Although wireframes and graphic comps can be visually appealing, they may fall a bit short in demonstrating the full UX potential of an idea. Products must be seen and understood in the context of how they fit into a user's personal or work life and how they help fulfill user goals. Whereas wireframes and graphic comps require the viewer to put himself in the shoes of the user and imagine what the user's experience will be, storyboards allow the view to be pulled back from just the application screens to show them in the context of a user's life, needs, and behaviors.

Storyboards are used to bridge the flow, motion, and experience gap between the script and the screen.

If you've watched the special features content on a DVD, you may already be familiar with storyboards. In filmmaking, the script alone communicates the story of the film, but generally fails to communicate or outline the flow, motion, and experience of the film. Storyboards are used to bridge the flow, motion, and experience gap between the script and the screen. Likewise, in software design, storyboards are a useful tool in communicating flow, interaction, and, again, the experience of the application.

Animatics

The term "animatics" is another one we borrow from the film industry. In film, animatics are an extension of storyboards wherein the static storyboards are built into rudimentary animations to better demonstrate the motion of the camera and the action in the frame. Animatics in software are essentially short films produced to further enrich the demonstration of a concept. If done well, they can be considerably more effective in winning support than storyboards because they can show an application's UX and interaction design with a much higher degree of fidelity, and can bring actual people into the picture to show them interacting with and reacting to the application. EffectiveUI has seen a significant increase in the number of clients who need animatics to generate buy-in more widely in their company, to the point that we've established a creative division in our company dedicated to this service.

The depth, quality, and approach of animatics can be widely varied. Some aim to demonstrate a broad vision with a lesser attention to specifics, whereas others are meant to sell a specific concept with a detailed, high-fidelity representation. Others are less concerned with the application itself, instead focusing on capturing a view of the user's experience with it.

Future vision

This approach is similar to the way car manufacturers produce concept cars in that, although they will never actually be produced, they are an effort to generate enthusiasm for the future direction of the brand. One of our clients, Wells Fargo, has a business unit whose purpose is to explore ways technology can propel their business forward, and they wanted to get the wider organization excited about some of the possibilities they were looking forward to. Combining live-action actors with computer-generated effects, we produced a 12-minute film that showed the future systems in action, being used by real people along a storyline written to show how these future systems could enhance the lives of their users. This video was shown widely through the company over the Web and in conference hall presentations, generating strong enthusiasm. That video is now publicly available through EffectiveUI's website at *http://www.effectiveui.com/index.html#/?env=consulting&pop=1&f=0.*

Microsoft has also produced something very similar that illustrates the "future vision" animatic style nicely: *http://www.istartedsomething. com/20090228/microsoft-office-labs-vision-2019-video/.*

Future vision video

UX showcase

Another client had a business unit that wanted to improve the UX of an existing business-to-business portal, but they were having difficulty getting others to buy in to the value of improving the UX of a system that already seemed to be working well enough. We worked with them to identify a few key interactions and tasks that would be dramatically improved by better UX and created some graphic comps of what those application screens would look like. We then used animation to bring those graphic comps to life, making a video that appeared to show a real application being used, showcasing how engaging the UX could be. At that time, the application didn't exist at all, but by simulating what it might be like, the business unit we were working with was able to quickly generate buy-in and a common vision for what would become a multimillion-dollar, business-critical initiative that redefined how the company interacted with its customers.

User experiences

Years ago, we worked with a client that was trying to sell a very innovative idea to an investor. To help build the case, they produced a short movie with professional actors who were acting as if they were using the proposed system. This segment was followed by one where the actor/users gave enthusiastic, positive feedback about their experience using the product and how it affected them.

This was an effective animatic approach, because the value of the application they were proposing to build was in the experience and learning it was meant to offer its users. Focusing on the anticipated experiences and reactions of those users was a more effective approach than one that might have highlighted the features of the system.

Other Strategies for Building Support

Exactly how you build the case for an investment in UX will depend heavily on the opportunity and the internal politics and goals of your company. The concepts covered so far in this chapter are the weightiest—but by no means the only—tools for building your case. Following are a few more strategies.

Start with something small

If you can find some small amount of funding and support up front, you may consider creating something small that helps to prove your point and reinforce your credibility. The various methods of materializing the concept are examples of this, but there are other options, including:

- *Do some business planning early. Business planning is the process by which you hone in on the business goals for the product and reinforce buy-in with your stakeholders, and it's the subject of Chapter 5. This can be a very powerful opportunity for building support for your project because it gets stakeholders involved in setting out the vision and goals for the product, and exposes them to the problems, opportunities, and user feedback that are driving the project. Stakeholders who participate in planning will tend to feel like they're involved in and partially responsible for a project, rather than seeing themselves as needing to manage or approve it from a distance.*

- *Build a proof of concept. Proofs of concept can take a lot of different forms, depending on the time and money you can put into them. Generally speaking, the higher the fidelity of a proof of concept's visual and interaction design, the more compelling a case it can make. EffectiveUI sometimes translates wireframes and graphic comps into clickable prototypes, which allow a person to actually interact with a narrow simulation of the system, to get a sense of what the experience of using it will be like, or of how certain problems will be solved. EffectiveUI uses professional designers working in Adobe Flash to build these, but if you have a decent design sense and more free time than money, a software product called OmniGraffle Professional can be a powerful tool for building rudimentary, interactive prototypes. Another option is to find an eager developer or designer who sees building such a prototype as an opportunity to improve her portfolio.*

Lean on the credibility of outside experts

EffectiveUI occasionally involves the support of financial planning partners who have deep experience in building the objective, financial case for investments in software and UX. Professional research and analysis firms such as Forrester and Gartner have published a lot of studies and whitepapers reinforcing the need for investment in UX, and these carry enough credibility and authority with executives that they sometimes allow you to bypass the need for ROI modeling.

Stay under the radar

One of EffectiveUI's strongest successes was its partnership with eBay to build a desktop version of eBay's application. The project was primarily to experiment with eBay's UX in a sandbox that didn't affect their main website, and the goal of the project was to study some ideas and opportunities more than it was to produce a marketable product. As a result, the project was generally outside the awareness of most people at eBay, and it was treated as an experiment rather than as a central priority for the organization.

Chapter 3
Effective Planning and Requirements

Planning and requirements are difficult subjects in the world of software development, and are often points of bitter contention between managers and project teams. It seems to be universally recognized that the typical approach to managing software projects hasn't been working particularly well, and projects are perpetually behind schedule and over budget. The development of software—especially innovative, well-designed, user-centered products—simply can't be planned and managed in traditional ways, and failure to recognize this and adapt properly can lead to grinding failures, misconstrued goals, and half-baked products.

Despite the need for unique management approaches, software development projects exist in the context of businesses where strong planning and risk management are critical. Publicized release dates, limited budgets, forces of competition, and other unavoidable pressures push managers to try to get certainty in what will be delivered, when it will be delivered, and what it will cost. That this certainty has never been possible before usually doesn't cause managers to reassess the overall approach. Instead, they tend to resign themselves to the belief that software projects are always dysfunctional, and account for that dysfunction by padding their own estimates and commitments.

> Balancing the realities of how software is built with the need for a sense of security by the business and stakeholders is a challenge that can be met successfully, but it requires a major shift in how managers and stakeholders perceive software development.

Balancing the realities of how software is built with the need for a sense of security by the business and stakeholders is a tremendous challenge. It's a challenge that can be met successfully, but it requires a major shift in how managers and stakeholders perceive software projects. That change in perception is, unfortunately, very difficult and counterintuitive, but it is so critical to succeeding in a software project that we've dedicated the majority of this chapter to trying to drive the point home. These changes in perception and approach, though initially they may be hard fought, can brush aside some of the issues that have historically made building software such a dysfunctional, brute-force, grinding process. They can improve your company's competency in building software products, dramatically increasing the chance of a successful outcome. In the end, whatever initial challenges arose from changing perceptions is more than made up for in the avoidance of worse difficulties and greater risk of failure.

So, while this book is dedicated to helping you build and apply good practices in your software project, much of this chapter is meant to first break you and your company of bad habits. The deleterious effects of a misguided approach to planning and requirements can easily negate any good practices and hard work. Trying to work with bad planning and requirements is like trying to plant flowers in concrete or ice skate uphill. It's possible, but it'll be very, very hard, and that undue strain will get in the way of doing anything successful or artful.

Uncertainty and the Unknown

Uncertainty and the unknown are enormous, unavoidable, and fundamental components of every software development project. Being at peace with this reality means you can approach the project in a way that adjusts and flows to account for the unknown. If you fight uncertainty and the unknown—or, even worse, if you suppose they don't exist—it's a path to defeat.

The mistaken belief that uncertainty can be entirely stomped out through upfront planning and everything can be known in advance is the root of many of the worst problems and errors in the management of software projects. This arises from the misapprehension that software development is comparable to and can be managed like other types of large-scale engineering projects—building a bridge across a valley, for example. Bridge building and software development both have components of science and engineering, and of art and craftsmanship. But the role of uncertainty and the unknown, and the way science, art, engineering, and craftsmanship work together throughout the course of the project are very different. Those differences demand a fundamentally different approach to management of the project.

The notion may seem discouraging, but it's much more accurate to compare software development to war than it is to compare it to bridge building. While the battle of software development is fought more with electrons and Mountain Dew than bullets and napalm, the battlefield is a complex, dynamic, unpredictable system of activity residing in shifting political and operational contexts.[1]

The Humility of Unknowing

I am the wisest man alive, for I know one thing, and that is that I know nothing.

—Socrates

To demonstrate how uncertainty and the unknown are inevitable components of a software development project, we'll examine why the bridge-building analogy fails and the war analogy succeeds. But even with the aid of analogies, it's extremely difficult to explain why uncertainty and the unknown are unavoidable to someone who's never been in the trenches of a software development project. Much of the understanding comes from seeing how design, creativity, and inspiration factor into every aspect of building an application. It also comes from having seen how false certainty, and the demand for it, can cause failure and lead to poorly designed products.

---

1 In the war of software development, the enemy is failed product design. The enemy is most certainly not the stakeholders and managers, though frustrated project leaders may slip into viewing them as such. Stakeholders and managers are allies, and like all alliances of forces, a certain amount of diplomacy is necessary to ensure that the allies are all pursuing the same goals and working in concert.

It's difficult to explain or prove this fact except to state it this way for now: *you understand your project far less than you think you do.*

And so do your stakeholders, by the way. For your project to be successful, you need to cultivate in yourself and in your stakeholders a certain humility and a recognition that, for as much as you know, you know very little, and that the essence of the project is to investigate and solve a complex problem and not simply to implement a known solution. Embracing this humility of unknowing isn't a resignation to defeat or admission of weakness, but rather is a state of wisdom required to allow you to succeed.

The Weakness of Foresight and Planning

The great uncertainty of all data in war is a peculiar difficulty, because all action must, to a certain extent, be planned in a mere twilight, which in addition not infrequently—like the effect of a fog or moonshine—gives to things exaggerated dimensions and unnatural appearance.

—Carl von Clausewitz, *On War*

Everything required to design a bridge to a valley is knowable in advance and can be planned to an extremely high level of accuracy before construction begins. All of the important goals, variables, and constraints can be accurately obtained before design begins.

Remember that, as we discussed in Chapter 1, design isn't limited to visual and artistic design. Just as an engineer is said to design a bridge or an airplane, a general can design a solution to a battlefield situation, software engineers can design a technical solution, and UX professionals can design interactions and workflows. Design is the application of thought and creativity toward the solution of some challenge or problem, and does not require that the output be of a visual or artistic nature.

Once those key considerations have been discovered, the design of the project begins and can be entirely completed before construction starts. With accurate and complete designs in hand, construction is then all about ensuring the pieces all come together as designed. Construction is not concerned with any remaining questions about the design and isn't burdened by the risk that the design will change during the course of construction.

By contrast, a general preparing for battle can estimate the strength and disposition of his forces, the resources and capabilities available to him, the attitudes and aptitudes of his commanders in the field, the lay of the battlefield, the strategic goals of the battle, the state of the enemy's forces, and the parameters for success. He also has history and personal experience to help him intuit how events will unfold. Based on this knowledge, he can formulate a plan for the battle.

But this plan, no matter how carefully devised, is inherently incomplete and imprecise. It is wholly premised on estimates of the conditions before the battle and entirely ignorant of the unforeseen conditions that arise during the battle. These unforeseen conditions are based as much on the vagaries of weather, emotion, chance, and uncertainty as they are on even the best-laid plan. This reality is the basis for the famous quote:

> *No battle plan survives first contact with the enemy.*
>
> —Helmuth von Moltke

The same is true of software development. No matter how well you think you understand the domain and no matter how earnestly you've thought through the requirements, there is still great uncertainty in the original facts and premises and a vast depth of the unknown still awaiting you. As with battle, the outcome will be determined at least as much by what comes during the course of the project as by what comes before it.

Not all unknowns are bad, by the way; it's in solving the unforeseen problems that great design and inspiration can take place. Some unknowns may be revelations about your customers and users that fundamentally change how your business interacts with them, or they may be undiscovered opportunities for progress, innovation, efficiency, and improvements to your company's bottom line.

A major reason why uncertainty is unavoidable is that software development, unlike bridge building, requires most of the design to happen at the same time as construction. Construction in the bridge-building business is the application of craftsmanship against the realization of the design plans made prior to construction. Construction in software development is everything from UX design to software engineering to quality assurance.[2] No amount of upfront planning can keep design from being an essential component of the development process. Since design is the process by which problems are identified and solved, it follows that if design can't be completed before development begins, many of the problems and solutions have yet to be identified and cannot be accounted for in any early project plan.

None of this should be taken as an argument for not doing any planning at all. The value and role of planning is still strong, but it should be approached and used differently in light of an understanding of its inherent weaknesses and realistic value.

Friction in a Complex and Peculiar System

Everything is very simple in war, but the simplest thing is difficult. These difficulties accumulate and produce a friction, which no man can imagine exactly who has not seen war…. So in war, through the influence of an infinity of petty circumstances, which cannot properly be described on paper, things disappoint us, and we fall short of the mark. A powerful iron will overcomes this friction, it crushes the obstacles, but certainly the machine along with them…. Friction is the only conception which, in a general way, corresponds to that which distinguishes real war from war on paper. The military machine, the army and all belonging to it, is in fact simple; and appears, on this account, easy to manage. But let us reflect that no part of it is in one piece, that it is composed entirely of individuals, each of which keeps up its own friction in all directions…. This enormous friction, which is not concentrated, as in mechanics, at a few points, is therefore everywhere brought into contact with chance, and thus facts take place upon which it was impossible to calculate, their chief origin being chance.

—Carl von Clausewitz, *On War*

2 The word "development" is often used to refer to what software engineers do in coding an application, but we'll be using it in the more general sense that constitutes everything that goes into bringing a project to life, which includes design and user research.

The job of the bridge designer is to build a fixed system that can span a certain distance and withstand a variety of forces variably acting on the structure. A bridge, one hopes, is a fixed and solid object. It is composed of bits of metal welded to other bits of metal, cables attached to anchorages, arrangements of trusses, and so on. Though the bridge is a system of individual pieces, it is a simple, static system because once those pieces are properly assembled, they can be viewed reliably as a whole and each piece interacts only with those pieces it is in contact with. When testing a bridge design against external forces, the engineer first tests each piece, then each connection, then each structure formed by each connection, then each larger structure formed by the connection of smaller ones, and so on, until she can test the bridge as a whole system. If the individual component tests are entirely reliable, the whole system tests are also reliable without needing to reexamine the component level.

In addition, the process of building the bridge is a strongly centrally organized system. Although there is great complexity to how the pieces come together and systemic ripple effects can be caused by a breakdown in one part of the construction process, the entire system is perpetually reorganizing itself to the same static, central goal: building the bridge explicitly defined in the designs.

Software systems and the development of them are, on the other hand, complex systems. Specifically, they're Complex Adaptive Systems (CAS):

> *A Complex Adaptive System (CAS) is a dynamic network of many agents...acting in parallel, constantly acting and reacting to what the other agents are doing. The control of a CAS tends to be highly dispersed and decentralized. If there is to be any coherent behavior in the system, it has to arise from competition and cooperation among the agents themselves. The overall behavior of the system is the result of a huge number of decisions made every moment by many individual agents.*[3]

Understanding why this is the case in software helps to further the understanding of the role of uncertainty and the unknown in software development.

---

3 John H. Holland, *Complexity: The Emerging Science at the Edge of Order and Chaos* (Penguin Books, 1994).

The CAS of software

In object-oriented programming (OOP), every element of code that goes into a product—every class, component, library, data connection, and so on—is a discrete "agent." That's what makes OOP an effective approach to software development: it allows a complex software system to be built out of individual, smaller, comprehensible pieces with their own instructions and behaviors. Because each of these pieces—these agents, like individual soldiers on the battlefield—acts and reacts according to its own situation and instructions, and according to the state of the system, the result is a complex system that's far greater than the sum of its parts. Whereas a bridge is the sum of its parts—the pieces of metal and welds and everything else all add up to a single, static bridge—a software system is the behavior created by the dynamic interaction of its parts. The complexity further multiplies when you consider that the human user is an agent in the system, and the system must accommodate a wide diversity of users who don't behave in predictable ways. Unlike with a bridge—where, no matter what variable forces are in play, it's always the same bridge—a single software system can produce a near-infinite number of possible different behaviors and experiences.

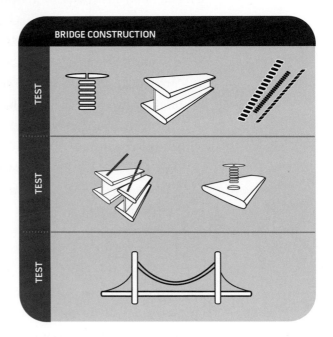

Software doesn't lend itself to discrete phases for testing in the same way that construction projects often do.

Returning to Clausewitz's thoughts on the complexity of the military enter-prise, if you recognize that software is composed not of large, static units, but rather a multitude of individual agents, "each of which keeps up its own friction in all directions," you can begin to understand why even the sim-plest thing can be difficult in unforeseen ways. The fact that the agents in the software system have the potential to act, react, and interact in unexpected ways is also the reason why bugs become an increasingly difficult problem as a product grows, because the complexity of the system and the profusion of potential interactions and behaviors are increasing nearly exponentially. In construction, as the staging area where you keep all the pieces empties as the project progresses, you're left with fewer and fewer questions; things become simple the closer you get to completion. The opposite is true in soft-ware. As you begin building, you start to realize how dynamic the system is and to see ways it might behave and ways people might use it that you hadn't considered before, and as you continue to build, the complexity and possi-bilities multiply.

The vast potential friction in the complex system of software is a key reason why the unknown bears so heavily on software development. Something that seems simple on paper is, in fact, difficult, and the scale and effect of that difficulty can't be accurately estimated or known in advance because chance, the unintended, and the unexpected are such strong factors, and a complex system can't be fully comprehended by any person.

The CAS of software development

It's fascinating, though perhaps discouraging, to consider that the process of developing software is itself a CAS. In this case, the agents in the system are not only the agents in the software itself, but also the members of the project team, the stakeholders, the development infrastructure, and even the office environment. With a team building a bridge, no matter what unforeseen com-plications arise (delays in materials, weather, poor workmanship, and so on), the entire system is constantly reorganizing itself around executing on the design since that design is entirely accurate, comprehensive, and stable. So, notwithstanding any happenstance during the construction phase, the out-come will always be the same: one predefined bridge.

The course of a software development project, on the other hand, is highly dependent on the idiosyncrasies of every agent in the system interacting with each other and the effect of happenstance, because there is no accurate, comprehensive, and stable plan around which to constantly reorganize. The conditions and progress of yesterday become the basis of what happens today, which determines what happens tomorrow, and ultimately shapes the end result.

This is easy to imagine if you consider assigning the same project to two different, equally qualified project teams. The initial conditions are essentially the same, but the agents—the people, their office environments, their infrastructure, and so on—are different. From the very first minute of the commencement of the two projects, they become divergent. Though equally qualified, the teams will nonetheless approach and solve problems differently, rely on different experience in decision making, and have different internal politics. They will also be subject to different happenstance events, such as having certain team members absent at certain times, getting different answers to the same questions by asking different stakeholders, and getting bogged down by different types of problems and bugs.

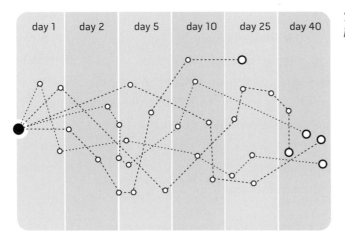

The conditions and progress of yesterday become the basis of what happens today.

Both teams will hopefully produce a working piece of software, but the two products will be very different from each other. This fact is not problematic in itself, but is a further indication of how strong a role the inestimable effects of chance and friction play in the course of a project. In other words, this is yet another reason why the unknown is such a huge and unavoidable component of a software project.

The peculiarity of the system

> *Further, every war is rich in particular facts; while, at the same time, each is an unexplored sea, full of rocks, which the general may have a suspicion of, but which he has never seen with his eye, and round which, moreover, he must steer in the night.*
>
> —Carl von Clausewitz, *On War*

The most reliable way to avoid uncertainty is to build products and solve problems precisely like others you've done before. This works strongly in favor of the bridge builder, who has the opportunity to use essentially the same bridge design to span a great number of different valleys. Though they may be different lengths and be subject to different forces of nature, the scope of the problem and the design is a lot less than it was the first time that type of bridge was designed. This allows a much greater predictability in the project and helps the bridge designer make accurate estimates of cost and schedule. It also makes it possible for her to point to the last bridge she built and say, "I'll make you one just like that one," which gives her client a much clearer picture than a written proposal, blueprints, or artist's renderings ever could.

Not so with software. Odds are, the product you're trying to build is very different from any other product that's been built before and certainly different from any you and your team have ever built, especially considering the role of emerging technologies, platforms, devices, and media. But even if you're trying to rebuild an existing product that your team is very familiar with, this go-around is nevertheless certain to be "rich in particular facts." If the original product were perfect, you wouldn't be rebuilding it, so the new version probably requires some significant improvements and changes or is operating under differing constraints and priorities.

Since software and software development are complex systems, a changed starting position means everything that follows will be different. Problems that have been solved before will have to be solved again under entirely new circumstances, and chance and friction will play out in new and unexpected ways. This is particularly the case with UX-focused products, because the mandate for better UX changes how every problem is approached and brings in the contributions of people and domains of thought that didn't exist for the previous version.

So, in short, every software project is unique and tremendously different from any other. Each project will have its own wealth of peculiar details, problems, solutions, and inspirations. This is what makes anticipating any approximations of scope and any corresponding estimates of cost and timeline impossible and unreliable, even for the most experienced and professional companies and teams.

But never fear; this doesn't mean that all commitments are impossible or inherently not credible. Solid commitments to schedule and cost are, within the right context, entirely possible. However, commitments to a certain scope are not.

Subjectivity and Change

Change is the inevitable consequence of uncertainty and the unknown. The more that's specified from the outset, the more change there's likely to be as discoveries are made. This change can come from within the project as opportunities, risks, and issues are encountered. It can also come from outside the project as the priorities of your company and stakeholders shift, changing the context and priorities for the project.

Change demanded by stakeholders, however well intentioned or valuable, can be especially pernicious. Here are a number of requests that our happy bridge builder never has to worry about getting midway through the construction process:

- *Can we move the bridge 17 feet to the left? It's only 17 feet, so that's not a big deal, right?*

- *Our CEO just read an article about how a cantilever bridge collapsed in Quebec in 1907, so he's worried about risks you failed to tell us about. Please change the bridge design from cantilever to suspension.*

- *We aren't very happy with how the bridge looks so far. Can you propose a change in the kind of materials you're using to make it more attractive?*

- *The natural gas pipeline that we ran under the bridge without telling you just exploded and partially destroyed the bridge. Why didn't you build it to withstand explosions? Please fix the damage and give it proper reinforcement, coordinate with our gas pipeline vendor, and have everything done within the original timeline and budget.*

- *Remember when you asked us whether the bridge would ever need to support vehicle traffic and not just pedestrian traffic, and we weren't sure, so we just settled on the cheaper pedestrian version? Well, we were wrong. What can you do to make this work for our needs?*

In short, every software project is unique and tremendously different from any other. Each project will have its own wealth of peculiar details, problems, solutions, and inspirations.

- *My nephew is majoring in civil engineering and he says the best, most advanced kind of bridge is a side-spar cable-stayed suspension bridge. I don't really know what that means, but why aren't we getting the most advanced bridge possible?*

- *We've hired an offshore company to start building from the other side of the valley so we can cut the construction time in half. They're making some improvements on your design, so please coordinate with them to make sure everything comes together ahead of schedule.*

In software, scarcely a week goes by without some comparable request coming down from stakeholders. Because most people don't understand how software is built and because it has no material, tangible presence, they don't have any basis for understanding what is hard and what is easy. They tend to think everything is easy. It's obvious that moving a bridge 17 feet to the left is an enormous undertaking, but a comparable change in software can be appreciated only by those building it.

It's also extremely important to remember that success in building software is defined in the minds of your stakeholders, not by the objective value of the product itself. A bridge is a success if it fulfills the original design, spans the valley, and withstands reasonable stressors. But software is often judged with much more subjective criteria by stakeholders. If the final product accomplishes 99 out of 100 goals, but the one missing goal was the pet feature of a key stakeholder, you may have failed. If the product exceeds expectations in every functional dimension but fails to integrate well with the visual standards of your company's brand, you may have failed.

This is why taking control of and maintaining your stakeholders' expectations is pivotal to your success. The one mitigating factor at your disposal, though, is that positive feedback from users can usually trump any stakeholder's misgivings and objections. Usually. Even this factor depends on your ability to cultivate a sense of deference to users in your stakeholders. Educating your stakeholders on the value of UX and user adoption doesn't end once you've gotten them to sign off on a budget for the project; their understanding must be continually maintained. Much of your project's success will depend on managing stakeholder perceptions and expectations, so each chapter in this book offers advice about how to work with stakeholders. The business planning and user research stages discussed in Chapters 5 and 6 are crucial to getting your stakeholders into the right mindset.

Lessons from Uncertainty and the Unknown

The art of war teaches us to rely not on the likelihood of the enemy's not coming, but on our own readiness to receive him; not on the chance of his not attacking, but rather on the fact that we have made our position unassailable.

—Sun Tzu, *The Art of War*

Having accepted that uncertainty, the unknown, and change are unavoidable, you can bring your project to a position of strength in its ability to accommodate them. In fact, you can turn them from threats into a source of value and strength. There are a lot of corollary lessons that become apparent with this new understanding. These lessons strongly underlie how we approach planning, requirements, and process.

The Further You Are in the Project, the Wiser You Are

The entire duration of the project involves the discovery of problems and their solutions and the constant contributions of design and inspiration. As progress moves forward, you gain greater and greater understanding of your users' needs and the possibilities, goals, constraints, and scope of the project as the window of uncertainty closes toward the completion of the project. That greater understanding includes a more complete understanding of and respect for the overwhelming complexity of the project that helps you put things in the proper perspective.

It follows, then, that the later you make a decision in a project, the more likely it is to be the best one by virtue of having been made from a position of greater experience. This is one of the reasons that attempting to comprehensively define the functional requirements of a product on day zero is absurd and futile; that's the day when you know the absolute least about the product, and any decisions you make on that day are very likely to be incorrect and eventually (hopefully) changed. Decisions taken too early and stated as fact rather than conjecture risk preventing informed thought and design from taking place for the betterment of the product.

This means that decisions that can be made later generally should be made later. We'll get into this more as we discuss how to approach realistic requirements, but this understanding demands that the initial requirements for the project be specific and concrete with respect to only what is actually known. They should be silent or permissive on any question that can be answered in the future from a more informed position.

Start Development As Soon As Possible

Development is where the majority of design happens, and design is the activity that discovers unknown problems and their solutions, so development should begin as soon as possible. Remember that, as we discussed in Chapter 1, development isn't the exclusive domain of software engineers. It's the stage where everyone on the project team collaborates to develop a solution. The sooner you begin, the faster the learning comes and the sooner unknown challenges and opportunities are discovered. This is an additional argument against spending a lot of time specifying and planning the project up front, because it means you're spending time and money guessing at the solution when you should be investigating and discovering it.

Written Functional Requirements and Specifications Are Inherently Flawed

Functional requirements and specifications are written before development begins, so they're immediately handicapped by having been made from the least informed perspective. It's also extremely difficult to make an effective language-based description of an experience, interaction, or visual design. And by virtue of their written form, they're never as fluid and dynamic as the project itself. It's pointless to try to keep the written requirements and specifications up to date (which no one ever does, anyway), because then you're just updating them to match what's already happened in development. That defeats the ostensible purpose of specifications guiding development, and there's no point in maintaining a written history of your product as it develops.

The production of detailed written functional requirements and specifications poses a number of other problems:

- *They're usually extraordinarily long and take a very long time to develop, so they delay the start of development and take budget and resources away from the building of the product.*

- *Being so long and so focused on the details and minutiae, they're rarely read in their entirety and make it difficult to see the forest for the trees.*

- *The focus on specificity and detail can in fact cause everyone on the project to lose sight of the big picture (if they had sight of it in the first place) and get caught up in focusing on the details.*

- *They tend to stifle thought and innovation by the development team because they can just follow the letter of the specifications without questioning whether they reflect good decisions and thoughtful approaches.*

- *They usually wind up being an unrealistic laundry list of every possible feature, rather than a studied, thoughtfully scoped product framed by reasonable constraints. This also means that every pet idea and feature of each of your stakeholders will be in the document and will therefore be apparently committed to, leading to potential conflict as unnecessary or infeasible ideas and features fall by the wayside.*

- *They tend to cause stakeholders to think, having spent weeks exhaustively laying out the specifications, that their work is done and all the questions have been answered. This leaves them with a false sense of certainty that you'll later inevitably have to defy, and also means they won't be around to participate during the development phase.*

Our new clients often come to us with a phonebook-size binder of documentation, or ask us to help develop one to satisfy a bureaucratic requirement in their organization. We've even seen clients spend more money on building the specifications than on developing the product itself. Invariably, when we finish a project and look back on the early documentation for it, the documentation and the product bear no resemblance to each other.

Putting together written requirements and specifications is not entirely without value, though, so long as it's perceived in the right way. The goal should not be to build a definitive description of the product, but rather to do a dry run of the product design, to get the team to start thinking through the problems that lie ahead. To quote another famous war strategist:

> *In preparing for battle, I have always found that plans are useless, but planning is indispensable.*
>
> —Dwight Eisenhower

Rather than thinking of early documents and planning as strict requirements, it's more correct and useful to view them as guidelines. They're the encapsulation of the best understanding that existed at the time. This understanding cannot stagnate at such an early stage; it must deepen and improve through the whole course of the project. Setting out initial guidelines from the perspective of the business and the user are the subjects of Chapters 5 and 6, which cover business planning and user research, respectively.

Commitments to Scope Are Untenable

Any estimation of scope, having been defined in the "mere twilight" of the project kickoff or contract negotiation, cannot possibly be accurate. And a comprehensive description of the scope of a project is so enormously complex that it simply can't be done; the only perfect description of a product is the product itself.

If the estimated scope is incorrect and incomplete, any subsequent estimate or commitment will be incorrect and incomplete. This is the root problem of the mistrust that often exists between managers and project teams, or between clients and their software services vendors. Managers look for certainty of scope, schedule, and cost—the so-called three-legged stool—and press for firm commitments to all of them. When scope inevitably changes, it makes the stool teeter off balance. More often than not, you find yourself either face-first on the floor or sitting on a much shorter stool than the one you thought you were building. Neither position is particularly dignified in the eyes of your stakeholders. In our experience, investing in UX yields such tremendous benefits that the period of uncertainty and the flexibility required with respect to the three-legged stool prove to be well worth it when the project ends.

Relish and Respect the Unexpected

Everyone carries a lot of preconceptions and assumptions into and through a project. The application of creativity and intelligence against the challenges, opportunities, and unknowns through the course of the project is bound to take the project down unexpected paths, and to challenge preconceptions about the product's users, its requirements, and the best solutions to key goals and problems. Those who put excessive faith in their own preconceptions or who are averse to the unexpected will find the progress of the project constantly clashing against their expectations and sense of security.

What you get back from the project team is often going to be significantly different from what you expected because the team has gone through an in-depth study and design process. If you have an intelligent, creative, professional team operating in the proper context, its discoveries and solutions should be much more solid than anyone's preconceptions and should therefore be respected and trusted. People involved in the project who are at peace with uncertainty and the unknown will actually come to enjoy unexpected turns and discoveries, because these offer lessons that are valuable beyond the product itself. They are evidence of innovation and effective, creative design at work. And in order to respond effectively to the unexpected without getting bogged down by new questions, the team must learn to respond to unknowns quickly and intelligently. This builds a strength and nimbleness that benefits the whole project.

Intolerance of Uncertainty Is Intolerable

People who oversee software projects have an entirely reasonable need to be able to plan for them in the context of the larger organization and to meet commitments of their own—and that need typically manifests as pressure for certainty. Some certainty can be offered, but some things are impervious to certainty. This is an immovable fact, as we've gone to great lengths to explain so far in this chapter. Unfortunately, it's extremely difficult to convince anyone who hasn't been in the trenches of software development of this fact. Too often, those people mistakenly view a person who humbly and wisely recognizes reality as being mealy-mouthed and resistant to accountability.

Intolerance of uncertainty causes very serious problems. It pressures project leaders to present things as certain when they should know they're not, setting up future conflict and injuries to credibility. It also tends to cause project leaders and team members to be overly optimistic in their projections as they try to offer pleasing answers to their stakeholders. As the project progresses and the weaknesses of their projections become apparent, the project team will often hold the stakeholder at a distance, in the hope they can scramble to pull off a last-minute miracle. This means that challenges to the project that should have been identified and disclosed as soon as they happened accumulate until the end. At that point, it's too late for the stakeholder to help or make adjustments, and they're blindsided by failure and disappointment.

> Intolerance of uncertainty can cause some serious problems. It pressures project leaders to present things as certain when they should know they're not.

It's certainly the responsibility of the project leader and team to act more responsibly than this, but it's very difficult to build a product in an environment of intolerance of uncertainty. Anything you can do to help stakeholders understand how to create the right climate of accountability and realistic expectations (giving them a copy of this book, perhaps?) will go a long way to ensure a successful project. The project's focus on delivering superior UX quality provides a helpful star by which to help people navigate. Ultimately, the project and your company are accountable to the needs of the user as an objective point of reference. Continually reorienting the team and the stakeholders to the UX goals of the project can help you slough off unreasonable expectations, focus on what's important, and take the best advantage of the unknowns as they arise.

Effective Requirements

Requirements need to be of a nature and in a form that allow them to adapt and remain useful and relevant through the winding course of the project. This is why the most useful approach is to think of the requirements as a framework for answering questions rather than a catalog of answers. The framework, if devised properly, will be stable because it will be composed only of knowable goals and constraints and not of solutions or designs that will be subject to future design and change. It should also be wide enough to allow room for a variety of successful outcomes (success is a range, not a single point) but narrow enough to fence out most unsuccessful outcomes. The framework requirements can be pictured as a frame describing the bounds of a successful solution.

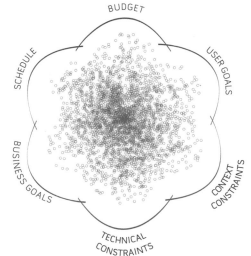

Figure 3-1. Framework requirements describing the bounds of a successful solution

In this visualization, the dense area represents the successfulness of the solution, while the constraining boundaries represent the framework requirements. This portrays a very effective set of framework requirements because the framework encompasses barely more than the most successful solutions, is wide enough that it encompasses all possible successful solutions, and is dead on center so that the tendency will be for answers to questions to also find their way to the center.

Throughout the course of the project, thousands of little questions and decisions will need to be made for which there won't yet be an explicit answer. These questions are like rubber balls tossed into the framework; they bounce from wall to wall and tend to arrive near the center. Thus a successful framework provides not the answers to every question, but the design parameters for how team members can themselves discover answers and make decisions, large and small, through the course of the project.

The framework requirements—being a set of constraining parameters rather than a list of answers—are a description of the problem and not of the solution. In our experience, most companies planning a new product haven't had a chance to develop a solid understanding of the problem they're trying to solve, let alone how they'll solve it. A phonebook-size binder of requirements documentation represents an exhaustive attempt to accurately define a solution. But, as you've learned in this chapter, that view of the solution is guaranteed to be inaccurate. This approach is an attempt to answer every question before the real work of design has had a chance to begin.

Recognizing that the purpose of requirements is to define the problem and not the solution, all efforts should be made to ensure that guesses at the solution don't wind up becoming parameters in the framework requirements. The framework parameters need to be entirely reasonable, accurate, and stable, but they also need to be flexible and restrained. When guesses at the solution are built into the framework, they risk being wrong and falsely limiting or misleading design decisions, undermining the value of the framework itself.

It's a hallmark of good framework requirements that they remain stable and unchanging through the project, because it means they haven't crossed the line into areas reserved for the design of the product. The closest analog for good framework requirements is the U.S. Constitution, because it's general and flexible enough to provide a framework for answering questions that the founding fathers could never have possibly foreseen, and yet remains a resilient foundation for democracy, stability, and the rights of citizens.

How Framework Requirements Are Built

The great news about framework requirements is that they don't require 12 weeks of Sisyphean planning efforts and documentation the length of *War and Peace*. While clients often come to us with their own first attempts at requirements, the first part of a project is still spent building the framework requirements.

The process of building framework requirements involves investigating each of its key parameters, and then distilling the findings of those investigations into a form that can be easily used and understood by everyone on the project. The parameters that go into a project's framework vary from case to case, but they generally fall into three categories:

- *The needs of the business*
- *The needs of the user*
- *The technical and infrastructural constraints*

The framework shown earlier in Figure 3-1, for example, was composed of six example parameters:

- *Business goals*
- *Schedule*
- *Budget*
- *User goals*
- *Context constraints*
- *Technical constraints*

In the next three chapters, you will learn how the business, user needs, platform and context constraints, and technical constraints are investigated, distilled, understood, and communicated to form a usable, realistic framework of requirements.

Extending the requirements

The essence of building a software product is an ongoing evolution and deepening of the team's understanding of the requirements through ongoing design, with engineering following close behind. The framework requirements are a starting place and become, as the project progresses, the exterior frame within which tighter and tighter frameworks of understanding are developed.

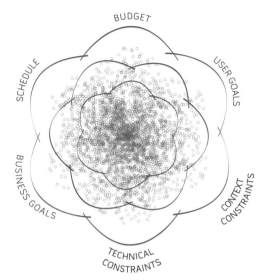

Figure 3-2. Extending the framework requirements

Each step of the project, including the design and engineering work that go into building it, are elements of an ongoing investigation of what the product should be. Every document that's produced, every meeting that's conducted, and every bit of design that's done is oriented at honing the collective understanding of the product. The result should be an increasingly narrow, multifaceted, and accurate view of the requirements with an ever-decreasing area of uncertainty. The final product represents the moment when all is known and all questions have been answered, and so would be a single, perfectly round point at the center.

Reexamining the Three-Legged Stool

The fact that commitments to scope are untenable seems to fly in the face of the managers' need to have a reasonable degree of certainty of what they'll be getting. But not basing commitments on a specific, early guess at scope actually gives them a greater degree of certainty, so long as they trust you and the project team.

Errors in and changes to a scope commitment can have a wide effect on a project. The scope may prove to be overambitious given the budget and schedule available, forcing the project leader to go back to his stakeholders to revise scope or get more money and time. Ambiguous or largely inaccurate initial guesses at scope can cause a project to run far off in the wrong direction, requiring scope to be cut or money and time to be added to bring it back on course. Overwhelmingly long and specific scope documents can fail to carry through the company's and the stakeholders' overall vision for the product, leading to a product that disappoints and may require more time and money to bring up to suitability.

So, in short, by forcing a commitment to an early guess at scope, managers are, in fact, contributing to the peril that all of commitments they were relying on will be challenged and changed. The reason for this becomes very obvious if viewed in the form a pseudo-equation for the traditional three-legged stool of committed scope, schedule, and cost:[4]

```
product = f( scope & schedule & cost )
```

The problem here is that whereas schedule and cost are known, scope is not. This means this equation is inherently unsolvable until scope is known. As we've said, the only true and full definition of the scope of a product is the product itself, a fact that would make this the case:

```
product = scope
```

And invoking the rule of equivalence, we end up with:

```
product = f( product & schedule & cost )
```

---

4 The ampersand (&) is a logical symbol, but is being applied very loosely here—as a placeholder, essentially—because the way the variables are related isn't knowable and isn't important to the argument being made.

The only way this equation is meaningful is if schedule and cost have no effect whatsoever. But schedule and cost are certainly key factors that will go to define and limit the product. In fact, it should be uncontroversial to leave scope out of the picture and say that the product will be some function of schedule and cost:

```
product = f( schedule & cost )
```

Then we follow a simple chain of logic that leads to a happier place:

```
product = f( schedule & cost )
    &
product = scope
    therefore
product = scope = f( schedule & cost )
```

In the end, the fact that scope is unknowable until the completion of the project means that the notion of scope is unusable as a defining parameter for the product. The project's requirements must be a function only of knowable variables, of which scope is not one.

This is a fact that's acknowledged and successfully addressed by the framework approach to requirements. The unknown value of product is ultimately solvable by a study of the parameters that represent its constraints, which are variables that all have known values. The example framework presented earlier in the chapter would, for example, have a pseudo-equation like this:

```
product = scope =  f( schedule & cost & business_goals & user_goals
    & platform_and_context_constraints & technical_constraints )
```

Every variable of which the product and scope are a function is knowable, and therefore the equation is solvable. Schedule and cost can be dictated by managers; business goals are fixed during business planning (see Chapter 5); user goals and context constraints are discovered during user research (Chapter 6); and the technical constraints are found during the initial product architecture stage (Chapter 7).

It's also somewhat of a change to view schedule and cost not as flexible factors influenced by scope, but rather as fixed, constraining parameters. Software projects can generally be made to fit within or expand to nearly any reasonable budget size; it's just a question of how ambitious you want to make them, how detailed you allow things to get, how richly designed you can allow them to be, how you choose and allocate resources, and so on. Clients often come to us with requirements documentation and ask us to prepare an estimate based on it, but everything in the documentation except the high-level business requirements is frankly irrelevant, because we know it will change. The more important questions are: how much are you willing to spend on this product, and when do you need it by? The answers to those questions give a much, much clearer picture of what the true scope of the project will ultimately be.

Approaching projects in this way requires a big leap of trust on the part of the client or stakeholders, though, so often it's not an option. We typically make cost and schedule estimates as best we can based on whatever constraining variables we've been permitted to know about, and then work with our client to hone the estimates to fit their actual constraints. Though these cost and schedule estimates may be based on early requirements documentation, once these estimates have been approved they supplant the requirement documentation as part of the framework requirements.

So what does this all mean for the three-legged stool? In the stool metaphor, the stool is the product, which is, as we've just demonstrated, also the scope. So to say the stool rests on scope, schedule, and cost is to say the stool is resting, in part, on itself. This is a paradox worthy of a mind like M.C. Escher's, but is hardly proper territory for a software product. The stool sits not on scope, schedule, and cost, but rather on schedule, cost, and any other constraining parameter.

Commitments You Can Live Up To

All of this may require an enormous mental shift for you, but once you do it, you'll find you can make commitments with a much greater degree of confidence and reliability. What you should be committing to is fidelity to the constraints—the framework parameters—for the product. Luckily, two of those constraints are cost and schedule, and being able to make confident commitments to those two will go a long way toward reassuring managers and stakeholders. The remainder of your commitment is not that the product will conform to some preordained scope, but rather that it will satisfy the needs of the business and its high-level criteria for success and will satisfy the needs of the user. Who could object to that?

The trick then becomes making sure that the needs of the business and the user have been well understood and are reasonably construed. Once they are, they become an essential part of the basis of your commitment. Rather than requiring certainty of scope, your stakeholders should hold you accountable to the project's fidelity to its business and user constraints. This makes it important that stakeholders are in agreement with and have signed off on those constraints, which is why we spend a lot of time discussing stakeholder buy-in throughout this book.

Effective Process

The process by which software gets developed is just as much guided by uncertainty and the unknown as the requirements are. This is for two principal reasons:

- *Design happens in the context of the unknown through the whole course of the project, so the project's process must support successful design that leads to correct decisions and outcomes.*

- *The actual destination of the project (the final product) is unknown up to the end, so the process must ensure that there is a minimum of off-course meandering before you arrive.*

We should be clear at this point to explain what we *don't* mean when we say "process." Some people seem to believe that the software development process is like an instruction manual; if you follow all of the instructions to the letter, you'll end up with a successful product. In our experience, that kind of "process" is a dangerous myth. Remembering that software and software development are complex and peculiar systems, no instruction manual could possibly exist that would cover every possible project. There's also a risk with this type of thinking that project teams will view their success not in terms of the success and quality of the product itself, but rather in terms of how well they followed the process and whether they did a good job of producing process-mandated documentation on time.

People are also often under the misapprehension that, as with an instruction manual, the software development process is a serial progression of discrete steps. This view is very appealing to managers and stakeholders because it gives them a sort of timetable for what progress and deliverables to expect and also lets them know when they need to pay attention. Unfortunately, it's just not that simple.

Good software development process addresses the effects of uncertainty and the unknown that we just identified. It supports successful continuous design to ensure good decisions and outcomes, keeps the project headed in the right direction with a minimum of course deviations, and keeps all of the key contributors participating in design through the full course of the project. These three goals are supported by combining proper methodology with effective tools and techniquess.

Development Methodology

It's perilous for us to tread into the realm of software development methodology, but there's no way around it. Software professionals often have very strong opinions on what constitutes good versus bad methodology, in some cases exhibiting cult-like adulation of some specific approach and complete intolerance of differing views.

In our experience, no one methodology suits every possible project. The infinite variety and peculiarity of projects makes this conclusion rather obvious. Every different, specific methodology has well-reasoned underpinnings. When you're acquainted with that reasoning, you can figure out what's best for a given project.

Waterfall

The waterfall methodology is the most familiar to people because it's the most widely employed and also seems to make the most intuitive sense. As shown in Figure 3-3, it proposes that software be built in a sequence of major steps—usually business requirements, design requirements, development, then deployment—each of which is entirely completed before the next one begins.

Figure 3-3. A basic waterfall process

The supposed strength of waterfall is that it seems to provide a great deal of clarity and certainty through each step of the project. It's appealing to managers because it suggests that once the brainstorming is done and the requirements have been built, everything else follows naturally.

The flaws with this approach should already be obvious, but before we get into that, it's worthwhile to point out that waterfall is actually an effective approach for some types of projects. Waterfall is efficient and effective for products that represent minimal design and engineering complexity, or that are cookie-cutter implementations of well-understood solutions. We would employ this approach if, for example, we were building a calculator application. A calculator is very simple to build, and there are very few questions that need to be answered about the calculator's features (what it should look like, whether it should be basic or scientific, whether it should include memory functions, and so on) before development begins. The answers to any design questions are readily obtained in advance and are highly certain.

But no one ever asks us to build calculators. If that's what you're working on, you should quit reading this book and just go build the darn thing.

For any other project, waterfall's fatal flaw is its total failure to account for uncertainty and the unknown. It presumes that each step can be entirely and perfectly completed before the next step begins. We've devoted a great deal of this chapter teaching you what a huge mistake this is; running down the list of problems with this approach would be beating an already quite dead horse.

There are, however, two other serious problems with this approach that we've touched on only briefly so far:

- *Because each step is entirely separate, each group of contributors is entirely siloed from the others. The people brainstorming and writing requirements for the product never collaborate with the people architecting and designing it. The software engineers never have the opportunity to collaborate with the architects and designers, let alone the business managers and stakeholders. Collaboration across all disciplines is absolutely critical to the building of great software, as we'll discuss shortly.*

- *This approach forces the engineering and quality assurance (QA) stages to absorb almost all of the effects of the risks and unknowns that arise during the project. Since the planning, architecture, and design of the product are already ostensibly complete, there's no option for changes to them because the money for them has already been spent and the resources have been allocated to other things. This leaves it to the engineers to figure out how to account for the inevitable unforeseen problems and unknowns—and to do it within the budget and timeline they were allocated before the problems and unknowns were identified.*

This is why it so often seems like a beautifully conceived and designed product gets hacked and compromised into severe mediocrity by the engineers. They aren't being lazy or incompetent; they're simply delivering what they can despite being left to absorb the full brunt of risk and the unknown on their own. That they are likely to have made compromises and hacks that the stakeholders and designers disagree with is just one more reason why waterfall's tendency to silo resources is such a terrible problem.

Big Design Up Front

The term Big Design Up Front (BDUF) is shorthand, often used as a pejorative for a sort of methodology that's similar to waterfall but takes a meaningful step in the right direction. As the name suggests, BDUF essentially involves large upfront design efforts before engineering and QA begin. It differs from waterfall, however, in acknowledging that not all design occurs up front and some design (in the form of resources, budget, and prerogative) must be reserved for the engineering and QA phase.

BDUF accounts for waterfall's tragic central fallacy that each step can be made perfect before the next begins, but it does so rather weakly: it suggests that the design step can be made nearly perfect before development begins.

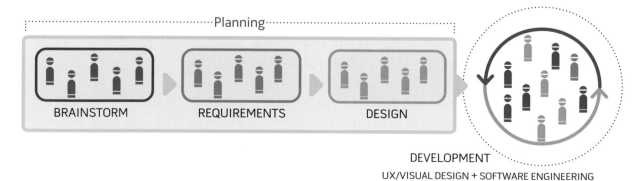

Figure 3-4. Big Design Up Front

Proponents of BDUF suggest that planning a product on paper and on whiteboards before engineering begins saves time and cost throughout the rest of the project because it's easier to change requirements and sketches than it is to change actual code. This is absolutely true; only proponents of the most anarchic, cowboy methodologies would ever argue that No Design Up Front is a sensible approach. The problem with BDUF, though, is in the "Big."

BDUF tends to require that too much design be done up front. It still treats design largely as a discrete phase that begins and ends before the actual development of the product begins. Upfront design efforts suffer from the absence of any of the understanding about risk, opportunity, and the unknown that come through the engineering effort, and through development more broadly. Upfront design is also typically done without the assistance of software engineers, who should be present to assess the cost and feasibility of certain ideas and to contribute ideas from their unique perspective. The early days of the project are when the least is understood about the project, so the more design work done during that period, the more likely that work will be off base. This all means that significant portions of the big upfront investment in design will be wasted, depriving the rest of the duration of the project of valuable design resources and budget, and delaying the commencement of actually building the product.

Like waterfall, this approach also promotes a false sense of certainty in stakeholders and siloes resources from each other. Stakeholders tend to participate only in the upfront design process, and UX designers participate in the development stage only to the extent that their budget and time weren't expended up front.

But the fact that experience designers participate in the development stage at all is a huge step in the right direction. It's an acknowledgment that unknowns and problems will be uncovered for which collaboration with experience designers will be beneficial, and acknowledges to a degree that the initial designs will need to be adapted and modified.

Truth be told, BDUF is a methodology EffectiveUI is frequently compelled to employ, despite our preference to do otherwise. This is because we are a professional services company that builds products for other companies, and those companies have a very reasonable need to understand what to expect from us and to be reassured that we understand their needs and know what we're doing.

In the absence of a trusting relationship built on a long history of partnership and successes, we can't ask a client to just give us a budget, timeline, and a high-level understanding of their goals and trust us to build them something they'll love. That approach can work very well—that's essentially how we developed an extraordinarily successful partnership with eBay to build eBay Desktop[5]—but it requires a degree of trust and latitude that's rarely available in any project, let alone a first engagement with a new vendor. Whether you're building your product for a client or for your own company, the same considerations of credibility and trust will probably pressure your process toward BDUF.

What BDUF offers in this circumstance is the opportunity to work intensively with stakeholders to translate their business and user needs into a comprehensive set of visual experience design requirements. At the end of the upfront design effort, the stakeholders are given a thorough stack of visually rich documentation that demonstrates that their needs have been heard and understood, that they're working with a professional and qualified team, and that the team has a strong understanding of the product's requirements and the road ahead. This stack of documentation is often what's used to unlock the remainder of the budget for the project or to seek buy-in from higher levels of the management ladder. BDUF projects are also easier to sell, because they allow stakeholders to sign off on a smaller design project before committing to the larger full project.

The problem with BDUF is that it generally keeps the engineers on the bench, in the dark, and out of the conversation for too long. A great number of unknowns, problems, and opportunities can be identified and solved through an exhaustive upfront design process, but until engineering begins, a vast, rocky sea of the unknown remains unexplored. Additionally, without the benefit of the engineers' input, promises and estimates can be made that will later prove to be impossible or unrealistic, leading to disappointments and increased tensions.

Like waterfall, BDUF also has the tendency to suggest a higher degree of certainty than can actually be obtained through early design efforts. In some

5 With an eBay account, you can play with this application by downloading it from *http://desktop.ebay.com*.

cases, managers and stakeholders try to use this apparent certainty as a means of "exposing" their engineering team—that is, of putting the engineering team in a position of being isolated and solely responsible for the completion of the project. This tactic is calculated to increase accountability for the engineering team, but its true effect is to make all teams less effective and put an undue burden of risk and strain on the engineering team.

As EffectiveUI's stature and commensurate credibility in our market have grown, we've been able to reduce the amount of upfront design required to reassure our clients. Your success in moving in this direction will also be dependent on your credibility, which is why so much of this book is dedicated to the subjects of maintaining enthusiastic buy-in and building credibility with your stakeholders.

Agile with a capital "A"

Agile is the name of a broad set of methodologies that arose from frustrated software engineers who were trying to find more effective approaches to their work than the traditional, failing ones. Despite its origins in software engineering, the concepts of Agile are very applicable to the entire product development process. The integration of UX design into Agile processes is a somewhat new frontier of thought in software methodology.

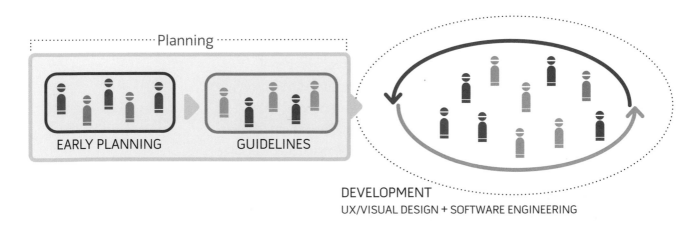

Figure 3-5. Agile processes in UX design

Unfortunately, some people already have a bad taste in their mouths left over from previous encounters with Agile devotees. The problem with Agile is that it has some very overzealous supporters who insist that Agile concepts are the panacea for every possible software woe. These people may dogmatically enforce some particular purist submethod of Agile to the great detriment of the project and the sanity of its team. There is no single right answer, no perfect methodology that can address the full range of projects and problems in the world. Just as software projects have no room for false certainty in features, they have no room for false faith and dogma in methodologies.

But notwithstanding its outspoken supporters, Agile concepts contain a great deal of wisdom born of a long history of experience. Many people have a passing familiarity with some of the offspring of the Agile movement, such as Extreme Programming (XP) and Scrum, but not with the Agile Manifesto itself. The fact that it's called a manifesto may seem to bode poorly (think Unibomber), but bear with it.

MANIFESTO FOR AGILE SOFTWARE DEVELOPMENT

We are uncovering better ways of developing software by doing it and helping others do it. Through this work we have come to value:

- Individuals and interactions over processes and tools
- Working software over comprehensive documentation
- Customer collaboration over contract negotiation
- Responding to change over following a plan

That is, while there is value in the items on the right, we value the items on the left more.[6]

This aligns very tidily with everything we've discussed so far in this chapter. At the heart of Agile is the acknowledgment of uncertainty and the unknown, which requires that flexibility, collaboration, and thoughtfulness be favored over rigid commitments and the stunting and segregation of design and thought.

6 *http://www.agilemanifesto.org/*

Effective development methodology

What, then, is EffectiveUI's solution to the methodology question? We've been successful in building superlative products using a broad range of methodologies, and that experience has brought about a lot of ideas from many of our team members. The difficulty in proposing an EffectiveUI methodology is the fact that no single methodology will work in every circumstance. We're also living very much on the cutting edge of this sort of thinking, and anything concrete we propose at the time of writing this book is bound to be outdated by the time the book goes to press.

We espouse, therefore, not a specific, patent-pending methodology, but rather a set of principles and best practices. Like the framework approach to requirements, good principles can guide successful thought and progress and stay relevant as the domain of thought progresses. The rest of this book is dedicated to sharing those principles and showing them at work, with a specific emphasis on development methodology (coming up in Chapter 8). If it seems like we've spent most of this chapter breaking you down without building you back up, please bear with us.

If you return to our discussion of the definitions of "design" and "development" at the end of Chapter 1, you'll note that we mean development to be inclusive of every professional discipline, including stakeholders, the project leader, UX architects, visual designers, and software engineers. A huge part of what makes taking a restrained approach to upfront planning and minimizing wasteful upfront design efforts so important is that it frees up room for a larger, more inclusive development stage. The ideal setting for building great UX is one where the business leaders, designers, UX architects, and software engineers are all working in tandem and actively collaborating to build the product. This can't happen if each group's contributions are segregated into discrete phases. Working closely together as part of one large development team allows everyone to benefit from the learning that occurs during its course, and to contribute to the decision making that responds to unknowns, problems, and opportunities.

For the sake of avoiding redundancy, we're leaving the greater part of the discussion of the development cycle for Chapter 8. But that chapter is very much a sister chapter to this one, since all of the concepts we discuss regarding how to handle the approach, methodology, and planning for the product are mostly aimed at creating a fertile ground in which development can occur. So, if you're curious and want to continue exploring this line of thinking in more depth, you may consider jumping ahead to that chapter.

Efficiency and the unknown

It may seem at first blush that a project at the mercy of uncertainty and the unknown will be inefficient to produce and, therefore, more expensive. Compared to the nonexistent project where all things are known and there is no uncertainty, a real-world project will certainly be less efficient. If you know exactly where you're going, you'll naturally take the straightest path there. But since that sort of certainty is never available, the efficiency of a project will be a function of how well you account for uncertainty and the unknown. Clinging to false certainty is a surefire recipe for enormous waste.

Consider again a project assigned to two equally qualified teams. One team is managed using a waterfall process and the other using a more nimble framework requirements–driven process. The course of each team's progress toward the same destination might look like what's shown in Figure 3-6.

Team waterfall's first step is to start executing an in-depth plan that, by virtue of having been developed in a "mere twilight," has them heading in the wrong direction. They don't discover this until they finish, present the results, and fail to please. They then do more extensive planning to identify how the product needs to be modified to reach success. That plan leads them closer to success, but not quite all the way, resulting in two more planning and building cycles.

Team agile, on the other hand, zigzags along the course to success. Each time they pause and assess the situation, they see that they are off course and make a correction. Further, each time they make a correction they're further along in the project and are therefore able to make better decisions about course adjustments, so the distance of each deviation gets smaller each time.

And this doesn't even account for the time team waterfall spends planning. Nor does this reflect the fact that it's much more time-consuming to refactor large volumes of code that were written over a long period of time than it is to make adjustments to small bits of code that were recently written. When you add this all up, the efficiency of an agile approach in the context of the unknown is clear.

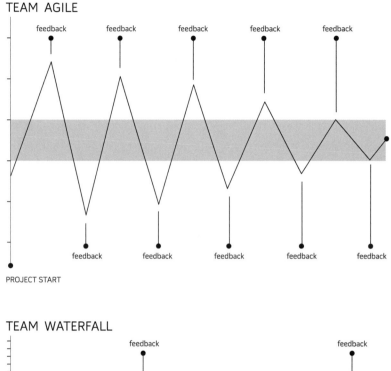

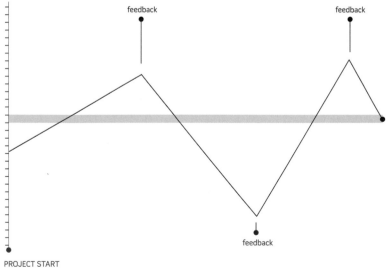

Figure 3-6. Comparing methodology development pathways

Chapter 4
Bringing Together a Team

Since the entire course of your project will involve the application of intellect to identifying and solving problems, the capabilities and aptitudes of your team members (stakeholders included) will be the single greatest contributor to the success of your project. No amount of process, no brilliant development methodology, and no force or aptitude of management can bring about as much success as a talented, driven team can. That is, unfortunately, one of the weaknesses of what we're able to offer through this book. We can provide roadmaps, strategies, and tactics to help you find your way through the project, but if the people applying those concepts and doing the design and development work aren't adequately creative and qualified, you'll be swimming against the current the whole time.

Of all the things EffectiveUI has figured out how to do well over the years, hiring amazing people was our first priority and has remained our principal focus. We've been very fortunate in being able to attract some of the top people in our field, because our company works on the cutting edge of this domain and is able to provide a more challenging, user-focused alternative to talented people. All of the learning that's described in this book has been developed through putting those people together in challenging situations.

But most people don't have the opportunity to access a pool of specialized, highly qualified individuals. You may be cobbling together a project team from various departments in an organization, or working with an IT team that is more accustomed to maintaining legacy applications than building new ones. The only designers available may be print and brand designers from your marketing department. You may have access to terrific developers, but no access to UX design professionals, or vice versa. The single most important thing you can do to help the success of your project along is to get the best possible team assembled, so vigorously addressing deficiencies should be a top priority.

That advice really bears repeating on its own and in boldface:

The single most important thing you can do is to get the best possible team assembled.

Given the difficult constraints you and your company are probably operating under, this may not seem like particularly useful advice on its face. Good people are expensive and hard to find, so the cost and scheduling constraints for your project may seem to prevent you from being picky about who you have working on it. But this is one among many ways in software development where it's easy to be penny-wise and pound-foolish.

Cheaper, more readily available resources are that way for a reason: they're less experienced and qualified. These deficiencies, in turn, cause the development of the product to be less effectively performed and less efficient. Less experienced people can't anticipate or address issues as effectively as pros. They make progress more slowly, produce lower-quality results, make more mistakes, and are less capable of making estimates and hitting goals. The burden of all of those problems accumulates over the course of the project, leading to a higher chance of low-quality results or outright failure.

It's important to appreciate the enormous complexity and difficulty of building a software product and not discount the skill it takes to succeed at it. If you're building a skyscraper, you wouldn't consider hiring a bunch of day laborers to do the job. Their progress would come much, much more slowly, and their lack of experience would lead to problems in the project that would cause massive ripple effects and impose enormous risk. It is exactly the same with software.

So if you're stuck thinking, "I can't afford to hire highly trained professionals for every position," consider whether you can afford less-qualified professionals who underdeliver, fail to meet expectations, develop an unstable system, overrun your budget, or simply fail. Experienced professionals may be more expensive per hour, but they'll require fewer hours to produce stronger, higher-quality work, and the six weeks you might have to spend finding them will be more than made up for by the risk and difficulty you will have averted.

The Project Leader

The role of the project leader is not well understood, so it's too often left unfilled. There may be a primary stakeholder who provides oversight and answers questions, or process-oriented project managers charged with managing the schedule and budget, but they aren't what the project needs as a leader. Effective project leaders have a unique and multifaceted role:

- *They are managed by the stakeholders, but they must manage the stakeholders.*
- *They manage the project team, but they serve the project team in their drive to make progress.*
- *They stand for firm fidelity to the business and user requirements, but they fight to preserve a rational approach to uncertainty and the unknown.*
- *They carry the high-level vision for the product and are a living encyclopedia of the cumulative knowledge developed throughout the project.*

The project leader is the standard bearer for the project, charged with ensuring its success, no matter what obstacles the project may face.

Relationship to the Product

An effective project leader fully owns the product—its requirements, its challenges, and its outcomes—by staying deeply immersed and engaged in the project through its entire course. No one else involved in the project will have the opportunity to consistently stay at this level. The project team will be busy solving specific problems and implementing specific functionality, so they can have difficulty keeping the whole product in mind and staying focused on its high-level goals, mission, and criteria for success. Stakeholders have many other priorities to attend to and can't keep their minds engaged with the project. They can't keep up to date with the project's day-to-day discoveries and challenges, which makes it hard for them to make informed decisions.

Only a person who lives in a state of high-level, long-view orientation with low-level, daily engagement can successfully hold the vision for the product together, liaise between the needs of the business and the practical realities affecting the project, and effectively guide successful decision making. This is a very time-consuming role that requires a passionate commitment to the project's success and a deep immersion in its minutiae.

Relationship to the Stakeholders

As previously mentioned, the project leader is in the unusual position of being accountable to and managed by the stakeholders, but also of needing to manage and exert a certain level of control over those stakeholders. To the stakeholders, who have limited contact with the project team, the project leader is the individual representative of the project. The stakeholders look to the project leader to provide them with an understanding of progress and to apply the pressures of accountability. To the project leader, the stakeholders are the guardians of precious information about the business's needs, the product's users, and specifics of different facets of the business that influence the product. Stakeholders are also the gateway to resources.

Stakeholders must participate wholeheartedly, constructively, and capably in the project, and they'll need prodding and guidance from the project leader to do that. If the project leader can't induce stakeholders to participate in a helpful way, the stakeholders will represent a huge source of risk for the project.

Because the project leader is the project's ambassador to the stakeholders, her credibility and trustworthiness with them is of tremendous importance. The stakeholders are entrusting the project leader with costly resources, with the task of solving a critical business problem, and with representing their interests through the course of the project. The better the project leader's credibility is, the more willing the stakeholders are to provide resources, to be deferential with respect to the project leader's assertions about the processes and constraints that guide the project, and to allow the project leader wide latitude in making decisions on their behalf. The project team must be able to rely on the project leader for quick and reliable answers to questions, which requires trust on the part of stakeholders to allow the project leader to make those decisions autonomously at times. There are many opportunities to build trust with the stakeholders through effective facilitation of the project, which we will discuss in the coming chapters.

The project leader needs to educate, guide, and manage the stakeholders through the product development process. Stakeholders will be experts in whatever field and domain of the business they're representing, but may have little or no experience in developing innovative software products. Since the process is often counterintuitive and requires patience and restraint, the project leader's credibility is again of critical importance to helping the stakeholders understand the project's progress and how to best support it.

Stakeholders usually don't understand how software is built and don't have an intimate understanding of the state of the project, so they can interfere in the project in inadvertently problematic ways and represent a source of risk. But stakeholder interference should never be an excuse for failure. The project leader is responsible for the project's success and must defend it from any source of friction and risk, even if that source is her own superiors. No excuse matters if a project fails or falls short of expectations. The project leader must recognize her comprehensive responsibility and accountability and seize control of everything influencing the project, stakeholders included.

The project leader may also act as a moderator and facilitator for events and exercises that involve the participation of stakeholders. Because of their differing positions and backgrounds, stakeholders are likely to have diverse and sometimes contradictory opinions. It's the responsibility of the project leader to corral stakeholders' opinions toward actionable consensus and ensure that stakeholders don't impede the momentum of the project.

If project team members are pulled from a variety of departments in the company, the project leader may also find herself accountable to the managers of those departments, regardless of whether those managers themselves are involved in the project. It's extremely important to the success of a project that the project team is working toward, and is accountable to, the project's goals. When the team is comprised of employees from different departments, they might act as agents of their departments rather than as members of the project team. Their responsibilities to their respective departments also might strain their ability to give the project the attention it requires. So it falls to the project leader to act as an intermediary between project team members and their respective departments and managers. The project leader must reassure managers that their resources are being put to good use and ensure team members feel free to focus on the project. As well, department managers who aren't active stakeholders in a project might nevertheless try to influence it by way of project team members. The project leader needs to recognize this and step between the team member and the manager to retain control of the project and stakeholder expectations.

Relationship to the Project Team

A project leader needs to be deeply immersed in the project and embedded in the project team. Stakeholders and process-oriented project managers tend to manage teams with a certain degree of distance and abstraction. The project leader, on the other hand, must be on the ground with the project team, working with them through every critical decision and staying abreast of the current state of progress, risk, thinking, uncertainty, and unresolved questions. It's only through this active level of involvement that the project leader can effectively guide decision making, keep the project team focused on the high-level goals, and have a total, accurate understanding of the state of the project. This total understanding is critical for her ability to make accurate commitments to stakeholders and to maintain the delicate alignment of expectations and reality.

The project leader is in yet another dichotomous position in relation to the project team. Because she is accountable to the stakeholders and to the success of the project, the project leader must manage and guide the project team toward a successful outcome, but she is also there to support to the project team. Designers and engineers working on innovative projects need quick, decisive answers to thousands of tough questions; many of those answers can be provided rapidly and correctly only by someone who is responsible to the stakeholders and the high-level goals of the project and is also familiar with the low-level details. As the project team wades deep into the details of the project, the project leader needs to ensure that they don't lose sight of the project's high-level goals and that their decision making is guided by the framework requirements.

Who Should Be the Project Leader

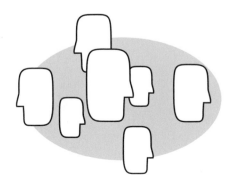

The nature of the project leader's role likely means there are few people in your organization who are both capable and available to do it. The person filling the role must have a strong degree of trust and credibility within the organization, and those people typically don't have time to lead a project. For most projects, the role of the project leader is at least a half-time focus.

Your project may already be spearheaded by someone who can fill this role, making the choice automatic. If that's not the case, you may look to someone from the department or business unit at the head of the project for someone who can fill this role. If your organization has UX or CX specialists on staff, they may also be a good choice.

A project leader should:

- *Have the time available to devote to the project*
- *Be passionate about the project and dedicated to its success*
- *Have the humility necessary to allow her to facilitate a process that will be guided more by other people's ideas and vision than her own*
- *Excel at motivating people and enabling their success*
- *Have the trust, credibility, or clout necessary to wrangle stakeholders*

The project leader's role is very much like that of an entrepreneur. It's a role that requires passion and an ability to preserve a focus on vision and goals while attending to all of the tiny details. The success or failure of the project is entirely the project leader's responsibility, even though other people do almost all of the work necessary to succeed.

If you're working with a third-party vendor for UX design and development services, it may also be an option to have one of their UX designers, interaction designers, or product managers fill this role. This can be a challenging choice, though, since the project leader must have credibility and trust with the stakeholders and latitude to make decisions on their behalf. Representatives from vendors are usually treated with cautious distrust if there isn't a strong history of partnership between the two companies. On the other hand, the representative's extensive experience in product development may be a credibility-strengthening quality that isn't available from within the organization.

As a matter of convenience, throughout this book we'll assume that "you," the reader, are responsible for helping to lead the project, whether as the project leader or as a key contributor.

The Stakeholders

Every project has a set of stakeholders, whether or not they're all immediately identifiable; many more people will try to influence the project than will be willing to actively participate in it. For professional service companies, stakeholders are almost always representatives of the client, but those representatives have their own stakeholders. For internal projects, stakeholders are those people who control the budget, the resources, the mandate, and the domain knowledge that fuels the product's development.

The participation of stakeholders is essential to a project's success, but there are many ways that stakeholders can unintentionally hinder the project. Most stakeholders aren't familiar with how innovative, UX-driven software products are built and can at times unwittingly behave in ways that derail progress or interfere with good decision making. It's important, therefore, that the relationship between the stakeholders and the project is set up for success, and that the stakeholders are aware of how they can best support the project's progress while still having their interests attended to.

The project team relies on stakeholders to provide a thorough and stable understanding of the project's goals and its user base. As the development of the product begins and design encounters unknowns, a steady stream of difficult questions arise. It's critical to the progress of a project that answers to those questions can be readily obtained and are firm and reliable. From the beginning of the project through its end, the project team relies on stakeholders (by way of the project leader) to provide reliable, steady direction for the product. Stakeholders need to provide clarity that diminishes uncertainty and risk, rather than increasing uncertainty and risk through frequent changes and unstable decisions.

Securing Authority

Since the decisions and direction provided by the stakeholders to the project team need to be stable and reliable, the authority of the stakeholders to commit the project along specific lines also must be stable and reliable. This may seem a strange concern, since stakeholders are typically higher up in the company and are ostensibly conveying their authority down to the project leader and team. But a lack of clear and secure authority in stakeholders is actually an enormous problem for many projects.

The stakeholders must ultimately speak as one voice and communicate a unified vision for the product, provide only one answer to a question, and choose only one favorite from any list of options. The project's success will be greatly jeopardized if:

- *There's uncertainty about the prerogative of the group to make autonomous decisions.*
- *Conflict amongst stakeholders leads to instability in their decisions.*
- *Higher-ups in the company can overrule stakeholders' decisions.*

The decisions made by the group of stakeholders actively participating in the project must be definitive and must be supported by stakeholders and influential people who aren't actively participating in the project. This degree of authority and support often isn't automatically in place, and if you don't secure it at the beginning of the project, you risk the bottom falling out of the project midway through. Your stakeholders might have their own stakeholders, but the project can't wait for or depend on decisions to be run up the management ladder. The active stakeholders on your project must have the necessary authority to commit to decisions that won't be overruled after they've been made.

Authority afforded by trust

The list of people interested in affecting a product's development is always much longer than list of people who have the time or ability to actively participate in the project. Some managers of involved departments or business units assign someone under them to participate in the day-to-day activities of the project, but then these managers will appear suddenly when they disagree with decisions or when the project grows in significance. The same can happen with managers who either declined to participate initially or who weren't initially actively involved but later decided to assert themselves in the project. Other stakeholders may participate in the original concept work on the project, disappear during the early stages of development, and then reappear later in the process.

This kind of behavior poses a number of serious problems for the project. From the project kick-off through to its end, the progress of a project entails a tremendous amount of thinking, design, decisions, and compromises. Anyone who hasn't participated actively in that progress lacks much of the context and information that is necessary for understanding why certain decisions were made. They also lack the perspective necessary to balance their ideas and individual agendas against the other priorities and considerations that are guiding the project. Late-arriving or on-again, off-again stakeholders, not understanding or appreciating the decisions that have come before, often challenge decisions or revisit basic premises that would shake the foundations of the project. As we discussed in Chapter 3, changes stakeholders may perceive as simple may, in fact, be enormously difficult and costly. These changes will probably be improper if they're imposed by stakeholders who haven't actively participated in the project.

So, although late-arriving stakeholders can be welcomed if they trust and are deferential to the progress that's been made so far, you should head off late-arriving and hidden stakeholders who might derail the project. This requires some effort up front to determine who should be active stakeholders on the project. The group of active stakeholders must consist of people who are in a position to contribute to the project; they must also be vested with the trust and authority of the other potential stakeholders.

This means that a manager who assigns a subordinate to represent her interests in the project must trust him to make decisions in her stead, must be available to him if he should want her input, and must be committed to working through him and never around him. It also means that departments and business units that decline to participate actively in the project must place trust in those who are actively participating. This usually means the group of active stakeholders needs to be strongly representative of the diverse domains and interests within the organization so all interests can trust that they will be well represented.

Authority in rank

It can be difficult when some of these hidden and late-arriving stakeholders are senior managers and executives in the company. Many projects start off as initiatives of lower-level areas of individual departments, but then grow in prominence as they near completion and their ability to significantly impact the business becomes more apparent. Senior managers tend to tune in to the project as it nears completion, and to have strong opinions and interests that weren't present as the project ran its course. They also hold prominent positions in the company, so existing stakeholders and the project leader have difficulty challenging their demands. Or they represent departments that want to take over management of the project and profoundly redirect its course. Companies that are large, highly political, and bureaucratic are particularly susceptible to these issues.

It's therefore important that the group of active stakeholders is backed up by sufficient authority in rank to insulate the project from this type of problem. If the project mandate is delivered by senior executives, the project is more likely to be well insulated against incursions by less senior managers. But if this isn't the case, you need to secure some high-level backup early in the project. This may be accomplished by seeking out the executives who aren't necessarily able to actively participate in the project themselves but are likely to be affected by the product outcome. Spend time with them to find out what practices, information, and people they feel must be in place in order for them to fully trust the process without participating in it. You'll need to get them to explicitly commit to trust the process and to lend their support, should other executives start to meddle.

Collaboration and Decision Making

Though stakeholder participation in the beginning of the project is mostly structured in the form of in-person workshops, their participation through the rest of the project is much looser. It's not necessary—though it may at times be useful—to bring everyone together in person for every decision. Stakeholder schedules are likely too busy to allow for many in-person meetings.

It's important to figure out early on how collaboration and decision making will work for the project. The momentum and success of the project depends on stakeholders rapidly answering questions, providing guidance, and deciding on course adjustments to respond to discoveries and risks. Some method of collaboration should be agreed upon and put into effect early in the project. It doesn't really matter what that method is, so long as your stakeholders will use it; orderly, consistent collaboration is the goal, and every company and stakeholder has a different approach to this. You need to make it clear that stakeholders must tune into and participate in the discussions and decisions that happen during the project. Stakeholders must understand that if they don't actively participate and respond, they're forgoing their rights to affect those decisions later on and they may begin to lose the context necessary to contribute to future discussions and decisions.

The Characteristics of a Successful Project Team

The raw materials that go into building a software product are the intelligence, ingenuity, and creativity of the team that builds it. So it follows that the strength of the project team you're able to assemble will have an enormous effect on the project's outcome. Modern, UX-focused software projects tend to be built by relatively small project teams, usually 5–15 people who won't all be working simultaneously.

This may seem obvious, but a strong degree of unity within the team is critically important. There's an energy and efficiency inherent to groups of people who are all thinking about the same problem and working alongside each other; this doesn't exist if they're isolated from one another. Unified teams share a sense of ownership in creating something valuable and reflect each other's enthusiasm, whereas members of fragmented teams just focus on handing off deliverables without embracing a sense of being part of something larger. Collaboration in UX-focused project teams needs to happen by way of discussions and design, not through deliverable hand-offs.

If people are brought together from a variety of departments or from a mixture of internal and external sources, they may feel accountable to priorities other than the project itself and may work from different locations. Bringing everyone together into one centralized office can help build a sense of unity around the project and also makes collaboration much easier. If you can't get everyone together in one space, you should try to provide team members at least one opportunity to meet face-to-face; it makes a remarkable difference in their ability to work together. EffectiveUI has multiple offices and we often work in distributed teams, but in our main office, all of the designers, engineers, project managers, and other project team members are together in one space. As we'll discuss in later chapters, the process of building UX-focused software involves constant and active collaboration amongst all the roles and disciplines involved in the project. Thus it's important that visual and UX designers aren't segregated from software engineers. Being together also helps the team members become better acquainted with one another's concerns and professions, which in turn helps everyone make better decisions. A software engineer who's had strong exposure to UX design does a better job of building components with good UX, and a UX designer who's familiar with engineering practices and constraints creates designs that are easier to engineer.

The need for the different professional disciplines to work together implies another important characteristic of a successful team: mutual respect amongst team members for one another's expertise and the value and constraints of each discipline. In settings where the visual and UX design staff and effort are segregated from the software engineering team and effort (as in a waterfall process, discussed in Chapter 3), there's a strong tendency for the UX and visual designers to be unaware of or to not heed the constraints imposed in software engineering. As a result, they specify things in their designs that are needlessly difficult to implement, or they offer only a small benefit in exchange for significant expense in engineering. A software engineering team that's segregated from the UX and visual designers also tends to undervalue the thought and time that's gone into the designs they're attempting to implement, so they'll compromise or change certain things to either suit their personal preferences or gain small engineering expediencies at tremendous cost to the UX.

For UX-focused projects, you need to have UX and visual designers who understand and respect the challenges presented through software engineering. You also need to have software engineers who appreciate the value of UX and visual design and the need to strive to honor the designs they're provided. The mutual respect for one another's disciplines is also necessary in the project team members' continuous, intensive debates (which constitute the overall product design process).

Another key attribute of successful teams is recognizing the primacy of the user's needs for the product. A culture of attentiveness to and empathy for the user is essential for the team to make appropriate decisions all along the way. Without a strong focus on the user:

- *Software engineers can let technical expediency or a desire for "elegance" get them off track.*
- *Designers can get too focused on making something pretty instead of first making it functional.*
- *Other contributors can forget to set aside their assumptions and defer to the guidance provided by users and user research.*

Getting Professional Help

We'll do our best throughout this book to equip you with an understanding of the components of a software development project and how everything is developed, but you also need to understand that certain things can be done only by a professional. Few would expect to develop software without software engineers; it's a highly technical and advanced field. But, unfortunately, the same care often isn't given to UX design, UI design, and user research.

Why? These disciplines deal in concepts and materials that are much more intelligible to nonprofessionals than software code and architecture are, so there's a tendency to undervalue them. Many fail to recognize that UX design, UI design, and user research are as advanced and as technical as software engineering. Failing to apply professional, experienced resources to UX and UI design challenges and in user research is tantamount to undervaluing the role of user-focused design and results in an inferior product. Our assumption is that your goal is to produce a product with a superior UX quality, and that goal is attainable only with professional help.

Get specialized, professional help

It's also important that professionals are properly specialized. Within software engineering, there's a wide range of platforms, languages, and sub-disciplines, and it's important to work with engineers who have extensive experience with the technologies you'll be using. Even if you have people in your IT department who are familiar with the right technologies, their experience may be limited to maintaining products. They may not be familiar with how to develop products from scratch, or they may not have worked on user-focused projects.

Visual and UX design for software is also highly specialized. The print and web designers from your advertising and marketing departments might enthusiastically volunteer to do UX and UI design, but their design experience does not translate well to UX and UI design. Likewise, user research for the purpose of building software is not the same as market research. It requires a special intuition built through extensive experience and not just "people skills." Like a radiologist whose training and experience allows him to see tumors and abnormalities where everyone else sees only a haze of gray, the experience of professional user researchers and UX specialists attunes them to the important observations and the areas in need of exploration as they progress through their work.

Cost considerations

The more capable, professional, and specialized a person is, the more expensive he is. When cost-focused companies are faced with expensive hourly resources, they tend to bring projects in-house, hire more junior staff, or offshore projects. But this is a penny-wise and pound-foolish mistake.

Hiring more expensive, professional resources will mean your budget will buy fewer hours, but that's more than offset by the benefit to overall efficiency. If developing software were more like manufacturing widgets, the more people you hired, the faster you'd pump out units of progress; there's a linear relationship between number of employees and rate of production. But because of the extreme complexity of software projects, using experienced resources has a nearly exponential effect on overall efficiency, not a linear one.

This is because the units of production, whether in UX and UI design or in software engineering, are not self-contained and independent like units of a manufacturing process, nor are they perfectly designed in advance. Each unit of progress is the application of intellect to a problem in an effort to build a solution. Each unit becomes part of the delicate latticework upon which the whole of the project rests. So the pace of progress depends not only on the speed of a person's ability to produce per-unit results, but also on the likelihood that those results are correct and reliable. If they're not, then the stability of the product is compromised and time must be spent returning to resolve old problems (and every other problem that spawned from them). The effects of many small errors can easily accumulate into grinding, intractable problems that undermine or sink projects. A more experienced resource can work at a quicker pace, and the results of his work are much more likely to be correct and stable. More experienced resources also require less supervision; organizations often underestimate the costs associated with supervising junior resources.

Using more professional and experienced resources radically increases the likelihood of the project succeeding. Ultimately, the only measurement that matters is whether you launch a successful project roughly on time and on budget—not whether you maximized the number of man hours that went into it. The use of experienced resources offers a much greater likelihood of ultimate success and also helps make the project itself a much smoother, more reassuring experience for you and your stakeholders.

EffectiveUI worked with a client that learned this lesson the hard way. The client engaged EffectiveUI to do some of the initial business planning, requirements gathering, and design work for a new product concept. But when it came time to build the product, the client decided to use an offshore company with hourly rates that were a fraction of EffectiveUI's. They thought they could spend the same amount of money and get a greater volume of results. The offshore company assured our client that they would succeed, then disappeared for about eight months to develop the product. At the end of the eight months—and after a number of change orders and cost increases—the offshore company came back to the client to inform them that they were unable to produce a product that functioned at all. It wasn't just incomplete or of poor quality; it was essentially nonexistent from a functional perspective. To make matters worse, they were convinced it would be impossible to produce a functional product without a great deal more time and money.

The client finally decided to engage EffectiveUI to rebuild the product from scratch, and we were able to build a very successful solution for less cost than the offshore firm had originally quoted. In the end, by taking the higher-risk approach of trying to save money on the hourly cost of development, our client wound up spending twice as much as they should have to get the product built.

Insourcing Versus Outsourcing

It's difficult to choose between building a project in-house versus using a vendor (or some combination of the two). There are obvious implications to cost and control. If the product is important enough to your company, many individuals and departments may be clamoring for control and participation. As a result, they might not be willing to hand that control to an outside firm. On the other hand, the resources needed to build a successful, UX-focused product may not be available internally, though there may be some misconception that they are. As we discussed earlier, designers in marketing and engineers in IT maintaining legacy systems don't add up to a UX-focused team for building new products.

We recommend looking to the preceding section to guide your decision to insource or outsource the project. You're in the fortunate position of having good options if you can build an internal team of professional, specialized resources who are able to work together with a unity of purpose, in the same space, and with mutual respect for one another's contributions, and if those people fit the other attributes we described.

But unless your company has a strong track record of producing UX-focused products, you'll be hard-pressed to find most of the key professional resources internally. Even if your IT department has qualified developers, it can be difficult to wrest control of them from their current accountabilities. Your only design resources may be marketing staffers who have the wrong specializations or who may already be deeply committed to other major initiatives. And the issue of management and technical infrastructure can also complicate things; each different type of professional requires their own software and IT infrastructural support and should be managed by people experienced in managing that specific type of professional and UX-focused projects in general.

UX-focused projects require strong teams who are working near the leading edge of software technology, so it's likely that looking at a specialized, third-party vendor will be high on your list of options (or it might even be your only option). The strong value you get out of working with a vendor is that the vendor should have all of the attributes of a successful team in place and available to you as a turn-key solution:

- *Qualified and engaged staff*
- *Unity of purpose and location*
- *The right kind of management and technical infrastructure*
- *Experience in UX-focused projects*
- *No complicated cross-accountabilities within the organization*

It's also possible to build a team out of a mixture of internal people and outside consultants. But you need to establish that same unity, mutual respect, and clear focus; that need places a greater burden on you to ensure everyone comes together properly. And if, for example, you have internal software engineering resources and have contracted outside design resources, neither group will likely be accustomed to working with the other. The software engineering people are used to being in their own department, and the design people are used to being segregated from software engineering (handing off designs as deliverables and disappearing to their next projects). You also might encounter hostility from the internal team, a sense of smugness from the consultants, or other culture clashes that you need to address to keep the team working together successfully.

Offshoring

There's one thing that's very important to state explicitly: innovative, UX-focused projects are not good candidates for the use of offshore vendors. Offshore companies tend to favor volume over quality, throwing large numbers of lesser-qualified resources at problems. As we've already discussed in this chapter, that approach is fraught with risk and not nearly as cost effective as it appears.

Offshore companies with highly talented and experienced resources do exist, but even they are problematic to work with. Progress in an innovative, UX-focused project relies on quick feedback cycles among stakeholders, the project leader, UX specialists, design, and software engineers. Time zone differences between your internal team and offshore companies hinder—if not outright destroy—timely and effective collaboration, and generally have the effect of segregating the offshore team, excluding them from the overall project and design process, keeping them focused on narrow units of progress, and obscuring their insight into the state of (and challenges to) their progress. If your goal is to produce something exceptional, this just doesn't work.

OVERALL PROJECT COST	MORE EXPENSIVE LOCAL RESOURCES	LESS EXPENSIVE OFFSHORE RESOURCES
ENGAGEMENT	$100	$100
UNITS PRODUCED	1.5	5
ACCURACY	80%	20%
SUPERVISION & REWORK	$10	$50
UNITS SHIPPED	1.2	1
COST/UNIT	$92	$150

Evaluating an outsource vendor

In selecting a vendor to perform some or all of the services for the project, all of the criteria used to define a successful team should be used to assess a vendor. For example:

- *Are their resources sufficiently qualified and specialized?*

- *Do they fully understand the relationship between UX design, visual design, user research, and software engineering? Have they created a setting where they can work together effectively?*

- *Are they focused on the user and the UX (rather than focused primarily on visual design or software engineering)?*

You should also review the lessons from previous chapters and ask the vendor questions to discover whether they've learned those lessons too. The way the vendor proposes to manage uncertainty and the unknown in a project will be very telling. Vendors are accustomed to being asked to provide formal, documented processes and to pretend that uncertainty is minimal. But ask them about how they dealt with unknowns and changes in other projects and how they propose to manage scope so you can see whether they provide an honest, realistic point of view. If they don't—if they tout their patented process as being universally and comprehensively effective, or if they put a great deal of emphasis on upfront requirements building and big design up front—then be wary. Vendors who use this approach tend to try to hold you, the client, at arm's length in an effort to conceal the internal details of progress. That approach doesn't allow your project to benefit from the wisdom available through the stakeholders and the project leader. It also prevents you from having a clear, unfiltered understanding of the state of the project. You also don't have immediate control over its course as the inevitable unknowns and risks are encountered. This leads to surprise disappointments, budget overages, and change orders.

The ultimate goal for your company and for the vendor should be to build a strong working partnership of mutual trust and respect.

The ultimate goal for both your company and your vendor should be to create a strong working partnership that is built on mutual trust and respect. Your company gains that trust and respect by:

- *Being reasonable about the realities of uncertainty and the unknown*
- *Being effectively supportive of the development process*
- *Keeping focus on the high-level goals*
- *Being clear-headed and passionate about the product you're building*

The vendor gains trust through transparency and a willingness to acknowledge and take responsibility for issues as they arise. It demonstrates its trust by allowing the project leader direct access to the project through development. If a vendor is resistant to this level of transparency, it may simply be because they have been burned in the past by clients who didn't reciprocate that trust. But they should at least acknowledge it as a goal and be working toward it.

You should also examine the role of the vendor's account management and project management. Good project management is crucial to:

- *Helping teams meet their commitments and goals*
- *Providing a level of order to the often-chaotic flow of developing software*
- *Providing you with an advocate in the vendor's company who can help foster a strong relationship between the two companies*

On the other hand, project management and account management are often used as layers to obscure the internals of the project from the client, translating everything into periodic, heavily packaged, diplomatically presented abstractions. This is a product of the vendor's experience working with clients who reacted poorly when presented with a direct view into the messy realities of a software project. So, again, although a certain amount of trust hasn't yet been earned at the beginning of a project, both you and the vendor should strive to build mutual trust and develop a more tightly integrated relationship. When you're trustworthy as a client and, resultantly, in tune with the project, the vendor won't feel compelled to hide reality behind pretty packaging and diplomatic account management. This mutual respect improves the overall efficiency of the project.

A deep examination of the vendor's portfolio of past work is also important. Portfolios—often represented as an impressive collection of logos of well-known, ostensibly satisfied clients—should never be taken at face value. It's important to gain a deeper understanding of what, exactly, the vendor's role was in any given project. You may find that in their showcase projects, they provided only the design services, or only the software engineering services, or perhaps they consulted only at a minor level. You're looking for a vendor with experience in bringing together all of the disciplines from UX design to software engineering, so the vendor should have several strong case studies of instances where they did just that.

It is possible to bring together the design services of one vendor with the software engineering services of another, but we'd strongly caution against it. This situation requires that trust be built amongst three parties instead of two. That trust can be difficult to build because the vendors will likely perceive themselves as being in a zero-sum battle for your budget. It also makes it significantly more difficult to create the setting of a unified, multidisciplinary team; rather, it creates a setting of segregated roles whereby the respective parties pass deliverables back and forth but don't necessarily collaborate on anything. This is why full-service agencies, though generally more expensive and in high demand, are most often the best option.

Be wary of engaging agencies that are focused primarily on marketing and advertising. It's often the case that if a project is part of a marketing or CX initiative, or if the product is web-based or has a strong online component, your company's first impulse will be to work with whichever agency has helped with past marketing or web initiatives. When asked whether they're capable of building the product, these agencies will almost invariably answer "yes"— whether it's true or not. If they don't already have the capability, they'll see your project as an opportunity to build that capability on your dime.

Besides their basic inexperience, the problem here is that marketing and ad agencies approach these types of projects as websites on steroids, beefing up their web design and development staff and applying web solution strategies to the project. But there are enormous differences between websites and software. UX-focused software, as we've discussed, requires specialized resources in UX, visual design, and software engineering. Web design and development skills do not translate to software design and development capabilities. As well, the technical infrastructure and management practices required for a software project are vastly different than they are for web projects. An in-depth investigation of the qualifications of the agency's resources and their contributions to their portfolio projects should reveal their true capabilities.

Also, it's worth doing some digging to ensure that the company you're hiring will actually be doing the work. Agencies that don't currently have the in-house capability to build your product may simply hire a more specialized agency to do it on their behalf. In those cases, you're needlessly paying a middleman. And an additional party in the middle of everything can only harm the unity of the team and the trusting, integrated working relationship that needs to be established.

The following are some additional questions you can ask of the agency you're evaluating to see if they'll be a good fit.

To see if they can do the work themselves

- Ask to see an example of a live project completed entirely in-house without the support of third-party vendors.

- Ask to be walked through the actual timeline and process for that project. It's OK if the initial plan changed along the way—that happens in every project—but pay attention to the sort of changes that came up, how the agency responded to them, and whether they seem to understand and are prepared for the way uncertainty and the unknown affect projects.

- Ask to talk to the client for the project they described to see if the client tells a similar story.

To see if they are good at the engineering but not the UX design

- Try to use a product they've built—preferably something created for a broad audience. Do you think it's easy to use? Trust your gut reaction.

- Ask for their recommended approach to creating a good UX. If they don't include a few methods for gathering input or feedback from actual users (interviews, observation, usability testing, and so on), they probably aren't familiar with how UX design should work.

- Ask who they think creates good user experiences. If they can't think of any examples other than Apple, they probably don't think about the topic as much as they'd like you to believe.

> **To see if they are good at advertising or marketing, but perhaps they aren't a true UX-minded software development company**
>
> - Ask to see sample wireframes or functional specifications from something they consider a highly functional project. If they can't some up with any, or can show you only visual designs without detailed notes and workflows, they probably don't know how to do that.
>
> - Ask to speak to a past client that the agency has built functional applications for.
>
> - Ask for someone from their engineering team to join in on a meeting. If they can't come up with someone, or if that person doesn't engage thoughtfully in the conversation, they may not have a qualified engineering team.
>
> - Separately, ask their project manager, engineers, and designers how engineering and design usually work together. If don't share similar perspectives, they probably don't work together very well.

Full disclosure

Because EffectiveUI is a full-service agency and we're essentially describing ourselves in this chapter, it's important for us to acknowledge the risk that our recommendations in this section will seem self-serving. This was unavoidable—this book is a compendium of our views on the best practices in this domain, and we spend our days (and a few nights and weekends) using these practices in our work. For what it's worth, it wasn't our idea to write this book. We were asked to write it by our publisher, O'Reilly Media, because they noticed we had been delivering strong results in UX-focused engagements where other, ordinarily competent agencies had failed, so they wanted us to help you understand how we've been doing it. There are a number of independent research papers, mostly by Gartner and Forrester, that have helped inform our views and can provide impartial support for our assertions, particularly for this chapter. Unfortunately, we're unable to quote or cite them directly in this book because they're proprietary works.

We've taken great care to ensure that this book is the source of credible, accurate information and not just a big perfect-bound advertisement for EffectiveUI. If you've sought out this book for the full range of advice it provides, then you're likely not in a position to hire a company like EffectiveUI anyway. You're probably looking for a roadmap of how to do it on your own—and that's precisely the information this book provides.

Chapter 5
Getting the Business Perspective

Business planning is the first stage of planning the project, when you start to explore and define the problem that needs to be solved. In Chapter 3, you learned that effective requirements are a framework of constraining parameters that guide decision making and design. Framework requirements convey a clear understanding of the problem to be solved, but leave the details of the solution to be worked out later when the development stage begins. The business's needs and goals will guide and constrain everything else in the project and are therefore the starting point in building the framework requirements. Though the focus of the project will eventually shift primarily onto user needs, meeting those user needs will always be a means of accomplishing the business's goals.

The result of this stage should be a clear statement of what the business absolutely needs and expects of the project—nothing more and nothing less. Since it forms the basis of a key part of the framework requirements, business planning must be restrained to just focus on defining the problem without attempting to prematurely define the solution. The needs of the business that are explored, clarified, and documented through this stage will stand as a faithful proxy for the interests of the business and the stakeholders through the course of the project. But they shouldn't interfere or intrude unduly in the product design process.

This stage is also a significant opportunity for the project leader to build trust and buy-in with stakeholders because the work done in this stage requires intensive stakeholder involvement. The project leader can gain credibility and reduce worries and uncertainty by taking competent charge of the business planning process and ensuring it leads to useful results. This is also the project leader's first opportunity to seize control of the stakeholders' expectations about the project. The differing perspectives of stakeholders must coalesce around a common understanding of the business's needs that is firm and stable. This solid understanding will guide the product's design and development; it will also help ensure that stakeholders' expectations remain in line with the project's original goals. This will be essential in ensuring the project remains focused and isn't subject to the big course changes that can occur when stakeholders lose sight of the original problem and goals. It also helps prevent stakeholder expectations from wandering, allowing the project leader to focus on and be accountable to goals that are fixed and definite.

Defining Success

Everyone involved in a project should be working toward its success—that much is obvious. But what does it mean to succeed? There's often a remarkable lack of clarity and consensus on this most basic of understandings. Left unguided, each participant in the project may have a completely different view of success:

- *Some project managers and stakeholders try to ensure a project is delivered on time and under budget, above any other consideration.*

- *Some stakeholders want to ensure the project succeeds in meeting their department's specific goals, but they aren't focused on how the project will affect the rest of the organization.*

- *UX professionals can focus exclusively on succeeding at meeting user needs without attending to the needs of the business.*

- *Project team members may view success as meeting the isolated demands imposed on them by managers, rather than delivering an exceptional product.*

- *Project leaders can get so focused on pleasing their stakeholders that they lose sight of the overriding quality and business goals for the product.*

If everyone is working toward different goals, it's guaranteed that those goals will come into conflict. And every narrower interest interferes with the greater interest of truly succeeding in the fullest sense. So, again, what does it mean to succeed?

Software projects are born to address business problems, to respond to business opportunities, and ultimately to drive value into the business. In short, software projects are meant to create a return on investment. It's the anticipation of that return that motivates a company to invest money into a project, and determines how much investment is appropriate. Meeting the ROI projections that were used to justify the project is the ultimate standard of success, because it is the truest reflection of the project's reason for being.

If you look at the previous list of the disparate, narrow views of success, you can imagine how each originated from the goal of helping the project meet its ROI goals. Working to ensure that a project comes in on time and on budget is an attempt to make key projections in the ROI model come true; meeting user needs is a stepping stone to meeting the business's needs. If, however, the relationship between these lower-level goals and an overriding ROI-oriented business goal is lost, the lower-level goals will pull the project in differing (and wrong) directions, and each of the narrow interests will come into conflict. Therefore, it is tremendously important to kick off the project with clarity about what success looks like, and strong unity of purpose in meeting the high-level objectives. This is the core purpose of the business planning stage.

As the project progresses, stakeholders won't be able to spend much time working on it. And as the team gets consumed in the details of designing and building the product, the focus of their day-to-day activities will be very narrow. But you cannot allow the team to lose sight of the high-level purpose of the product. And as the project progresses, even the stakeholders can forget the original purpose for the project and divert their attention to narrower goals. You must not let the product deviate from its founding business goals, because those goals were what justified the investment in the project and it is to those goals that you should ultimately be held accountable. This means that practices and mechanisms must be in place to preserve their memory throughout the project, and to ensure that everyone is working toward the same objective all along the way.

Creating a Project Mission Statement

Almost every company has at some point tried to formulate a mission statement for itself. Mission statements are meant to help people keep sight of why the company is doing what it's doing and why each person is doing his work, instead of leaving people to live just in the day-to-day without a view of the big picture. Mission statements are a fixed but flexible point of reference for people to judge whether their efforts are effectively propelling them and the company in the right direction.

A mission can offer the same advantages to software projects. It's easy to get caught up in the features, design, and technology going into a product and stop thinking about why it's being built and how it fits into the larger organization.

Keeping a keen focus on the mission is especially important for projects where that mission is centered on good UX. High-quality UX is a diffuse, general goal that must ultimately be translated into a specific product with a concrete feature set. It's too easy for project team members to focus on narrow details of the implementation while forgetting that better UX is the central priority. A concise, high-level mission statement becomes part of the framework requirements. Members of the project team will refer back to it as they make decisions and judge progress, asking, "Are we being successful in fulfilling this mission?"

Mission statements are best created through direct collaboration among your stakeholders—if you can get their time for it. Mission statements should be just a few sentences or paragraphs, but those can be hard to arrive at. If you can't get your stakeholders together, prepare a first draft and pass it around among the stakeholders for feedback until you arrive at something that meets with general approval. It's again important that every stakeholder approve of the mission statement, since it will be the basis of many future decisions. The project mission will be a point of reference for them to return to as a reminder of the goals as the project progresses.

This is a mission statement from a product we've been working on that is meant to help marketing professionals reach their customers through multiple channels more easily:

> *Our mission is to help businesses better communicate with their customers in ways their customers prefer and appreciate, while also helping businesses spend more time on marketing strategy instead of the logistics and tactical details of executing on their marketing plans.*

The company building this product thinks it can find success in expanding the capabilities available to marketing professionals and improve their effectiveness through high-quality UX that makes the new and existing capabilities easier to perform. The mission has a clear user orientation; it's stated in terms of the benefit the product can offer its users. This was possible because the company had drawn a clear connection between its own business success and user needs. Project missions (especially those for internal projects) can focus a bit more on the business's own needs than this one does, but not exclusively. If UX quality is a high priority for the project because it's the means by which you except to accomplish some business goal, the project's mission should carry the UX focus.

Note also that this mission makes no attempt to define specific aspects of the solution. It doesn't say, "help businesses better communicate with their customers through email," though email channel capabilities will certainly be part of the product. The mission helps the project team decide whether certain ideas and features should be implemented. If an idea furthers the product's mission, it's included; if it offers some benefit that doesn't further the mission, it's omitted. The mission also informs design decisions. There are, for example, many ways to approach email channel marketing capabilities, but only some of them will align with the project's mission.

Determining Project Success Criteria

Success criteria are the end of the sentence that begins with, "We will have been successful if we...." The best way of settling on success criteria is to return to the financial and business models that you used to build support for the project. The ROI proposition in the models will revolve around certain key variables, such as "percent change in customer retention" or "percent change in call center volume," that are at the heart of how the company proposes to make or save money on the project. So, the degree to which the project meets projections for these key variables will also be the degree to which it succeeds in bringing about the anticipated ROI.

Success criteria are much more specific than the mission statement, but maintain a focus on the high-level, overriding *raison d'être* of the project. They translate the key variables from the financial justification of the project into clear, explicit goals. For example:

- *Reduce call center volume 10–20 percent over a six-month period.*
- *Increase customer retention by 15 percent or more as measured over a one-year period.*
- *Reduce the incidence of data input errors by 50 percent after a six-month period.*

Each of these example goals would have arisen from some key variable in the project's ROI model. For a project to succeed in meeting its ROI objectives, it must meet projections for its key variables. Success criteria are best when they're specific and clear, readily measurable, and "timeboxed"—that is, they have a specific period over which they will be measured.

There are numerous benefits to identifying success criteria:

- *They provide another point of reference for project team members to use in decision making and give them concrete goals to aim for.*

- *They help ensure, when the project is over, that stakeholders judge the success of the product based on its original goals and mandate and not based on personal, subjective misgivings.*

- *They give people outside the project a quick understanding of how the project is meant to affect them and the company without having to understand the product itself.*

- *They amount to a commitment on your part that you can be held accountable to, which can be very helpful for your credibility.*

Once the mission statement and success criteria have been identified, agreed upon, and documented, make sure that they remain present and relevant in the day-to-day progress of the project. They shouldn't just be documents that are produced at the beginning of the project and never looked at again. Every stakeholder and member of the team should receive a printout of the mission and success criteria at their desks, and every significant decision and design concept should be filtered through them. Members of your team should be able to tell you what mission and success criteria they're working toward without having to look at notes, since they should be thinking about the mission and success criteria every day. And each time you engage stakeholders to review progress and offer advice, you need to first reorient them to the project's mission and success criteria, to ensure that their reactions and advice are framed by the project's goals.

Exercising Restraint

As you examine the business goals, your greatest challenge is likely to be encouraging a discipline of restraint in yourself and your stakeholders. In the early days of a project there's a tremendous amount of valuable thought and enthusiasm. But left unguided and unrestrained, all of the ideas and enthusiasm can run amok. This causes projects to be founded on unreasonable goals and expectations—clearly a setup for failure. At the same time, care must be taken to exercise restraint without quashing any of the enthusiasm or discarding any of the early ideas.

Therefore, much of the work of discovering business goals is a progression of techniques that help you parlay all of the ideas and enthusiasm into business goals that are reasonable and thoughtfully restrained. The process involves coalescing the information and value brought by your stakeholders, and getting their expectations unified and their progress pointed in the right direction. Getting the various perspectives of stakeholders to align around a common vision can be a challenge, but you should encounter less difficulty than you might expect. At the outset of a project, stakeholders are typically concerned about the risk, uneasy with the scale of and lack of clarity surrounding the problem, and unsure of how to proceed. The techniques and restraint employed during this stage, and the focused objectives that should result, do a lot to allay their uneasiness. Restraint helps eliminate a lot of the complexity and noise, which in turn helps the project seem less difficult and less risky.

Just as perfection is the enemy of the good, over-ambitiousness can set a project up for failure—failure to launch, failure to meet expectations, failure to engage users, and so on. There's usually a strong impulse at the beginning of a project to throw in every possible feature, and to dream up a product that will appeal to every possible market or demographic. But the more sprawling the initial conception of the product is, the harder it becomes to actually build. And overlarge concepts leave too much room for stakeholders and project team members to have very different mental images of and preconceptions about the product.

So, in the interest of restraint, you should be continuously asking the question: "Is this truly necessary for our product to succeed for our business?" This is a useful filter for preventing guesses about aspects of the solution from being confused with actual requirements. A concept is a requirement only if the project would be considered to have failed to some degree if that concept isn't reflected in the finished product. Surprisingly few things actually pass the test of being truly necessary; many are just ideas for features that are means to a more fundamental business goal.

Though it may seem like we're asking you to give up hopes and dreams before you even begin, we're just encouraging you to exercise restraint at the beginning of the project, to ensure that there will be room for those hopes and dreams when their time comes. If you strive for something too ambitious from the outset, you risk overstretching your resources. You typically don't fully recognize you've overreached until the project is too far along to make adjustments and you either run over budget or underdeliver. Broader goals mean broader susceptibility to change and risk. If you overreach in your original conception of the product, you risk finding yourself in a position of having to make cuts and compromises at the end of the project. This is costly and difficult to do; it forces you to renege on prior commitments, which damages your credibility with stakeholders.

It's much easier to add in features and refinements after you've delivered a successful, thoughtfully restrained first release (which may just be an internal demo release). By virtue of having gained the experience of having built an actual working product, you'll be much better prepared to decide which of the earlier ambitions are actually worth pursuing. You'll also be much more practiced at estimating how far your remaining resources can take you.

A restrained first version of the product also requires less time to develop, which means you can get it in front of actual users sooner. Those users will be much better judges of what's missing or problematic in the first version of the product than you and your stakeholders; you, your stakeholders, and your project team are too intimate with the product to have a clear perspective. If you exercised restraint, you'll be grateful that you have leftover time and money to make changes in response to user feedback. Also, releasing something acceptable and functional (even if it isn't 100 percent of what everyone wanted from the outset) relieves a tremendous burden of pressure and risk. It's far better to have something releasable and imperfect than something that endeavored for perfection yet never got to the point of being releasable. Too many projects die under the weight of overblown expectations and requirements. There will always be more you could have done, but for a product to see the light of day, some sacrifices will always have to be made.

The mindset of restraint, like that of the humility of unknowing, is both difficult and crucial to instill in your stakeholders. They need to understand that restraint is a key discipline of risk reduction, and that "not now" doesn't mean "never." It just means that you're keeping your options as widely open as possible and giving everyone the opportunity to gain experience before making difficult decisions. As a military commander said to the president in the TV show *The West Wing*, "A proportional [restrained] response doesn't empty the options box for the future, the way an all-out assault does."

Applying the Pareto Principle

The Pareto principle, more widely known as the "80/20 rule," is a useful cognitive tool for the exercise of restraint. Although some people believe it means that one should focus on the 80 percent and not worry about the other 20 percent, it actually means that the 20 percent portion is quite often the cause of 80 percent of the effect. This suggests that attending to the pivotal 20 percent is the most effective use of resources. Retailers, for example, may recognize that 20 percent of their offerings represent 80 percent of their revenue and focus their inventory and marketing investments accordingly.

With user-focused software, it's often the case that a product built to do an excellent job of satisfying the needs of a small set of users will also work well for almost every other user. The process of describing target users therefore involves identifying the 20 percent of users who can serve as good ambassadors for the rest.

What Not to Restrain

The practice of restraint should be a filtration and distillation of ideas that happens in a collaborative environment. It should not be a self-censorship of ideas and enthusiasm before they have a chance to enter the group conversation. Creativity and inspiration shouldn't be headed off before they're shared, nor should ideas be discarded before they've had a chance to be considered. Restraint is exercised through the process of deciding what ideas to include in the framework requirements, not when initially generating those ideas.

Also, if you've identified some way your product is going to significantly differentiate against the competition or drive compelling value and change to your organization, that aspect should be given wide latitude. The proper exercise of restraint should never dilute the core value and anticipated ROI of the product. Restraint is meant to keep all of the other stuff at bay so the core goals have room to breathe.

The nature of the solution you're trying to create may demand that it be a sprawling and complicated product and greater measures of restraint just aren't available. In cases like this, it's useful to compartmentalize the product into smaller concepts and approach them as separate projects, to make the domain of your team's focus narrow enough to keep them effective.

Refocusing Product Objectives

It's typical for competing companies to try to retain their competitive edge by matching and then outdoing each other's feature lists. Product objectives are set by what will look the most impressive on a feature matrix in comparison to competitors and what marketing thinks they can message most effectively. But getting into a feature parity war with your competitors puts you on a long road to nowhere. The best you can ever hope for is to be a few months ahead of your competitors with a number of features they're already working to replicate. The intrinsic usefulness of the product suffers as it grows into a Frankenstein of fragmented features that render the product feature-complete but a nightmare to use. And the more that gets bolted onto the product, the harder it is to change, so companies get committed to a trajectory they can't control, because the inertial mass of the product is too great and simply maintaining and supporting it is consuming all their resources.

It's no wonder, then, that scrappy, focused startup products built by college dropouts in their parents' basements pose a serious challenge to previously well-established products made by large companies. Unburdened by the need to tilt against the overwhelming friction of an existing behemoth, these startups are free to build products that differentiate on quality. They focus on the intrinsic value and usefulness of the product, rather than on a long list of mostly irrelevant features. Smaller projects are also easier to design and build, because they can be held in one's head all at once more easily. And the less complexity there is in a project, the more thought and attention is available to each of its details.

vs

If your company needs to offer a comprehensive range of capabilities in some area, consider breaking the efforts into smaller standalone products to be developed separately. Apple took this approach in building the suite of products that includes Mail, iCal, and Address Book. Those products handle many of the capabilities that Microsoft crammed into its incredibly complex Outlook and Entourage products. By breaking up the functionality into separate products, Apple was able to keep the development efforts smaller, more focused, and less prone to risk. Smaller products generally do one thing very well, whereas larger products tend to do a lot of things not as well. Smaller products also make it possible to bring the suite to market in smaller increments rather than one big one. This lets you get something out sooner, to build a base of customers and receive real-world user feedback. That feedback can be applied to improve the quality of the subsequent products in the suite that you develop.

As you investigate the business needs for your new or remodeled product, don't allow feature parity to control the conversation and product direction. If you commit to matching a competitor's feature from the outset, you've limited the resources and latitude you have to pursue other avenues of differentiation. Matching a competitor's features ultimately may be the right decision, but don't let it pass by as an unchallenged assumption. Do some research and try applying the Pareto principle to your feature list. You may discover 20 percent of your features account for 80 percent of the product's usage, or that 20 percent of your features are the reason why 80 percent of your customers use your product. There are many other ways to differentiate your product than just feature lists—better UX, for example—and those options need to be given due consideration.

Omissions Aren't Permanent

Rich internet applications (RIAs), software-as-a-service (SaaS) deployment models, and desktop software auto-updaters allow software to be updated much more easily, so product managers can breathe much freer. Decisions to leave certain features out of a given release aren't permanent. If user feedback ends up demonstrating that a decision to omit something was a mistake, that missing feature can be added in an automatic update.

What is permanent, however, is any expenditure of time and resources that occurred before the release. This is another argument for exercising restraint in the product's objectives. Whereas you can add a feature in response to user feedback, you can't undo the expense of building one that wasn't needed or doesn't succeed. If restraint saved you from building an unsuccessful feature, the time and resources you didn't expend will be available to build something else in response to user feedback.

Describing the Product's Users

Unless you're catering to a very narrow and well-defined customer base or audience, there's a tendency for companies to try to build products that work well for every possible user. Our UX architects call this the problem of designing for "everyone with a neck." Overly inclusive target user populations are just as problematic as overambitious feature goals. Good UX happens when software is built in a way that's attentive to the specific and unique needs of its users. That attentiveness and specificity is impossible if you're trying to cater to an overly broad group of users. This understanding is the basis of the following aphorism:

> *If you try to build software that works for everyone, you'll wind up building something that works for no one.*

Designing for an overly broad set of users can cause you to design a product for the lowest common denominator in the group or for all of the disparate weaknesses within the group. Here, again, is where some thoughtful restraint can prevent your well-meaning ambition from bringing about poor results.

And so a key goal of the business planning stage is to reduce "everyone with a neck" down to a more practicable understanding of who your key users will be. This understanding will be applied in the user research stage to determine what users to bring into the research. It will also help simplify and guide the remainder of the discussions about the business perspective, giving participants a narrower set of potential users to bear in mind as they think about the product.

The identification of key users is more of an art based on experience than something that can be learned from a book, so if it's possible to involve a UX professional, your project will be better off for it. The principal goal is to provide a thoughtfully restrained starting place for user research as they select as their sample users. By providing them with a diligently restrained view of who the key users are, you avoid undue cost and loss of time in user research. Be careful not to take the restraint too far, though; the key users you describe should be a broad enough group to allow user researchers to address a complete sample of users without inappropriately ruling any out in advance. The group must also be broad enough that your stakeholders are confident that user research will be based on the full diversity of potential customers or users.

User Attributes

You will define your key users by discovering and describing their attributes—the attributes of their lives, of their home or work environments, and of their attitudes that affect how they will relate to your product. We've generally found that the important attributes are different depending on whether you're building a business or enterprise application or you're building a consumer application. Business users tend to come to an application through the context of their business and of their specific role within it. Consumers, on the other hand, generally relate to an application in the context of their own lives and the goals they've set for themselves.

Some examples of attributes for business or enterprise user types might be:

- *Marketing directors who oversee staffs of 10–50 people and have budgets of over $2 million*
- *Network administrators who either oversee a large internal network or oversee multiple smaller ones for clients*
- *Call center operators who manage first-tier customer service requests*

Attributes of the organizations the users work for also strongly influence user types—for example, which industry or vertical their company operates in, its size, how technology is integrated into the organization, and so on. Attributes of the users' personal lives usually aren't material to business or enterprise application user types, though. Whether users have children or cats, or whether they live in condos or houses, etc., has little influence on their jobs, so these factors don't influence how they will use a product. People adopt a different persona when they walk through the office door; they are guided much more strongly by the demands of their job than by their personal lives.

User types for consumer applications, on the other had, can be strongly influenced by personal and demographic information. It's relevant to online tax software, for example, whether many of its key users have children. Parents have to puzzle over the complexities of family tax credits and juggle tax preparation in their free time with other demands such as ballet lessons, work, and family meals. Their individual attitudes toward technology and data security will also play an important role.

As well, use of software for personal purposes is voluntary, whereas in a work environment it tends to be a required part of the job. Software in a business setting generally has a clear-cut function and relationship to the job, and the decision to use a given usually isn't up to the individual user. Users of consumer products, on the other hand, decide for themselves whether to buy a product and how it will fit into their lives. These decisions are heavily influenced by personal attributes—age, gender, income level, and so on.

Your company's existing marketing research and market segmentation can be a good starting place for kicking off the discovery of user attributes. This can provide a preliminary understanding of the broad categories of individuals who will use the product. But a user and a customer are not the same thing, even when the user is also the customer. Marketing seeks to understand and influence customers' purchasing behaviors and brand affinities; UX design is concerned with a user's interactions with the product. The attributes that influence these two concerns are different, and the approach to researching them is also different.

Exercises to Identify Key User Attributes

It's essential to collaborate with stakeholders during the process of identifying key user attributes. They bring a variety of perspectives that reflect the complexity of your company, and their buy-in will be crucial as you move forward. Involving them to help craft the user types helps produce better results and instills a sense of ownership and understanding in your stakeholders.

This is also a good opportunity for you to build your own credibility. You need to exercise effective leadership in helping the group distill noise and complexity down to actionable, consensus-driven results. You may find yourself in a room of higher-ranked people with differing attitudes and goals who will all be looking to you to provide reassuring leadership and bring everyone to a good outcome.

First exercise: Getting to something narrower than "everyone"

As we've said, though it's tempting to try to build software that works for everyone, it isn't a reasonable goal. Even if in your situation "everyone" is a smaller group than "everyone with a neck," it's probably still a pretty expansive group—everyone who follows financial markets, for example. You'll need to winnow this down to a more manageable size.

The first step along this path is a collaborative exercise conducted with your stakeholders in a meeting room. The exercise is simple; you just pose the following question and encourage unfettered thinking:

Who is everyone?

Everyone in the group should start rattling off the attributes that they think describe the full range of potential users of the product. In a group setting, the ideas typically come out fast and furious and then peter off toward the end. The role of the facilitator (either you or a UX professional) is to write all of the attributes and ideas on sticky notes and post them on the wall. We recommend using large sticky notes and writing with a Sharpie® for better readability across the room. Encourage people to speak up and explore territories that are being hinted at but missed.

By the time the brainstorming has finished, you're likely to have an entire wall plastered with sticky notes. We've conducted sessions like this where we came close to running out of space on three walls. Even though the ultimate goal is restraint, an overabundance of attributes should be encouraged at this stage. For one, it ensures stakeholders have an opportunity to get their ideas out and aren't being frustrated, censored, or self-censored so early in the project. It also helps stakeholders recognize the need for restraint; a room covered from floor to ceiling with widely scattered attributes makes clear the need to narrow the focus.

Even if hundreds of attributes are identified in first exercise, it should nevertheless also be clear that the group of target users is much more finite than just "everyone." Getting all of the attributes up on the wall makes the collective understanding of the product's users feel much more concrete. This concreteness is reassuring to stakeholders who may be overwhelmed by the scale of the undertaking.

Second exercise: Consolidating similar attributes

If the brainstorming in the first exercise was fast and free, many of the attributes identified will be similar or substantially overlapping. The differences between "VP of Marketing," "CMO," or "Senior marketing executive," or between "very busy," "little free time," or "many pressing demands" usually aren't meaningful enough to be kept separate.

This is where using sticky notes in the first exercise will come in handy. Ask the group whether any of the attributes can be consolidated. Participants will scan the wall covered in attributes and throw out suggestions. There's usually a lot of disagreement about these suggestions among stakeholders. You can step back and allow the group to negotiate among themselves over whether a certain set of attributes can be consolidated. As attributes are identified for consolidation, take their sticky notes off of the wall and replace them with one that describes the consolidated group.

With very large groups of people, consolidating attributes through open discussion and negotiation can be cumbersome. As an alternative for any size of group, you can do this type of exercise using collaborative mind mapping. We often use the software tool MindMeister (*http://www.mindmeister.com*). This web-based tool lets participants collaborate over a single mind map instead of editing and emailing different versions.

The consolidation needn't be too exhaustive. The goal is simply to ensure that there aren't redundancies or superfluous concepts remaining to complicate progress. If possible, it's also best to conduct this exercise immediately after the first one. The ideas will still be fresh in everyone's heads, and the sticky notes will still be up on the walls in the same locations. Additionally, writing with Sharpies on sticky notes forces complicated attributes to be abbreviated, so doing this exercise right after the first one helps everyone remember what the abbreviations mean. Before leaving the room for the day, make sure to take notes on the abbreviated and complicated attributes for future reference.

Third exercise: Distilling it to key user attributes

In the third exercise, you apply the Pareto principle to the collection of attributes identified in the previous exercises. For this exercise, the group dynamic can be very useful in quickly getting to a definitive result and strong consensus. It's very hard to apply the Pareto principle on your own, and every individual who attempts it will come back with different results. As a group, however, you can focus and clarify the process by running a spending exercise.

Spending exercises

Spending exercises are a great way of facilitating tough prioritizations and choices for small and large groups and can also be useful to individuals who have a hard time making up their minds. These exercises work by helping priorities and decisions become apparent from the aggregate of all the participants' opinions. Participants are given a limited amount of "currency" (votes, essentially) to spend in favor of the options on the wall. The amount of currency people have should be far less than the number of options before them, so they're forced to prioritize. In large group settings, the currency can take the form of the little round color-coding stickers you can get from office supply stores. Each person comes to the wall where the options are posted and puts stickers next to his preferred choices. In smaller group settings or when the options are fewer, it may be simpler to have participants vote by raising their hands.

So, with the consolidated sticky notes from the previous exercises still up on the wall, pose this question to the group:

Which of these attributes describes users whose needs we can directly address and in so doing will also address the majority of the needs of the majority of all of our users? Or, in other words, which are the attributes of the 20 percent of users who will be good representatives for 80 percent of our users?

Then run the spending exercise. Participate in the exercise yourself, but also make sure to observe how stakeholders are making decisions and negotiating aloud with themselves and each other. Make note of who may be favoring user attributes that aren't favored by the rest of the group.

Determining the amount of currency to distribute can sometimes be tricky. If you're not sure how much is appropriate, try giving every participant a number of votes that's one quarter of the number of options. If it later seems that too few votes were distributed, you can give people more. If it turns too many votes were distributed, you can run a second spending exercise on the results of the first round with more limited currency.

At the end of one spending exercise, there should be a clear set of key user attributes and some important secondary user attributes. If you find there's a large group of favored attributes but no clear primary priorities, you probably distributed too much currency and should run another spending exercise. You should also repeat the exercise if the list of primary and secondary user attributes still seems too large or unfocused. When running another spending exercise, it should be limited to just those attributes that survived the first round.

Also, if the results don't make it obvious, it may be useful to decide as a group where the line between primary, secondary, and remaining attributes will be. This question may be solved through simple negotiation, or may require another quick spending exercise to give a more focused picture of the distribution of priorities.

Each of the dots represents a vote for that item.

Fourth exercise: Adding depth to the user attributes

Once you've identified the key user attributes, work with stakeholders to bring an additional dimension of clarity and definition to the understanding of the key users. Pose the following questions to the group:

- *What are the triggers that are bringing these users to the product, or what are the considerations that cause them to need the product?*
- *What do they expect out of the product?*
- *What would pleasantly surprise them?*
- *What would potentially disappoint them?*

Encourage the group to consider the questions in light of the different key user attributes. The attributes describe a range of users rather than a single, unified user, so there will be many answers to the same questions. As with the previous exercises, capturing these ideas in a group setting on sticky notes is best. If you wind up with large collections of notes, you can use the same consolidation and spending exercise techniques to hone the lists down to something manageable.

Deepening the understanding of the key users in this way has value beyond giving greater clarity to the rest of the project team. This exercise can help draw out some of the assumptions and expectations that your stakeholders may have about the users. This will be useful to know as you begin user research and find yourself disproving or running counter to those assumptions and expectations. Discovering unexpected things in research is a sign of effective research, but it's also a warning sign that the project may begin grating against stakeholder expectations. The project leader must be on alert for issues like this that may challenge stakeholder support so she can proactively address them.

Documenting the results

At the end of these exercises you'll still only have a wall covered in sticky notes and stickers, so the results will have to be reduced to documentation. The documentation of this process has two audiences: the people performing user research, and your stakeholders.

For the stakeholders, the goal for the documentation is to ensure that the apparent consensus generated through the exercises is real and lasting.

Documentation is something stakeholders can hold onto as a reminder of their decisions as the memory of the thought process behind those decisions fades. For the user researchers, the documentation provides a condensation of all the thinking that took place during the exercises and a general description of the range of users they'll need to work with in their research. The documentation should be simple so you can produce it quickly while the exercises are still fresh in your stakeholders' minds.

The main content of the documentation will be a catalog of the primary and secondary user attributes. These can simply be listed. But the documentation is also a good opportunity to record the basis of some of the more difficult decisions, to serve as a reminder for your stakeholders if they start to drift back toward wanting a product that works for everyone. This extra detail also gives the user researchers deeper insight into the thinking that went into the selection of key user attributes.

If there were any big or contentious debates during the exercises, note the opposing arguments and the reasoning for the conclusion. If a collection of attributes was consolidated into a single, complicated one, offer some explanation of that consolidated attribute. In addition, if you noticed that any of your stakeholders had particularly strong opinions on a given subject or stood against popular opinion on some particular issue, seek out that person to get his thoughts on the subject and include them in the documentation.

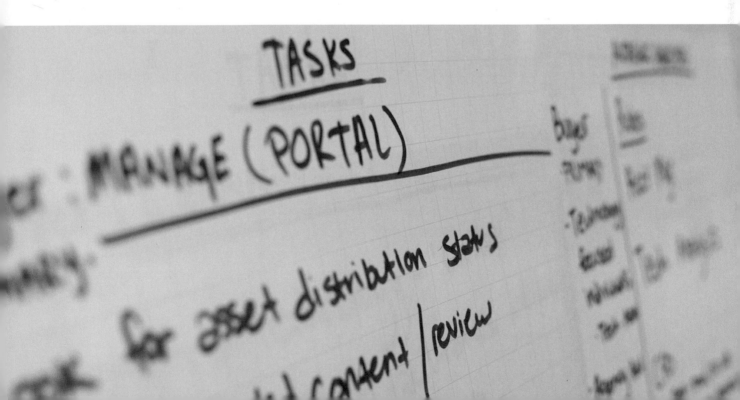

This may or may not be useful to the user researchers, but it will help ensure that those stakeholders feel listened to and will support the results of the effort. It can also be useful to include a list of the attributes that didn't make the cut at the end of the documentation, just to ensure that those thoughts aren't lost.

Check back with each stakeholder individually before distributing the documentation to make sure they all feel comfortable with the results. If anyone has concerns or objections, include a summary of them in the final draft of the documentation. Stakeholders who don't support the conclusions of this stage probably won't support anything that follows from them. You'll need to obtain a definitive assent to the results from each of your stakeholders to be able to move forward with confidence. Ensuring that the final documentation reflects their thoughts and concerns will help keep them on board. Whether and how the user research team uses those thoughts is up to them.

BUSINESS USERS

Pizza Ordering System Administrator
Adds/edits/deletes stores
Maintains global food offerings
Maintains global coupons and discounts
Maintains global pricing rules

Store Manager
Adds/edits/deletes employees in the system (for his store)
Maintains prices in the system (for his store)
Maintains food offerings in the system (for his store)
Maintains coupons in the system (for his store)

Order Taker
Takes the order over the phone (writes on paper)
Enters order info from paper into the pizza system

Pizza Maker
Reads the order from the system
Produces pizza, etc., according to the order

CONSUMER USERS

College Student
Orders pizza about twice a week
Usually orders for self, but may also order for several people
$ is very tight, but generally doesn't use coupons
Very comfortable with web, mobile devices, etc., and has access to and uses all of these very regularly
Low tolerance for poor/dated interfaces
May not have or want to use a credit card

Mom
Orders pizza about twice a month
Always orders for the family—never just for herself
$ is always a consideration, but not the only consideration. Will use coupons
Comfortable with web, somewhat less so with mobile devices, prefers phone
Has credit card, may prefer to pay cash

Office Administrator
Orders pizza once or twice a month
Orders for the entire office of 60
Comfortable with web, prefers it to calling
Uses company credit card. Needs an itemized receipt

Creating Business Requirements

The term "requirements" is often applied to those phonebook-size binders of detailed specifications that attempt to exhaustively define the solution. But effective business requirements are instead an elaboration on and elucidation of the needs of the business. As part of the framework requirements, they provide a fuller description of the problem from the business perspective, but do not attempt to specify a solution.

Once again, there's need for restraint on the part of those defining the business requirements. The business requirements should include only those things that are absolutely required. The rest will be worked out later during the development stage. As with the selection of key user attributes, restraint is essential. There will be a strong temptation to set a vision for an expansive product with broad capabilities. But unless a given capability is clearly necessary for the product to meet the business's needs, it shouldn't be listed as a requirement. The less that's specifically required from the outset, the more room there will be for capabilities and requirements to be built when there's a much greater understanding of the user and the product. It costs less money and political capital to add capabilities to restrained initial requirements than it does to make cuts to overambitious ones.

Defining "Requirement"

There's a tendency to treat "requirement" as being synonymous with "feature," but they're quite different. *To describe a feature is to describe an aspect of the solution, but to describe a requirement is to describe a facet of the problem.* This understanding encapsulates the essence of the restraint necessary to developing business requirements as a component of effective framework requirements.

We took this approach with Herff Jones in creating their web-based yearbook creation tool, eDesign. Three of the key business requirements for the product were:

- *Make it easier for students and schools to create successful yearbooks.*
- *Help Herff Jones representatives provide better ongoing and active customer service and support without having to go on-site.*
- *Make the yearbook creation process integrate better with the production process to reduce the operational burden and risk of errors.*

Notice that these requirements are expressed as goals and desired outcomes and not as features. Requirements should stay within the realm of business goals and avoid getting into product design specifics. This leaves room for user research and professional product design to translate these business requirements into specific functionality.

Had the stakeholders on this project been overly exuberant and unrestrained, they might have put forward ideas for functionality as requirements. For example:

- *The application must have email capability that enables students and Herff Jones representatives to exchange emails within the application.*
- *The application must have social networking capabilities to allow students to share ideas and build community among students at their school and other schools.*

In the minds of the well-meaning stakeholders, these two "requirements" might seem like a natural extension of the business requirements in the previous list. But it's not a given that supporting better customer service means having built-in email capabilities. And including social networking capabilities may be in vogue these days, but in this case it's a catastrophic requirement. Students don't need yet another narrow-purpose email account to pay attention to, nor do their social networking proclivities extend to yearbook class and the community of people working on other yearbook committees, nor would email or social networking really make it easier for them to build better yearbooks.

But if these feature ideas had been expressed as requirements, the project team would have been forced develop them. Money and time would have been spent on functionality that never had an opportunity to be vetted. User researchers would have spent time looking into how to make email and social networking work best for the users instead of looking into how to best support the simple goal of better customer service. Design and engineering time would have been consumed by useless functionality. And other, more important features would have been crowded out.

A business requirement is an elaboration on the business problem the application is intended to address, expressed in terms of goals rather than functionality. To be a successful part of the framework requirements, business requirements must be concrete and certain about only what's known for sure—the business goals for the product—and restrained about everything else. This leaves room for creative, effective product design to occur and avoids mandating wasted efforts.

Exercises to Develop Business Requirements

As with the selection of key user attributes, the development of business requirements must be done in active collaboration with stakeholders. The business requirements stand as an ambassador for the stakeholders' interests throughout the project, so stakeholders must trust that they are complete and correct.

The role of the facilitator (again, either you or a UX professional) through this process is to encourage the free flow of participation, but also to help keep everyone within the bounds of proper restraint. Stakeholders need frequent reminders to think in terms of goals instead of features. This is again an important opportunity for you to reinforce your credibility by exercising leadership and influencing stakeholder expectations toward reasonableness.

The process of developing business requirements must be done with a constant regard to:

- *The key user attributes*
- *The product mission*
- *The success criteria*

Keeping these considerations always in mind helps ensure that the business requirements are consistent with and don't stray beyond the existing constraints. They also provide a very useful early framework for answering questions through this process. They provide a means for determining whether a given requirement serves the needs of the target users, whether it's consistent with the project's broad goals, and whether it supports meeting the success criteria.

First exercise: Getting it all out there

The first step is to draw out everyone's ideas and get them on sticky notes on the wall. Kick off the exercise by asking this question:

What goals and capabilities would we like to see this product support?

Send your stakeholders this question a week or two before you conduct the exercise to give them plenty of time to explore all of the corners of their ideas and expectations. If you can get them to send you notes of their ideas ahead of time, too, you'll be better equipped to ask clarifying questions and encourage the exploration of overlooked areas as you conduct the exercise.

This first exercise should be a mostly unrestrained brain dump on the part of your stakeholders, and you should be liberal in accepting ideas. Try to avoid letting anyone in the group dismiss ideas or argue them away so you can keep up the momentum of the brainstorming and prevent politics or bruised egos from impeding progress. It's also OK at this point if the ideas are about specific features and functionality, because those ideas can be reduced to goals later.

As the flow of ideas peters out, you'll again find yourself in a room completely covered in sticky notes. The presence of lots of ideas is a positive sign that your stakeholders have had a chance to fully engage and be heard. An overabundance of ideas also makes it easier to convince everyone of the need to apply restraint moving forward.

Second exercise: Group things together

It's likely that the first exercise produced a ton of ideas that are described at a very granular level with many overlapping concepts. Also, many of the ideas will have been expressed in terms of specific features and functionality instead of as broader goals. Affinity diagramming exercises are useful to begin to distill the ideas down to requirements.

Affinity diagramming

Affinity diagramming, also known as the KJ Method, is a technique that helps bring order to large numbers of ideas. Presented with a large collection of unorganized ideas, participants are asked to identify ideas that are similar, overlapping, connected, or logical siblings of the same parent concept. Participants negotiate among themselves about whether two ideas are sufficiently related or whether they deserve to stand apart. Having the ideas on sticky notes makes it easy to organize them into logical groupings.

With the sticky notes from the previous exercise still up on the wall, ask the participants to physically group logically related ideas. The goal of the exercise is to group all of the ideas under headings that are clearly expressed in terms of business goals. While grouping similar and overlapping items together, participants also should try to identify categories for these groupings. These categories should be expressed in terms of business goals instead of functionality. Returning to the Herff Jones example, you might consider grouping these ideas (which are a collection of lower-level goals and specific features) together:

- *Proactive customer service*
- *Ease workflow between schools and account managers*
- *Built-in email system*
- *Faster responses to support requests*

These could all fall under the high-level goal of "help Herff Jones representatives provide better ongoing and active customer service and support without having to go on-site." This is a clear expression of a business goal that's specific enough to be actionable (as opposed to just "improve customer service") but flexible enough to allow a range of interpretations during user research and professional product design. Fulfilling on the goal requires specific functionality to be designed and implemented, but those specifics are left to be determined at a more appropriate time in the project—the development stage.

Allow stakeholders to suggest groupings and negotiate and argue over them without giving them much prompting. Your role is to ensure that ideas are being given a fair hearing and that no one is allowed to either dominate or drop out of the conversation. You should also work to ensure that ideas ultimately fall into groupings expressed in terms of goals instead of features. If the discussion needs a little nudge or certain areas are staying in the realm of specific features, you can simply ask, "Why do we want this?" All ideas are descendants of some business goal; asking "why?" allows you to work your way up the chain of thought to the goal.

As you group and restate ideas, make sure the original ideas are preserved. You can do this simply by making sure the sticky note holding the original idea stays with the grouping it falls under. Even though the end purpose of the exercise is to state everything in terms of business goals, the ideas that lead to those goals and the feature ideas that resulted from brainstorming can be tremendously valuable to the project team. They can also be useful in planning subsequent versions or iterations of the product.

Third exercise: Prioritize

Even if the group has been successful in reducing every idea and feature to the business goal it reflects, you might still find yourself with an excess of business goals. The number of business goals needs to be well aligned with the time and budget you have available. An excess of goals spreads your resources too thin and causes you to build a larger number of capabilities that are all only partially baked. Unfortunately, that alignment is extremely difficult to assess before development begins.

This is therefore another occasion for the exercise of restraint. The overall risk in the project is greatly reduced if the initial focus of the project is on only those business goals that are of core and utmost importance. The entire focus of the team and resources should be on doing an excellent job of fulfilling those core critical goals. Successfully meeting those goals may require all the time and resources you have available. If nonessential goals are included in the initial focus of the project, then resources will be committed to them; those same resources might have been necessary to deliver fully on the core goals. But if secondary goals are acknowledged as secondary, you allow yourself the flexibility to bring them into the project only when you know that doing so won't force you to compromise the core goals of the project.

Determining the relative importance of business goals can be tricky. The goals are reflections of the diverse interests of your stakeholders; each person's assessment of priorities will be different. Bringing the project's mission statement and success criteria back into the center of the conversation helps refocus the group. Ask the group to look at the list of goals they've assembled and think about how essential each goal is to fulfilling on the project's mission and meeting its success criteria. After they've had time to consider the question, run a spending exercise.

In this case, the amount of currency distributed should be more than the amount distributed the first time. Some stakeholders may feel that nearly every business goal needs to be a top priority, so they should have the opportunity to distribute their votes evenly over a larger number of options. Other stakeholders may be inclined to a more distinct prioritization, so they should be able to cast multiple votes for a given goal to give it greater weight. At the end of this exercise, you'll hopefully have a clear picture of the weight of priority and a good idea of where to draw the line between core, secondary, and tertiary goals.

Alternatively, you can ask the group to sort the business goals into three groups:

- *Essential (must have)*
- *Helpful (nice to have)*
- *Defer*

This approach can work in smaller group settings and may be preferable to a spending exercise because it forces the group to discuss and negotiate every decision rather than allowing them to rank things without having to share and justify their thinking. Again, every participant should consider this prioritization with the project mission and success criteria foremost in their minds.

As with everything else you do with your stakeholders, the end result must reflect a genuine consensus. There may be disagreements within the group, but those disagreements should be discussed and resolved; don't allow individual stakeholders to be overruled by the majority. If the outvoted stakeholders don't assent to being overruled or aren't brought around to agreement, they'll begin to hold the project in negative regard. This will cause them to tend to disagree with future decisions, because the decisions will be based on conclusions they don't agree with.

Documenting the results

The process of documenting of the results of these exercises is very similar to the process used for documenting user attributes. The documentation is intended to inform the project team, but also to memorialize the decisions and thinking that occurred for stakeholders. This helps them remember why certain decisions were made and helps ensure a lasting assent to the results.

Besides documenting the final prioritized list of goals, the documentation should also include summaries of the basis of the more important and contentious decisions. As you prepare the documentation, seek out each stakeholder to ensure they feel that their interests are properly taken into account in the results. You'll need to address specific concerns that they still have before the documentation is finalized. Even if a stakeholder's opinion is in the minority and isn't represented in the results, that person's assent to the results is nevertheless essential. Documenting their opinions along with everything else can go a long way toward reassuring them that their concerns have been heard and will be taken into account.

Maintaining Stakeholder Buy-in

Though the main purpose of this stage is to gain a clear understanding of the business goals, you also need to use it as an opportunity to build and maintain stakeholder buy-in. The process of investigating the business perspective is the first and perhaps most important opportunity for you to build your credibility. You need to help stakeholders understand how uncertainty affects the project and why restraint is such an important discipline. You also need to work hard to obtain their enthusiastic buy-in. If their buy-in is only tepid or skeptical, the project faces almost certain crises down the road.

You have an opportunity to build some early credibility by simply showing up for these meetings and exercises with a clear plan and an informed understanding of how everything should work. It's likely that the stakeholders will feel a bit overwhelmed as they contemplate what needs to be done, so you will earn a lot of respect right out the gate if you bring clarity, focus, and a sense of confidence to the group. And you will gain trust by going out of your way to ensure that everyone's views are heard and individually seeking their approval.

A thoughtful, attractive packaging of the final documentation can also go a long way to build credibility. Sloppy, rushed summaries of the work done in this phase might belittle their contributions. A little attention to the quality of the presentation will go a long way toward ensuring the documentation will be treated as professional and complete.

Much or all of the thought and decision making that happens during this phase will happen in a group setting, so remember that some people, whether for personal or political reasons, don't do very well in groups. People might be quiet, easily talked down, or generally deferential—but they still have strong opinions. Stakeholders who don't feel they've been heard or who think their ideas were unfairly dismissed or overlooked can lose trust in you and potentially derail the project.

Chapter 6
Getting to Know the User

The UX quality of your product will be determined by how successful you are at making the user's needs the central focus of the product's development. Though the broad scope of the project is set and constrained by the goals of the business, attending to the needs of the user is the means of accomplishing those goals. The needs of the user must be a priority from day one and must be central to the work of the whole project and team. Responsibility for attending to the user's needs is not isolated to a single phase or a specific few members of the team. An understanding of and empathy for the user must suffuse the project at every level, informing prioritizations and decisions made by all members of the team. The framework for this kind of decision making is what user research brings to the project.

User research discovers information about the user needs that is necessary to form a key part of the framework requirements. You learned in Chapter 3 that framework requirements are an elucidation of the problem, not an attempt to define a solution. They serve as a flexible but fixed framework of constraints that help answer questions as they arise during the course of the project. Accordingly, the end result of user research isn't a set of complete designs, nor is it a complete catalog of answers—in other words, it isn't a depiction of the solution. In user research, actual users are studied in order to build a framework that will help the project team solve problems and answer questions in the best interests of users during the development stage.

Recognizing the need to think about the user's perspective is an important first step—one that's overlooked all too frequently. But just thinking about it isn't enough; the team's understanding of that perspective must be supported by researched specifics. The details of user behaviors and goals help the project team understand how users will approach the product, how the product will fit into their lives, and how the product can successfully meet their needs. This allows the project team to see the product from the user's perspective, and to determine answers to questions and solve problems in ways that best honor the user's needs.

As you proceed deeper into the project lifecycle, the need to employ specialized professionals to do the work gets more and more important. It's possible, though not advisable, for a project leader to conduct the exercises described in the previous chapter without the support of a UX professional. But trying to perform user research without the support of professional user researchers is very risky. Misleading results from user research can be a bigger problem than no research at all. User research serves as a key part of the framework requirements, so getting user research wrong means that your project will be built atop a weak foundation. Our goal in this chapter is to equip you with an overview of how user research is performed, so ideally, you can understand and support the work of professional user researchers.

Valuing User Research

With a UX-focused product, the needs of the user should trump nearly any other consideration. Meeting user goals is an essential stepping stone to the achievement of business goals. User research is an opportunity to verify or challenge assumptions that the company, stakeholders, and project team have about the users and project priorities. Whether they realize it or not, people inside your company likely have a poor understanding of actual users. They think users want the same things they want and think the same way they do, but in most situations users are quite different from company employees. And the understanding of customers that arises from interactions through sales and marketing differs from the understanding of users needed to build a software product. User research challenges and validates assumptions and offers often surprising insights that help the team overcome false preconceptions or a lack of information. Without research, the assumptions become the basis for decision making and design all throughout the project, and weaknesses in the assumptions will diminish the quality of the product.

User research is also a very useful tool in building and maintaining stakeholder buy-in. Much of what you learn through user research is revelatory and unexpected; it can give stakeholders insight into their customers that they'll appreciate. That will, in turn, help them to value the user-centricity of the project. User research is also helpful as an objective point of reference for resolving disagreements among stakeholders and project team members. In every decision, the user should be the final arbiter of what's right and wrong; compelling user research makes it possible for the user's perspective to be represented in decision making.

User research benefits everyone involved in the project, including the UX professionals; they aren't immune from false preconceptions and assumptions. Users are diverse and frequently surprising, and revelatory discoveries found through actual user research can affect the course of a project in unforeseen and positive ways.

We recently worked with a large company that engaged us to build a new, radically improved portal for business-to-business (B2B) sales and account self-management. Among the six major capabilities they wanted to build, high on the priority list was a product configurator that would support advanced configuration of their extremely complicated product suite. Our client also wanted people from their customers' companies to be able to use the B2B portal to collaborate with other people in their companies as well as with the client's sales reps and technical support agents. The collaboration system was given a lower priority (to the point of being considered optional) for the first version of the product, but it was included in early planning to begin plotting how these systems would eventually be integrated in the portal.

The configurator made a lot of sense to us, because their product suite was so complicated that assisted configuration seemed necessary, and also because we'd built a number of successful configurators for other clients. On the other hand, we were very skeptical of the value of and need for the collaboration system. We couldn't figure out why business customers buying this particular product suite would need a specialized collaboration system specific to this one vendor's product suite. We were also wary of the fact that collaboration and social networking have become "me too" buzzword concepts that we're often asked to add in even when they make no sense at all for the product at hand.

This particular client understood the importance and value of user research wholeheartedly and had allocated a great deal of money and time to an extensive user research phase. As we started talking to real users, we made a number of interesting discoveries. First, the people who would be using this portal were very experienced professionals. They knew exactly what they wanted, what kinds and configurations of products their businesses required, and all of the technical terminology and nuances associated with the domain. Their intensive professional concentration and specialization meant that they didn't need any help when it came to configuring new product solutions.

But despite these customers' deep professional experience, they weren't in a position to make independent decisions for their companies. In developing a recommendation for a new configuration of the product, they had to bounce all types of information and requests off of other decision makers in their companies. They were also responsible for constantly communicating the status of their purchased solutions and connecting the billing for the product to their companies' purchasing processes. And they were constantly spending time on the phone and collaborating with the product's sales representatives, sales engineers, and other support agents.

Based on these observations, it became clear that our initial assumptions were dead wrong. The users of this new portal needed much greater assistance in facilitating the volume and complexities of collaboration and communication over the ordering and management of our client's products. They needed little or no help in designing configurations for the product. As a result, emphasis of the project—in the form of attention, time, and money—was shifted away from the configurator and onto the collaboration system.

Had we just proceeded based on our own assumptions, we would have taken our client down the wrong path and wasted resources and time. But part of the discipline of building user-focused software products involves a cultivated humility and acknowledgment that users are full of surprises. Products built on the assumptions of a few technical professionals or businesspeople—instead of on actual user feedback—suffer in quality and success.

Combating Pressure to Skip User Research

The tendency of insights arising from user research to be revelatory and unexpected should be welcomed and expected. This is part of the reason why you should never dismiss user research. Proceeding without the benefit of serious user research means that all of the subsequent design decisions in the project will be based on assumptions about user needs instead of factual findings. This means the quality of the product will be a function of the quality of the assumptions. And, as we've just said, even UX professionals and domain experts often get those assumptions very, very wrong.

But at the beginning of any project, there's typically a strong impulse to save time and money by skipping user research and immediately diving into building the product. This is a result of the misconception that user research is a "nice-to-have" component that increases costs, creates delays, and adds only marginal benefit to the project. In our experience, however, spending time and money on user research generally doesn't increase the amount of time and money the project requires. Good user research helps the project proceed more rapidly and minimizes mistakes. It helps you set out on the correct initial course and stay on course. It makes it easier for the project team to determine the best solutions to problems, to make correct decisions, and to keep the project focused on what is actually important instead of what was presumed important. This has the general effect of improving your project's efficiency and pace of progress, which saves as much cost and time as you expended in performing the research in the first place. And a product built with the benefit of good user research will have a much better UX.

When you realize that allowing room for user research doesn't add cost and time to the project and results in higher-quality products and a greater chance of success, the argument to skip user research is an argument to spend the same amount of time and money for a lower-quality product at greater risk of failure.

We recently worked with a large consumer-oriented financial institution that was looking to modernize their online channel experience. During the research phase, they were concerned about the time (about a month) that was being spent on user research and worried that it was going to delay the initial design deliverables. We reassured them that the user research would reduce the time needed for the design phase. They allowed us to complete the research, and after only two weeks of initial design, we delivered the first concepts for a large portion of the product. This delivery came much more quickly than our client had expected; they even requested that we slow down to give them more time to respond to deliverables. We've found that user research does nothing to delay a project because it allows designers to make decisions much more quickly and accurately, shortens review cycles, reduces churn, and ultimately leads to a higher quality of products.

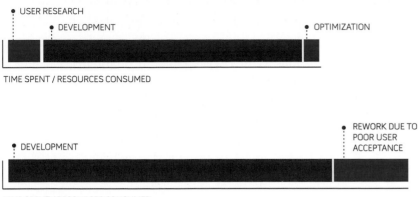

TIME SPENT / RESOURCES CONSUMED

TIME SPENT / RESOURCES CONSUMED

The time and cost of user research can make the overall project more efficient by reducing churn and avoiding poor user acceptance.

Key Concepts in User Research

User research is more than just an exercise in collecting statistics, trivia, and demographic information about users. Although that type of information is useful, it provides an incomplete and overly flat picture of users. Your project team needs a deep, rich understanding of users to be able to make correct decisions from the user's perspective. Since most members of the project team won't have the opportunity to get to know actual users, user research needs to provide the team with a means of seeing things from the user's perspective.

Empathy

By "empathy," we don't mean, of course, a sense of teary-eyed compassion for the plight of the user (although bad software UX definitely has the capacity to reduce users to tears). Rather, we mean it in the sense of the ability to understand, on both an intellectual and intuitive level, the users' needs and to see things from their perspective.

> *Sometimes when we suggest that the experience of interacting with software can be emotionally pleasurable and engaging, people (usually engineers) act puzzled at the idea of software having anything to do with emotion. But emotion underlies every human behavior and interaction, and software is no exception. It's often easier for people to imagine negative emotional experiences with software than positive ones, which indicates not the impossibility of positive experiences but the relative dearth of them so far in the history of software.*

Just as with every other component of the framework requirements, the goal in user research isn't to answer every possible question about the user's needs and perspective in advance, but rather to provide a framework for the team to answer those questions as they arise. Empathy on intellectual and intuitive levels allows them to take thoughtfully focused but relatively sparse information about users and use it to judge things and answer questions from their perspectives.

User Goals Versus Product Features and Tasks

The concept of "goals" is particularly significant in user research and UX design. To stakeholders and members of the project team, a product can seem to be a collection of features that gives users access to a set of capabilities. But to users, a product is a tool used to accomplish some higher-level goal. Those goals are accomplished using the features and capabilities available in the product, but the user's intention in using the product is to achieve his goals, not to simply employ the product's features and capabilities. Even with games, which are a type of software that has no strictly utilitarian purpose, the user's primary goal is to be entertained. He accomplishes that goal by operating the controller and progressing through the storyline, which are features of the game software. The use of those features isn't his goal, per se; they're the means by which he accomplishes his goal of being entertained.

Goals are also different from tasks. Tasks are the steps a user goes through when using the product to accomplish his goals, but the tasks themselves, like the employment of the features, aren't the end goal. The desire to achieve the goals is what motivates the user to employ a given set of features of a given product to perform a series of tasks that ultimately accomplish the goal. The meaningfulness of these distinctions is best demonstrated through the following example.

Essentially every official business activity is at some point discussed and formalized in some written form of communication: interoffice memos, sales proposals, contracts, legal demands, letters of introduction, tickets for business travel, and so on. Time is of the essence in almost every type of correspondence and documentation, so the goal of quickly exchanging this documentation has long been an important goal in business. The means by which that exchange has been facilitated—the features and capabilities of services and products that have been employed to accomplish the tasks required to achieve the goal—and the standards for quickness have changed dramatically over the last couple of hundred years, although the goal itself has not.

As an example, consider that a business in St. Joseph, Missouri, wants to send an agreement for the sale of a plot of land to its purchaser in Sacramento, California. This is a business scenario that was as normal and plausible in 1860 as it is today. The two high-level tasks required to accomplish this goal are first to prepare the agreement, and then to convey it to the purchaser. The means by which these tasks are accomplished have changed dramatically over the past century and a half.

In 1860, the agreement would likely have been written in longhand. A couple of decades later, it would probably have been prepared using a typewriter. Many decades later, it might have been prepared on an early computer and printed out on a dot-matrix printer. In slightly more recent times, it would be prepared and printed with more sophisticated computer equipment and software.

In 1860, the handwritten agreement might have been delivered by the famed Pony Express on a 10-day horse ride across the country. Later, the agreement might have been conveyed across the country by the U.S. Postal Service using a combination of trains, horse carts, or early automobiles in a matter of about five days. Fast forwarding past the era of the dot-matrix printer, the agreement might never have been physically delivered; it might have been faxed for near-instantaneous delivery. There was—honestly—a time when 14,400 bits (yes, bits) per second was considered basically instantaneous. More recently, that agreement might have been delivered in digital format as an email attachment with no physical copy ever trading hands.

Though the nature of the tasks involved in achieving the goal of conveying a legal document from one party to another has changed tremendously over the years, the goal has remained the same. The tasks have required typewriters, fax machines, PCs, the Pony Express, the post office, and email. Each has its own peculiar features and tasks required to successfully operate them, but the goal has remained the same.

Because user goals are constant and knowable while everything else is in flux, they are the ideal conception of the user perspective for the framework requirements. They exist at a high level and stay consistent through a long history of changes in technology and product capabilities. Each new product development effort entails tailoring the current technological capabilities and business considerations to user goals. It also requires a fresh examination of user behaviors, which do change over time.

Qualitative Versus Quantitative Research Methods

It's difficult to describe a person's conscious experience in the form of quantitative data. Demographic research can yield quantitative results about the target market segment or user base (62 percent are men, 14 percent spend two or more hours a day watching television, and so on), and certain types of ultra-clinical usability research can result in quantitative or quasi-quantitative results. But there are limits to the value of this type of approach in user research and design for UX.

Some researchers try to dress up all information collected through user research in the clothing of quantitative results (for example, 47 percent of people thought our product was 30–70 percent better than our competitor's). The appeal of this approach is that these points of data make a beautiful line on a graph and hold greater credibility because of their apparently solid, scientific quality. But representing qualitative feedback from users in numeric form doesn't change the nature of that feedback from qualitative to quantitative.

Another reason why it's appealing to portray qualitative feedback in a numeric form is that it seems to suggest that statistical analyses could be done on the data to expose new information, but that's generally not the case. If you discover that 18 percent of users rate your product's UX at 2 or worse and 45 percent rate it at a 3 or worse on a scale of 10, you've learned something vaguely interesting but not terribly useful. You can't extrapolate any new information from these findings; they just let you know that improvements are needed...somewhere. This kind of information can remind you that you're on a damaged ship in a darkened sea full of rocks, but offers no map or illumination to help you navigate safely to shore.

The principal goal of user research is to communicate findings about a limited sample of users to give the project team to the ability to understand the broader user base and see things from the user's perspective. As a result, the information that user research produces must allow the project team to make inferences and extrapolate from it. This would seem to be an argument for more numeric data, but in fact, the opposite is better.

Qualitative research on a sample of users, even if converted to numeric form, cannot be extrapolated, interpolated, or inferred from using statistical methods. Most of it can't even be plotted on a graph in any truly meaningful way. Although there are formal methods of analysis (Grounded Theory, for example) that are useful in building from qualitative research, in practical reality anything that rigorous is seldom in the budget. Rather, the most effective mechanisms for making inferences from user research are human intuition and empathy.

Members of the project team can look at stories about users' lives and their experiences using the product and, using intuition and empathy, make accurate projections about the user's point of view regarding things not specifically addressed in the research. The empathetic and intuitive capacity of the team is what allows research on a limited sample of users to be used as an intelligent, expansible, and flexible part of the framework requirements.

So, although at first blush, qualitative user research might seem to be less scientific and therefore less credible, it's actually much more useful to the team. It gets closer to the core of the user's subjective experience in a way that allows the team to make the best intuitive and empathetic inferences. This makes it possible for every member of the team to represent the user's interests, ensuring that the user's goals—and, therefore, UX quality—are kept at the center of decision making.

The apparent precision of quantitative data can also give the false impression that it's the most simple and direct route to answers. Back in 2000, when tools to gather website analytics were relatively new and expensive, people were just beginning to understand the effect of "banner blindness"—the tendency of website visitors to unconsciously ignore anything that looked like a banner ad. A large online travel company conducted a study to find out how people were using their site. Through quantitative analysis of the site's analytics, they discovered that a significant percentage of users were not getting beyond the home page. But the quantitative data offered no explanation of why this might be.

Usability experts (as they were called back then) were able to convince the travel company's executives that a qualitative study would shed better light on the situation. The first research participant who attempted to book travel online didn't make it past the first page. The "call-to-action" (the all-important button that advances you to the next stage in the purchase or conversion process) looked so much like a banner ad that the user simply did not see it. After the second and third consecutive users had this same problem, it was obvious that banner blindness was interfering with the site's success. This made both the problem and its solution quickly and plainly obvious. It was a win for the usability team, but more importantly the user struggling to book travel won relief and the business won increased revenue through radically improved conversion. The qualitative approach was cheap, fast, and offered an immediate answer to the question, "Why?" There are many cases like this in UX design where quantitative data might indicate that a problem exists, but a qualitative study is needed to know how to respond.

Who Should Be Involved in the Research

So much of user research is a combination of art and science that, as we've said, you'd be hard pressed to get through it successfully without the assistance of a professional user researcher. If you must press on without the aid of a professional, spend some time reading books that go into significantly greater depth on the process and discipline of user research than the high-level view we present in this book. If this is the route you take, you'll need to acknowledge that the results of your user research will be less robust, since it will be missing everything that the deep experience of a professional brings. Ensure that the project team is aware of this as they make use of the research results so they'll be prepared to identify and respond to weaknesses in the research. For the rest of this chapter, though, we'll assume that you'll have professional assistance.

You should be present for much or all of the user research process. This helps you get acquainted with the users directly and develop an early empathy for user needs. During the research process, keep quiet and simply observe. This prevents you from affecting the course of the discussion and the discoveries that result, and allows the one-on-one, comfortable interaction between the researcher and the user to proceed undisturbed.

It can also be helpful to bring stakeholders along for some of the interviews. It gives them an opportunity to see the process, listen to the questions, and understand the approach taken in user research. This reassures them that the research is valuable and is representing their customers' interests effectively. Stakeholders often become very engaged during the process, helping to ask questions and explore tasks that shed light on the problem. It's also a good opportunity for team building between the project leader, the researcher, and the stakeholders. It typically has the effect of getting everyone energized about the project and very considerate of the user's needs. This has obvious value as you continue through the project, and can also produce engaged stakeholders who will help you keep the other stakeholders on board.

There are risks, however, in involving stakeholders in user research. It's helpful when they constructively engage in the interview process, but some stakeholders might use it as an opportunity to push a particular agenda by asking leading questions or trying to direct the course of the discussion. Also, stakeholders who were involved with the previous version of the product can get very frustrated when they see users having trouble using the old system. We've seen some instances where a stakeholder intervened to try to educate the user on how to use the old system rather than simply observing the problems. There's also a risk that a stakeholder might seize on one particular challenge or observation of one particular user that might be minor or atypical and use it to try to push some personal agenda. But stakeholder support is such an essential element of a successful project that any risks to the research tend to be worth it. Good user research professionals know how to accommodate stakeholders in their research processes while maintaining its quality. You can also avoid many of these problems by preparing the stakeholders properly about the goals and practice of research ahead of time.

Finding Research Participants

In the business planning stage, you worked with stakeholders to produce a restrained set of key user attributes. The task of assembling the sample user set involves finding individuals who are good representatives of the key user attributes and who are currently using or are likely to use your product or one similar to it. The key user attributes will be useful in constraining the possible field of sample users into a manageable set, but within those constraints it's important to find a relatively diverse range of users. If your key user attributes describe, for example, marketing executives who manage budgets of $5–15M, then you might seek out:

- *Users working for companies in different industries*
- *Users managing budgets scattered throughout that $5–15M range*
- *Users representing a mixture of men and women*
- *Users of varying ages*

This practice leads to more roundly representative research. It's not always the case, by the way, that industry, gender, or age are the key variables of diversity. This will vary by project.

Stakeholders, salespeople, marketing managers, and other customer-focused colleagues help you identify potential research subjects. If the product is meant for internal use, then the job of finding sample users can be as easy as working through your company staff directory. Although it might seem like an imposition to ask someone to participate as a subject in user research, people often feel honored that you're interested in their perspective. Most participants are eager to help shape a product to better suit their own needs and to get a peek behind the curtain of software development. You can also promise a free copy of the final product to customers who participate in research, and people are usually more than happy to help out if there's a free lunch involved.

Determining the Research Sample Size

While quantitative research tends to require large sample sizes (usually in the thousands), qualitative research usually succeeds with surprisingly small sample sizes. This has been noted by the usability and UX experts Jakob Nielsen, Jared Spool, and Allen Cooper in some of their books and articles, and is something we encounter consistently in the user research we do. During business planning on a recent project, we determined that the following types of people would be the primary users of the product:

- *Network administrators in large businesses*
- *Billing analysts in large businesses*
- *Business owners in mid-size and smaller businesses*
- *Help desk agents from the product company's staff*
- *Sales representatives from the product company's staff*

We spoke to about 8–10 people in each group, for a total of 40–50 users in the sample. Working with a sample of this size, the user research stage took about three weeks.

There's no rule of thumb for determining how many people you need to work with; the size of the sample is dependent on project-specific considerations. The number of key user attributes identified through your work with stakeholders is a major factor. If only a small number of attributes were identified, then you need only find a representative diversity within the narrow constraints of those attributes. More user attributes will mean, of course, a larger sample. You needn't be overly meticulous when it comes to finding a diverse group internal to a given user attribute. Looking back to the example in the previous section, you needn't ensure that you have one male and one female marketing executive from every possible combination of industry, budget size, and age bracket. Often just a few people representing a given user attribute will suffice.

User research needs to balance expedience with thoroughness, and there's a rapidly diminishing return of value as you start to work with more and more people. This is particularly the case with user research for enterprise products, where we've found the user feedback is typically surprisingly homogeneous. The jobs found in large businesses—administrative assistant, help desk agent, network administrator, and so on—are often very similar across many companies. The reasons enterprise product users use the product, the demands imposed on them by their jobs, and the environments they're using the product in are relatively consistent.

For consumer products where the user's experience is guided less by standardized roles within organizations and more by personal considerations, more (but not dramatically more) research subjects are valuable. The target user attributes for consumer projects are typically strongly based on market segments, which are broad categories of people. You may have as a key user attribute, for example, the market segment "housewife." Housewives aren't a homogeneous group of people. Their backgrounds, home lives, motivations, brand loyalties, budget constraints, technical savvy, routines, and other wide-ranging factors will influence their relationship with a software product. Since "housewives" is such a broad user attribute, you'd need to plan to work with more research subjects to get a full understanding of the group. User researchers need to keep researching users until they notice and then confirm consistent patterns in the feedback.

The point where researchers are able to establish and confirm patterns is called saturation. It's the point where researchers start hearing the same things over and over, and stop identifying anything new or eye-opening. As we've said, researchers will usually hit saturation faster in enterprise products than in consumer ones, but in either case they may hit saturation sooner than they had originally expected. In these cases, it can be sensible to end the research early.

When choosing the size of the sample, be careful to consider your stakeholders' expectations and the effect on the credibility of your research. Your stakeholders' trust in and deference to the user's perspective as discovered and represented through user research will be critical to the project's success, so their expectations must be taken seriously. Sometimes talking to just eight users will be entirely sufficient from a research perspective, but won't seem thorough and compelling enough to garner the trust of your stakeholders. Small samples might also inadvertently exclude specific user or customer types that one of your stakeholders cares deeply about. Before starting the research, share your user researchers' plans with your stakeholders, whether individually or as a group. You need to ensure that they understand how user research works, that they support the research approach, and that they think the research sample is sufficiently representative. It's critical that the stakeholders support and respect the results of user research. You'll be pressing them to think about the product from the user's perspective and to be deferential to user needs, which are represented by the research results. If they're going to support and respect the research results, they first need to support and respect the way the research is conducted.

We recently went through an extensive user research phase for a huge enterprise product where we'd scheduled dozens of user interviews over a period of several days. We started hitting saturation very early, but we still continued on to complete over 60 hours of interviews. In this case, our client was very sensitive to the size of the research sample and keen to ensure all possible customers were included, so we continued on. Though the research itself yielded rapidly diminishing value for the project team, the value of our client's confidence in the results of the research and our diligence in respecting their interests trumped simple expedience.

Making Recordings

It will be useful all throughout the research process to make recordings of the time spent with users. The recordings are useful as reference material during the subsequent analysis and documentation of the research. Recordings are also a good way to share the user research process with stakeholders. They're more effective in building emotional buy-in and deference to the user's needs than documentation of the research findings alone. In the research stage of a product redesign effort we were involved in, we captured video of a user who got so frustrated and angry trying to use the product that he actually screamed and smashed the keyboard with his fist. When this video was shown to stakeholders, the product redesign suddenly acquired a much higher priority and budget.

How you record the sessions will depend on the situation. For the purposes of reference and stakeholder buy-in, video is preferable because it's more engaging and records more information, including the user's actual activities and workspace. You don't need a person in the room operating the camera; this is overkill and distracting. Just put a camcorder on a tripod in a position that lets it capture as much of the user's behavior and reactions as possible. One downside to video cameras is they can affect the way people behave and their comfort level in the conversation. Getting authentic information and putting users at ease are more important goals than capturing video. In some cases, placing the camera where it's easy to forget about it can mitigate this effect. It also helps to spend a little time with users and just have a casual conversation with them while the camera is running to get them acclimated to the environment and the presence of the camera.

If a video camera is too disruptive or intrusive, an audio recorder can work just fine. Audio recorders are much less conspicuous and are easily forgotten, even if they're sitting on the desk next to the user. People don't feel the need to give a performance in quite the same way as they do when they're on camera.

Whether you're recording video and audio or just audio alone, the quality of the audio capture is tremendously important. It's very aggravating to try to work your way through noisy, unclear recordings to try to find that one nugget of insight you're looking for. It also detracts tremendously from the emotional buy-in value to your stakeholders and makes the project look less professional. When setting up the video or audio recorder, consider the audio dynamics of the space and use decent quality equipment. When using the equipment in a new environment, make sure to test it to ensure that the recording will be usable. If positioning the video camera inconspicuously leads to bad audio capture, consider using a separate audio recording device as well. Also, be careful to keep audio recorders away from keyboards, air conditioning vents, and other sources of ambient noise, and also away from cell phones, as they cause interference in microphones even when they're not on a call.

Research Through Speaking with Users

Getting direct feedback from users is the primary mechanism of user research. It has its risks and drawbacks—users often misunderstand and therefore misrepresent their own interests and activities—but skillful user researchers can glean valuable insights through simple structured and unstructured discussions with users. As with everything that's done in user research, the goals of these conversations are to:

- *Alert researchers to key points of difficulty and opportunity in the product from the user's perspective*

- *Find the facts and stories that will help communicate the user's needs and interests down the line*

- *Develop an intuitive understanding of and empathy for the users that will be useful in conferring the same to other members of the project team*

User Interviews

We rarely conduct or recommend user research through group sessions or focus groups. The dynamics of the group and the difference in people's behavior within the group tends to lead to overly general or skewed information. The best information comes through one-on-one interactions with the users in the space where they will actually use the product. User interviews should also be comfortable and conversational, rather than formal and rigid. The goal is to elicit honest and insightful information from the users in whatever directions that might take you—not to simply work through a predetermined set of interview questions.

The user researcher will prepare interview questions based on what they know from the project's mission, business requirements, and key user attributes. The questions are open-ended and flexible, and during the interview, the researcher invites meandering discussions. This openness allows the user to introduce subjects and questions the researcher might not have anticipated, which enriches that interview and all subsequent ones. The researcher is there to listen and nudge the user occasionally to get important insights into the user's goals, the context in which the user uses the product, and the user's primary concerns and pain points. The researcher will also be trying to establish an empathic rapport with the user and get herself into the user's shoes in preparation for the task of helping the rest of the team get into the same position.

As the researchers complete more and more interviews, they'll start to get a clearer picture of the problem and know better what questions they should be asking and what issues they should be exploring. If they find something interesting midway through the interviews and start asking questions about it for the remaining interviewees, they'll probably want to go back to the prior interviewees to confirm the pattern and strengthen the data. So it's valuable to ask each research subject at the end of the interview for permission to contact them again to follow up. This can be as simple as making a phone call or sending a brief survey of follow-up questions.

Ten Typical Questions We Ask in User Interviews

Understanding the Steps

- "How do you do [a certain task]?"

- "Where would you start?"

- "What would you do next?"

- "What information do you need to complete this task?"

- "Can you show me how you do that?"

Understanding the Experience

- "Is any part of this process difficult or frustrating?"

- "Did that seem slow/fast/normal?"

- "Is that what you were hoping for?"

- "What's the most enjoyable part of this process for you?"

- "What's a successful outcome?"

Structured Interview Techniques

Although user interviews generally allow the user's thoughts to wander broadly and remain open-ended to ensure that everything has a chance to be said, there are a few structured interview techniques that can help pull out additional insights and information. They help get to a deeper level of detail than comes naturally through informal conversation, and uncover things that are often missed in interviews.

Guided storytelling

Guided storytelling is a useful technique in getting a specific picture of how a user finds his way through tasks or attempts to achieve his goals in working with a product. The researcher prompts the user with a question like: "Tell me about the last time you tried to check out your investments online," or "Tell me about the most frustrating experience you've had working with this product." The user will tell the story of that situation and what issues occurred along the way. Being near the user's computer can be useful in this sort of exercise, as it helps the user recreate the experience or refresh his memory by looking back to the product. Because the user is being prompted to tell a specific story rather than to make generalized statements about his experience with the product, he'll reveal more specifics, helping researchers detect unexplored avenues.

Task analysis

Task analysis is a means of getting into even greater specifics with key or problematic tasks within the system. The interviewer works with the user to either list or diagram all of the steps required to complete a particular task or accomplish a particular goal, including any steps or tasks that might occur outside of the software product itself. This kind of detail can reveal a lot about how users think, how they interact with systems, and how they might have developed unique workarounds for problematic interactions. It can also expose opportunities to consolidate or simplify tasks, helping you mold the product to operate more consistently with the way users approach tasks within the system.

Research Through Direct Observation

After speaking with users, there's still much to be discovered about their interests, challenges, and behaviors that they didn't think to tell the researchers. Users can be surprisingly unaware of certain details of their interactions with a product because they've grown so adept at operating it and sidestepping its problems that they're not actively conscious of what they're doing.

To illustrate this outside the context of software, try telling the story of what you do after you leave work for the day. Your story will likely be something like, "I drive home, take the dogs out for a walk, cook and eat dinner with my family, help the kids with their homework, watch some TV news, and then go to bed." What you will have omitted from this story, however, is a ton of specifics.

For example:

- *I jiggle the steering wheel while trying to start my car because the wheel lock always makes the key stick.*

- *I turn down Fourth Street, then Broadway, and then onto the frontage road, avoiding the freeway because it's always too congested at rush hour.*

- *I park in the driveway because my garage is too full of tools and junk to park in it anymore.*

- *I spend a lot of my walk trying to keep my dogs from entangling me in their leashes and trying to find a trash can to throw their poop bags in so I don't have to carry them all the way home.*

- *Either I or my spouse does all of the cooking because there's only one sink and not enough counter space for two people to work.*

- *Half the time I spend helping my kids with their homework is spent trying to understand the cryptic instructions given by their teachers and my kids' hazy recollection of what they're supposed to do.*

- *I watch CNN for about 20 minutes before nodding off on the sofa.*

If a researcher were charged with trying to help you have a better experience of life after leaving work, these details would be immensely useful. But it's all so routine that these tasks are performed without thought and without much memory of having performed them. This is where direct observation can step in to capture the useful details.

In direct observation for software, the researcher watches users operating the product to accomplish real tasks and goals. The researcher looks for a number of things the users won't generally report themselves and also observes the context in which those tasks are performed. The researcher is watching in particular for tasks that users perform repeatedly; even if the tasks aren't dysfunctional, it's still useful to know where users' time and mouse clicks are focused. The researchers are also watching for tasks and behaviors that are common across most or all users, as well as specific idiosyncrasies or workarounds that certain users might have consciously or unconsciously developed. It's also interesting to note how users are physically interacting with their systems—whether they're always sitting or often moving around, or where they've positioned their screen and keyboard, for example. While the researcher is trying to be unobtrusive, she might occasionally ask a user questions about peculiar behaviors she notices, being careful to ensure that the questions don't sound judgmental and don't suggest solutions to problems the user is encountering. If a user is doing something repeatedly or unexpectedly, it's valuable to learn why he's doing it.

A lot of valuable information and cues can be taken from looking at the users' workspaces, too. For example, users often tape cheat sheets to their monitors or tack notes to the wall reminding them of important keyboard shortcuts, account numbers, support phone numbers, and other information they use daily. These cheat sheets are usually a coping mechanism for something that's problematic with the product. We were doing research for a client that has franchise customers that manage a lot of individual locations and stores. Each location and store had a name, but our client's product used an account number—not an account name—to identify each location and store. As a result, people using the product had spreadsheets taped to their walls that associated account numbers with store and location names. This observation made it clear that we could help reduce some mental anguish, workspace clutter, and unneeded steps for users simply by adding the ability to nickname accounts in the product.

The user's experience of interacting with the product is also influenced by factors that come from outside the product itself. Stakeholders and users often don't think to alert researchers to external factors that are integral to the product experience, so researchers observe what external systems, materials, and cues influence and accompany the user's experience of the product. These observations can indicate the ways in which the product can be more broadly useful or simplify greater swaths of the user's work life. For example, if users frequently have to retrieve information from documents on the company network to accomplish tasks within the product, those documents might need to be brought within the scope of the product or the product might need to provide an alternative means of accessing the same information.

Cheat sheets provide clues about what's important or hard to remember.

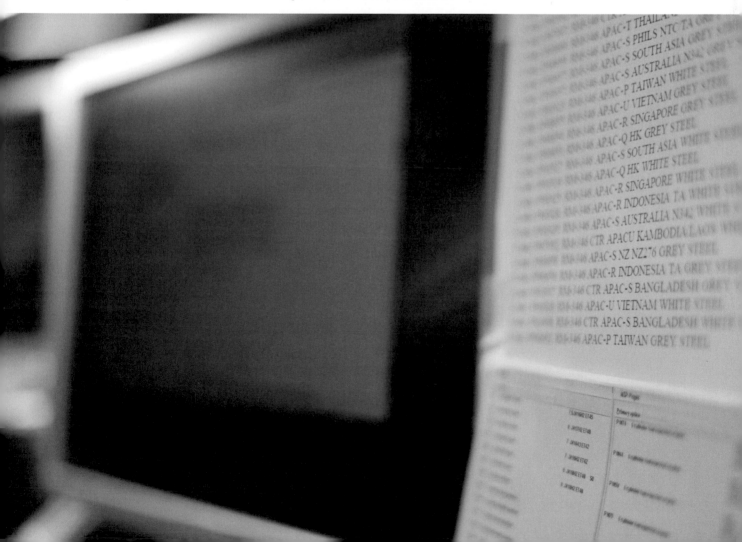

Analyzing the Research Observations

The user researchers' interviews and observations will reveal some clear patterns of behavior, challenges, and opportunities that will be apparent on at least an intuitive level. Throughout the research process, researchers will gather far more information than you can deliver to the project team or incorporate into the framework requirements. Therefore, it's necessary to analyze the research observations to generate usable results for the rest of the team.

This analysis involves taking all of the raw research observations and looking for meaningful patterns. These patterns are used to identify archetypal users, which deepens the project team's understanding of the target users. This analysis also helps identify common patterns in interactions, problems, and opportunities.

Discovering Personas

The concept of personas might already be somewhat familiar to you if you've had exposure to UX design, CX strategy, or certain modern types of marketing research. For the purposes of UX design for software, a persona is a fictitious, archetypal user who—remembering back to the Pareto 80/20 principle—can stand as a good ambassador for the interests of a large portion of the rest of the users of the product.

The documentation of a user persona is often itself called a persona, but it's important to remember that a persona is a significant and complex concept and framework for thinking that is much deeper than the documentation that represents it. The tendency to think that personas are simply documents is consistent with the dangerous belief that software development is just a series of processes and deliverables, rather than a complex, flexible system. Persona documentation is not the goal per se, but is rather an artifact of the goal of identifying, understanding, and conveying that understanding of archetypal user personas.

User personas are usually the aggregate of a number of similar actual users encountered in user research rather than just one individual who typifies the rest. User researchers draw on their experience and various techniques to identify trends and commonalities that can be used to bring together the attributes, behaviors, and observations of a set of users into a single, roundly representative persona. Researchers devise multiple personas to represent the full diversity of the users in a distilled, thoughtfully focused form.

Example Persona: Mike S.

Mike is a recent **college** graduate. He still has the part-time job that he held while he was in school, but no immediate prospects for full-time employment. He's **worried** about paying off his student **loans** now that getting a higher-paying job is such a challenge due to the current state of the economy.

Mike and searches **Monster.com** and **Craigslist** frequently for jobs and applies online for anything that seems to have potential. Understanding that he will likely have to work from the bottom up, Mike is mostly concerned with the **reputation** of the company that he's applying to. He researches the company online before he applies and won't apply to most postings unless he knows who the employer is. If there are indicators of **growth potential**, he may contact them for more information.

Mike shares a three-bedroom apartment with a roommate near downtown. Having a roommate isn't ideal, but the high cost of living makes it necessary. Mike likes living near the city because there's more **nightlife** and better job **opportunities**. He loathes the idea of commuting, and keeps his late-model Civic around to use only when it's **convenient**.

Mike uses a Motorola Razr to **text** more often than he talks on the phone. He's confident that his next phone will be an **iPhone**. He has an Apple MacBook and loves everything Apple. He's been trying to convince his parents to buy an Apple computer to replace the current one that Mike is often called upon to fix.

Mike plays **games** on his XBox almost every night. He plays with friends online and sees it as a great way to stay in touch with his **buddies**. He is beginning to download videos more frequently, and gets excited about **convergence** of all things digital. The more things that can connect to each other, the better. Mike says that if his Xbox had a web browser he would probably stop using his computer.

Facebook is his primary online social app, but he's starting to use **Twitter** a bit and has a profile on **LinkedIn**. He had a blog for a while, but didn't feel he had time to keep it updated. There are some people he doesn't allow to see his Facebook page (coworkers, parents) but still wants to be able to communicate with. **Privacy** is still important. He is using email less frequently.

Mike's Goals:

- Find a better job at an established company
- Work his way into a good position
- Stay connected to friends

Specific Considerations:

- Mike's job-search skills are basic
- Mike is very convenience-motivated
- Mike will likely adopt a mobile platform soon
- He has an increasingly high consumption of media on multiple platforms and a variety of touchpoints
- His personal social media strategy is intermediate

"Pretty soon it's just going to be about screen size. Either you get it on the little screen in your pocket or the big one at home."

Brand affinities

The main goal of personas for software UX design is to help the project team develop empathy and accurate intuition for the needs of the user. And so personas need to be rich with details that help people put themselves in the shoes of the user. Many marketing personas you might have already encountered are limited to information such as the user's name, job title, age, income level, and a blurb about the challenges of their work. That superficial level of information does little to help the project team develop an empathic understanding of the user's perspective.

Weaving User Stories

Your research should produce a tremendous collection of information about the user's goals, needs, insights, behaviors, idiosyncrasies, solutions to problems, and so on. This information will be scattered throughout the interviews and direct observations, and you will need to assemble it in a form that's both usable and compelling.

Presenting this information in the form of a bulleted list can be give the project team some insight into the user's perspective, but it's a weak way of communicating the information; it just gives the information without trying to organize or make sense of it. The information needs to be conveyed in a way that connects the dots and reveals the implications of the findings to tell a richer story. The aim is to turn the tidbits of information into something with an emotive quality that generates a good response from stakeholders and instills the necessary understanding and empathy in the project team. To do this, researchers weave the tidbits together to tell user stories.

As the name suggests, user stories are narratives—either in written or storyboard form—of select aspects of the users' lives and experiences that have bearing on their relationship to the product. Like personas, a single user story can be woven together from observations of multiple individual users whose experiences have a common thread. These stories describe things like:

- *How users try to achieve their goals*
- *The issues and difficulties users encounter*
- *The user's frustrations and hopes*
- *The way the product fits into the user's broader work or home life*
- *A day or moment in the life of a user*

A user story in storyboard form

By virtue of their form, user stories convey an understanding of the users' interests and experiences to the team and stakeholders in an engaging, emotionally appealing way. User stories are inherently richer than simple lists of user factoids. This richness makes it easier for the project team to gain an understanding of the user's perspective and build the empathetic framework that they'll need during the project.

Discovering User Priorities

Since you developed the business requirements for the product, you'll already have a sense of user priorities. The sample users will also provide you with a strong perspective on what the product's priorities should be. You'll have learned the users' perspectives on the problems, opportunities, and likely goals for the product. Some opinions on priorities will have been directly expressed by users, whereas other opinions can be inferred by looking at the patterns and trends in the users' behaviors and feedback.

Affinity diagramming exercises like the one you learned about in Chapter 5 can be a useful in getting a clearer picture of the relative priorities of issues, goals, tasks, and opportunities. Take all of the tidbits of information and observations that were collected from each user interview and put them on sticky notes, and then cluster together the similar ideas. Clear priorities will start to emerge. The size of any collection of similar ideas indicates how important that idea is to users. This helps you determine how the importance of that particular idea for the project. You can do your affinity diagramming with just the researchers, or you can do it with your stakeholders in your ongoing efforts to build their buy-in and understanding of the user.

Guerilla User Research

Sometimes, despite your best efforts and an abundance of expert advice, you still won't garner the support, time, or money you'll need for a full user-research phase. Your project will surely suffer as a result, but it doesn't mean you should bypass entirely the end goals of user research. You'll just be forced to take a more scrappy, enterprising, and perhaps surreptitious approach—what we call guerilla user research.

User research that's fraught with assumptions because it lacks actual data is still better than no user research at all. It helps keep the entire project focused on user needs rather than ignoring the user's perspective altogether. And the assumptions you can build as a project leader will be more focused and consistent than the various assumptions software engineers and stakeholders might make themselves if you don't provide them with any common point of reference.

It might be possible to significantly shortcut the field research rather than skip it altogether. Smaller sample sizes can be used, or the field research can be approached with less detail or formality, allowing you to get through it more quickly. Shortcutting it in this way might allow you to get some valuable research data without spending much time or money, possibly even enabling you to do the research without your stakeholders being aware of it. This approach can also make user research appear less wasteful to skeptical stakeholders because it's performed rapidly and isn't as thoroughly packaged or polished.

Field research can also be simplified by conducting focus groups rather than individual interviews. But people behave differently and say different things in groups than they do one-on-one. This puts an extra burden on the researcher to mitigate the effects of the group dynamic during the focus group. It might also be possible to accomplish some level of research through simply emailing surveys and follow-up questions to a sampling of users. If it's just not possible to speak to any actual users, there are nevertheless some useful sources of insight into the user's perspective that can be found in your company. Spending some time speaking to customer-facing departments and colleagues (such as customer support, sales, and marketing) can give you some valuable insight into what users are thinking and saying.

However you manage your guerilla user research, you must finish it off with personas and user stories—just as if a full research phase had been completed. These personas and user stories will still be focal points of the design and development of the product. They're still critical to keeping the team focused on the user's perspective and needs and to providing a framework for developing empathy and intuition for user needs. But you and your team need to remember that the personas and user stories were based on incomplete research. As you progress through the project, you and the project team will have opportunities to gain a better understanding of the users than you were able to during the research stage. This will afford you valuable opportunities to revise and enrich the personas and user stories, and to recheck old decisions and designs to ensure that you made the correct choices.

Stakeholders who were unwilling to approve full user research must be made aware of the problems caused by their disapproval. They must be constantly reminded that major decisions about the product are being made based on assumptions rather than on research. As a project leader without access to real user research, your ability to produce a product that satisfies users will be hindered. It's unfair to hold you accountable to meeting actual user needs if you never had a chance to discover those needs.

Some things we've done to learn more about users:

- *Used ourselves as guinea pigs on travel sites, web-based layout tools, shipping applications*
- *Asked our mothers to try to use it*
- *Shown up at an oil change franchise and interviewed customers in the lobby about their process for choosing an oil change place*
- *Asked relatives how they decided to open a particular franchise over another*

- *Lurked on b-boy message boards to get a sense of the b-boy language and culture*

- *Toured a tea production factory, coffee shops, and book clubs to get inspiration for an online "tea experience"*

- *Shoehorned a prototype feedback session into a sales seminar for investment brokers*

- *Surfed the blogs and Facebook profiles of college-age advocates of a certain energy drink to better understand their personalities and motivations for promoting the drink*

- *Mocked up a UI in Flash for a laser waypoint measuring device and shown it to engineers (the users) to get early feedback*

Stakeholder Buy-in Through User Research

The user research phase represents another critical opportunity to build stakeholder buy-in. It's also a chance to cultivate a sense of stakeholder deference for the user's perspective. That deference depends on the stakeholders' views of the credibility of the research and their sense that their interests—and the interests of their customers—were represented in the results.

Much of the advice we gave in the previous chapter also will be useful as you wrap up user research. The stakeholders' first exposure to the methods and findings of the research shouldn't come when you drop the documentation on their desks. Their buy-in needs to be cultivated from the outset, and the documentation should be a reflection of information that has already been thoroughly sold to and understood by the stakeholders.

Involving stakeholders directly in the interview stage of the research, or at least showing them some video of it, can help you gain their support. Seeing that the research was performed professionally should help them to respect the quality and authoritativeness of the results. Exposure to the research recordings also helps them develop a real understanding of and empathy for the user, which in turn helps them overcome any assumptions they might have had and be deferential to the needs of the user.

As you compile the research findings, check back in with each stakeholder to talk about the users you spoke to, how they were selected, and the methods that were used to get valuable information from them. This is also an opportunity for you to confirm that stakeholders are satisfied with the size and scope of the group you interviewed. You should also confirm that stakeholders feel the right questions were asked, and you should answer any concerns they might have about the research process.

This check-in is also a good chance for you to review the findings for anything the stakeholders might see as unexpected or revelatory. By spending time with stakeholders individually and discussing the research findings and their implications, you give them a chance to air their concerns. Ultimately, though, stakeholders should appreciate that the research uncovered differences between the user's perspective and the stakeholders' assumptions and preconceptions. Such discoveries are early indications that your efforts are successfully paving the way to better UX. Stakeholders need an opportunity to discuss the findings with you; don't leave them alone with their thoughts. This will also give you the opportunity to help them better understand the research, allowing them to use it to constructively channel their thinking about the project.

Though researchers will have uncovered a ton of tidbits of information and user statements, it's best to keep this level of granular detail out of your stakeholders' view. Personas and user stories are representative aggregations of a large amount of information that has been studied, filtered, and focused. While much of the user feedback will be carried through in some form within the personas and user stories, some of the extraneous information will fall by the wayside. If they're exposed to too much detail, stakeholders will sometimes overemphasize some specific observation or user statement that was properly omitted or subsumed into a larger theme to press a personal agenda.

Chapter 7
Initial Product Architecture

In preceding chapters, we've argued against big upfront planning and design efforts, using bridge-building as a counterexample. So you might find it puzzling that we're now presenting you with a chapter titled "Initial Product Architecture." What is architecture, after all, but a large upfront design effort aimed at solving all of the design problems before construction begins?

UX and software professionals have needed to rely on analogies to other fields to convey an understanding of their fields. Software development is often compared to major design and engineering undertakings like building architecture and bridge design because the comparison is actually apt in a number of ways. The problem with the comparison isn't that it's completely incorrect; the problem is that it isn't completely correct, but people nevertheless swallow the analogy whole. The ways that the field of software development differs are subtle yet fundamental, but the differences are too often overlooked when considering the similarities.

So the practice of calling these stages "architecture" and calling the professionals involved "architects" descends from the similarities, and you just need to keep the differences in mind. It's also a practice that has been in place for a while and predates EffectiveUI, so we're inclined to defer to tradition.

Through the business planning and user research stages, you created the framework requirements: the constraints around the problem that arise from the user's and business's perspectives. The task of continuing to refine the understanding of the problem and narrow the constraints continues in initial product architecture. It is, in fact, the fundamental task of the entire process of building software.

No matter how much planning you've done, you must always recognize that more of the unknown lies ahead of you throughout the entire course of the project. The scope and magnitude of that unknown diminishes as the project progresses because you continually improve your understanding of the problem and its solution through ongoing exploration and development. The error in the waterfall methodology is in supposing that the exploration of the problem and design of its solution end after the first big design phase. In reality, they don't end until you decide to slap a "v1.0" sticker on the product and call it a day.

So while initial product architecture is a recognizably discrete stage in software development, it is neither the beginning nor the end of the design process. It is the first big effort on the part of professional UX and technical architects to elaborate on the framework requirements—to build on the results of business planning and user research to develop a richer understanding of the problem and to begin to frame out its solution.

What makes the initial product architecture stage distinct from the rest of the project is that one of its goals is to provide stable answers to the big questions that would be difficult to reverse course on later in the project. To lean on the architecture analogy, these would be questions like:

- *Are we building a garage, apartment building, or skyscraper? In software, scale and ambition are important to define early.*

- *Are we building on a floodplain, mountainside, or a swamp? The platform context in which a product exists determines what's possible and how hard it will be.*

- *Are there existing structures nearby that we'll need to consider or connect to, and will they need to be rebuilt to meet our needs? If so, how will that rebuilding affect existing tenants of those structures? The need to rely on and respect neighboring and dependent resources can be the single largest constraint and risk factor in building a product.*

- *How will all of the major components come together to form a single, stable structure? It's important to understand how the various high-level components of the system will come together, and to find ways of simplifying the process by relying on existing components, much in the way buildings are often constructed using components that are prefabricated off the build site.*

- *How will people use and move through the spaces we create? In software, an early understanding of the basic workflow and the high-level organization of data and interactions helps organize and focus design efforts.*

- *What kind of building materials should be used to meet the structural requirements? The choice of which software engineering languages and frameworks to use should be determined by what best serves the product's requirements.*

- *Will the external facade have a modern, art deco, gothic, or Roman-influenced style? In software, broad style guidelines can be set early that set the tone for future visual design on the product, ensuring everyone shares the same understanding of the stylistic "mood" of the product.*
- *Does the design demonstrate strength and integrity on paper and against a range of theoretic tests and stressors? Software architecture is an opportunity to continue exploring the problem and trying to identify weak spots and risks ahead of time so they can be bolstered, worked around, or otherwise accounted for.*

The answers to these questions become part of an enriched, deeper understanding of the product's requirements. They provide further understanding of the problem and narrower constraints for the solution, and they begin to suggest solutions to the biggest questions. The initial product architecture stage won't answer all of the questions—just the big ones that need to be stable and certain. This restraint ensures product design solutions can be determined later during the development stage when the team is in the best position to make the right decisions. But it will provide a more refined framework for all of the remaining questions to be answered in their own time.

The Initial Product Architecture Team

Two types of software architects should be involved in the initial product architecture:

- *UX architects, who deal principally in design, interaction, and workflow issues*
- *Technical architects, who plan the technical underpinnings of the product*

We've far passed the line where you can hope to do any of the work yourself without the aid of professionals. There are software tools that can help you create seemingly passable interface wireframes or to make system, data, and flow diagrams. But the real work of software architecture requires specialized experience, creativity, and training. The software tools are useful in documenting ideas but do nothing to turn a novice into a pro.

It's crucial that the UX and technical architecture professionals are properly specialized. Experience preparing graphical interface designs does not in itself qualify a person to be a UX architect, nor is a usability expert necessarily a UX architect. The discipline of UX architecture involves a range of experience and skills, including the following, among many others:

- *Usability*
- *Information architecture*
- *Graphic design*
- *Interaction design*
- *Human factors engineering*
- *Business process analysis*
- *Psychology*
- *Client or stakeholder management*
- *Deep exposure to software engineering practices and constraints*

Good UX architects are rare and highly sought-after, but the value of their contributions when contrasted with nonspecialists or nonprofessionals cannot be overestimated.

Similarly, someone with experience writing software code isn't necessarily qualified to be a technical architect, nor is technical architecture experience on one software platform necessarily an indication of qualification to be a technical architect on another platform. Every software platform has its own abundance of idiosyncrasies and a wide array of available libraries and components with which only experience can acquaint a person. And writing the code for the components of a product doesn't require the same skills as figuring out what components in what configurations will be necessary. Experience as a technical architect maintaining an existing product doesn't necessarily qualify a person to build the technical architecture for a new product from scratch. Poor decision making in technical architecture has profound and disabling ripple effects through the whole project, so working with a specialized professional will save you from a tremendous number of headaches and potential catastrophes.

Your role as project leader during the initial product architecture stage is also very important. Though you're not doing the substantive work of this stage, your role is, as always, to keep the project on the rails. Ensure that the UX and technical architects strongly understand the project mission, success criteria, and existing framework requirements. You must also enforce respect for the primacy of user needs. It might also fall to you to ensure that the UX and technical architects are exercising proper restraint. They shouldn't attempt to define more of the solution than is required at this stage, and they shouldn't allow the perfect to be the enemy of the good.

Since stakeholders and users generally aren't available during this stage, you also serve as the ambassador of their interests. If it becomes necessary to consult stakeholders on certain key questions, you'll need to ensure this is done in the best way possible. Every contact with stakeholders needs to be viewed as an opportunity to improve their buy-in and maintain their expectations. Professional UX architects should be adept in the role of acting as a liaison between the project team and stakeholders, but since you're ultimately accountable, you should control the situation. If you involve stakeholders in initial product architecture questions, you'll need to educate them about the purpose and limitations of the initial product architecture stage and make sure their input is properly restrained and consistent with the existing framework requirements.

We will assume that you will be employing professionals in the UX and technical architect roles. Our goal in this chapter is to provide you with an understanding of what goes into UX and technical architecture, to help you better supervise, interpret, and communicate the value, process, and results of this stage.

UX Architecture

UX architecture sheds greater light on the problem, further refines the framework requirements, and defines solutions to the pivotal problems. UX architects do this by looking at the problem through a variety of lenses, and using a number of techniques that are effective at building clarity and suggesting solutions. We use the words "lenses" and "techniques" to highlight the fact that UX architecture, like software development, is not a stepwise process. The organization of this chapter shouldn't be interpreted as an ordered list of steps as in an instruction manual where, if followed precisely, success is guaranteed. It is an overview of techniques and methods of viewing the problem (lenses) that are used by UX professionals to deepen their understanding of the problem and begin to propose aspects of the solution.

Contextual Scenarios

Contextual scenarios describe the product's requirements from the user's perspective through narrative descriptions of the tasks users will undertake to achieve their goals when using the product. They are a sort of storytelling technique that's meant to give a clearer picture of how the product will need to behave and what tasks it will need to support, without enumerating them down to the tiniest detail. Much as user personas provide a framework for making decisions through inference and empathy, contextual scenarios tell a story in broad strokes, leaving the details to be filled in through inference in the minds of the project team. UX professionals write them by intersecting business goals with user stories, user goals, and other information discovered in user research.

This is a contextual scenario pulled from our work with Herff Jones to produce an online yearbook editing tool:

> *Tina is assembling the homecoming page of the yearbook. She logs in to the site and sees the pages she is assigned to. This makes it easier for her to navigate directly to the homecoming page. It's mostly blank, but the template her class worked on together over the summer has already been applied, so all she needs to do is pick out some photos and arrange them on the page in a fun and creative way. Tina opens the photo browsing panel and sees lots of photos the photographers have taken. She filters the images by "homecoming" and sees about 30 photos that have been tagged that way. Tina clicks on a thumbnail to zoom in to see the image more clearly and pages through the collection of full-size photos. This is Tina's favorite part of working on the yearbook. She selects an image and the photo browsing panel goes away. The image she selected is now on her layout and she resizes and crops it carefully.*

To illustrate why contextual scenarios are a strong means of describing requirements, let's look at just one sentence from this example: "She filters the images by 'homecoming' and sees about 30 photos that have been tagged that way." This sentence alone implies the need for many features and capabilities, including:

- *Photos are digital assets in the system.*
- *Some mechanism for importing digital photos into the system must exist.*
- *Photos can be tagged with properties that describe their subject.*
- *Some mechanism for tagging photos must exist.*
- *There must be some facility for browsing photos.*
- *The photo browsing facility must support filtering of photos based on tags.*

Notice that the first four implied requirements fall outside the view of the user's activities described in the contextual scenario. The photos have been imported and tagged before Tina's activities begin. This demonstrates the power and effect of designing products around the user's perspective; attending to the user's needs implies requirements and functionality that the user might never be aware of or personally encounter.

End result of the "homecoming" scenario

The practice of describing tasks using contextual scenarios that imply but don't specify details is in keeping with the discipline of restraint and the acknowledgment of the weakness of written requirements. UX architects allow decisions about the specifics of the solution to be made during development (when the problem and possible solutions are better understood) by leaving it to the project team to read between the lines from contextual scenarios. By leaving out specifics, it becomes possible to create a form of written requirements that are comprehensive in their breadth and are entirely reliable because they describe only what's known at only the level of detail that's available.

Contextual scenarios are an effective means of elaborating on the framework requirements because they have the trademark characteristics of framework materials:

- *Fixed, reliable, and certain about what's known*
- *Flexible, inclusive, or permissive about what isn't known*

The sample scenario requires, for example, that a mechanism for filtering photos based on tags exists. But the scenario doesn't attempt to specify exactly how filtering will be accomplished, the nature of and constraints on tags, what other activities might also be available through the same photo browsing screen, and so on. The specifics are left to be decided when things are better understood and when specific solutions are more apparent.

Contextual scenarios can be created in storyboard form in addition to textual form. Storyboards are useful in creating an even more emotionally appealing and implication-rich view into the user's life and needs. They also help keep the project team focused on the wider context and environment in which the user is using the product.

Mapping High-Level Workflows

A workflow is a sequence of steps the user will undertake to perform a task or accomplish a goal. Workflows can be high-level (pertaining to major sections or functions of the application) or low-level (pertaining to a specific, narrow task). For example, the high-level workflow for sending an email is something like this:

- *Enter recipients in the "To," "Cc," and/or "Bcc" fields*
- *Enter a message subject in the "Subject" field*
- *Compose a message in the message body editor*
- *Optionally, choose which email account to send the message from*
- *Click "Send"*

Note that each step in this workflow is presented and organized in a single application screen (the message composition window).

The Herff Jones example implies a number of different interconnected workflows. Let's focus on just one part of it:

> *Tina opens the photo browsing panel and sees lots of photos the photographers have taken. She filters the images by "homecoming" and sees about 30 photos that have been tagged that way. Tina clicks on a thumbnail to zoom in to see the image more clearly and pages through the collection of full-size photos.... She selects an image and the photo browsing panel goes away.*

At a high level, this describes the workflow for placing a picture into a year-book layout. In the email workflow example, all of the workflow steps are presented in a single application screen. In this contextual scenario, however, the need for multiple application screens is implied:

- *A photo browsing "panel" comprising (at least):*
  - *A photo thumbnail viewer*
  - *A text-input filtering mechanism*
  - *The ability to select a photo to view it full-size*
- *A full-size photo view comprising (at least):*
  - *A single photo viewer*
  - *A means of paging through full-size photos*
  - *A means of selecting the image in view for placement in the layout*

So, the high-level workflow implied in the contextual scenario itself implies that certain application screens exist. Because the existence of application screens is implied in a workflow, it's premature and unnecessary to try to figure out the organization of application screens at this stage. So, the job of mapping high-level workflows involves identifying those workflows, figuring out what steps they comprise, and determining an order or organization of the steps that's the easiest and most efficient for the users. Most high-level workflows comprise a number of low-level workflows, too. But unless a low-level workflow is very complicated, innovative, or represents an unusually high degree of uncertainty, initial product architecture is typically only concerned with high-level workflows.

The Herff Jones example shows how contextual scenarios can be very useful. They describe what features need to be available to the user, they imply sequences of tasks users will go through to accomplish goals, and they tell stories that suggest how the functionality of the application needs to be grouped and presented. The story of how a user uses the application should clearly suggest the pathways she'll take through it.

It's useful to document the high-level workflows of the application early so the project team can understand how the application's functionality should be logically organized from the user's perspective. The goal here is to map the workflow from the user's cognitive perspective rather than from a systems design perspective. The UX architects also shouldn't start making guesses about what application screens need to exist or start detailing low-level workflows; this should be done later during development.

The following figure is an example of a high-level workflow that shows a single point of entry and several possible outcomes. The primary path is highlighted.

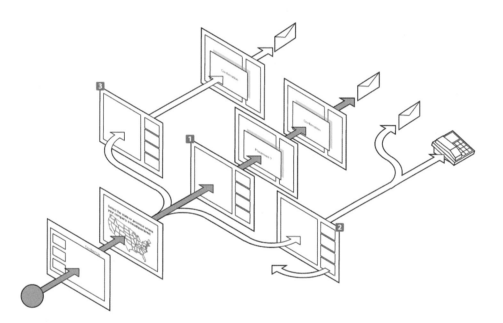

Sketching Low-Fi Visual Representations of Requirements

A full understanding of how functionality might be exposed to the user can be elusive until you start to visualize it. Although the bulk of the work of building detailed wireframes and mockups of application screens shouldn't occur until development begins, early sketches on a whiteboard or low-fidelity "paper prototypes" can be useful as a technique for deepening the understanding of the problem.

Sketches can be—and often are—simply pen and ink drawings on the back of napkins and on scrap paper. The goal of the sketches isn't to produce detailed requirements or firmly suggest how screens should be organized and composed, so they needn't be detailed, polished, or even accurate. Again, these sketches are simply a technique that can be used to explore and build a better understanding of the requirements.

This picture shows some of the early thinking done for asset management in the Herff Jones eDesign application. There are rough interface elements shown in different arrangements and control clusters shown in different positions on the "screens."

Examining Key Features and Interactions

Though the initial UX architecture stops short of examining and specifying low-level details of the solution, there might be some details that call for early exploration. You might be planning a feature that has never been done before, presents a significant challenge, or that introduces a radically new approach to its workflow or interaction design. You might also be contending with stakeholders who are skeptical or having difficulty picturing how key components of the product will work. Anything that's new, innovative, or challenging is bound to come with more than its fair share of unknowns and risks, and these should be examined during the initial product architecture stage.

The success and viability of the product often depends on finding a good solution to these key problems. You'll want to proceed into development with the confidence that they can be solved within the constraints of the project. To reduce the degree of risk and uncertainty surrounding these problems, UX architects can do a much deeper exploration of the problems and their potential solutions than would ordinarily occur this early in the project. These explorations can take the form of some basic wireframing to illustrate interactions on paper, but might be as complex as a building a working prototype of the feature. Success in an exploration might be in proving the technical feasibility of something, in receiving stakeholder approval and support, or in receiving positive feedback on the feature from sample users. The more risk there is in a given detail, or the more dependent its success is on user acceptance, the more important it is to create a higher-fidelity prototype.

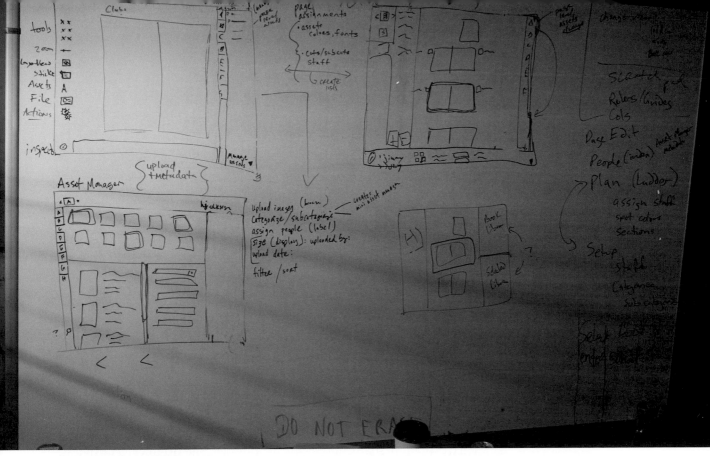

Lo-fi sketches on a whiteboard

Setting a Style Vision

The visual design of a product's UI can have different tones, moods, and stylistic genres depending on the product's audience and the purpose. Some software—educational applications for children, for example—are resplendent with candy-colored interface elements, use happy or goofy text styles, and emphasize fun, simplicity, and accessibility. Products made for professional stock traders tend to have very subdued tones and a relatively austere aesthetic, focusing on effective delivery of information without distractions from the interface design itself.

This doesn't mean that UI design is important for the children's application but unimportant for the stock trader's application. UI design considerations are critical to the experience of using the application, no matter what the intended experience might be. Many people believe that in enterprise or heavily data-focused applications, the UI design needs to "get out of the way" and isn't an important concern. But even in cases that demand an extremely austere UI design approach, the design still significantly affects the subtleties that create the experience of using the application. Stock traders don't need an application that will entertain them, delight their budding senses, and seize their fickle attention like children do. But they do need to feel that the application is high quality, professional, reliable, and sophisticated. So, one of the goals in initial UX architecture is to set out a mood and style vision for the product that sets the right genre and purpose associations for users.

Like art and fashion, software UI design has distinct genres as well as design trends that change over time. Modern UI design trends are recognizable even to people who aren't actively paying attention. The Web 2.0 trend has been accompanied by its own relatively distinct genre of web design. As long as Web 2.0 is seen as cutting edge, design styles from the Web 2.0 genre will be associated with modern, sophisticated software. We're frequently asked to design interfaces that are "clean" or "airy" or "crisp," using "friendly" UI elements and iconography. Clients requesting this are typically expressing the desire that their application UI look modern and sophisticated, because at some conscious or subconscious level they've noted that those characteristics are present in many of the cool new things. The product UI design is also a means of expressing the brand goals of the product or of the company generally.

It isn't important during UX architecture to lock down the precise color palette, iconography, or other specific elements of the UI design for the product. But it is useful to begin with a general sense of the mood, genre, and experience that the UI design will ultimately need to convey. The attributes of the experience or of the brand that you're trying to create are difficult to express in words. In setting the style vision for the product during UX architecture, vague understandings and expressions of visual ideas can be made concrete. That will give clear direction going forward and ensure stakeholders are all imagining and expecting the same things. This initial style vision will be the framework within which future visual design work is done. It also helps members of the project team visualize what the product will eventually look like so they have an easier time imagining their contributions in context of the whole product.

To begin developing a style vision, UX architects often ask stakeholders to make lists of other products, websites, print advertising, and brand design that stakeholders feel are representative of their style goals for the product. There's rarely an existing product that exactly represents the stakeholders' goals for their own products, but with enough examples, UX architects can get a clear sense of them. UX architects and UI designers are deeply immersed in the genres and design trends of software UI design, so they can readily support stakeholders through this process. They can help stakeholders clearly express subjective concepts, provide illustrative examples of ideas, and work to corral opinions to an outcome that their professional experience suggests is correct.

Based on the suggestions from stakeholders, and using some of their own materials, UX architects and UI designers document a vision of the design goals for the product using what are called mood boards. *Mood boards* are essentially collages of images, colors, and designs pulled from various sources that, in aggregate, give a clear suggestion of the product's design mood, genre, and approximate color palette.

Mood boards can also be a useful tool in getting some early user feedback on the design direction. On the Herff Jones eDesign project, we had internally arrived at a visual direction for the product that was consistent with other professional design applications. The interface was intentionally dark to boost contrast with the lighter content that users would be developing. But we began to worry that this approach might be off-putting to the primary users of this app—teenage girls. We were both right and wrong. The users we tested the visual concepts with appreciated the contrast but needed some deeply saturated colors interjected to maintain their interest. A new set of mood boards that balanced high contrast with very saturated colors in the controls seemed to resonate well right away when we tested it with users.

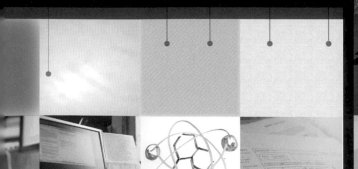

Developing Nomenclature

The decision of what to call certain objects and features within an application, or how to label its buttons and data, can be surprisingly difficult. Users look to the names and labels of elements of the product for cues in understanding how to operate the product and what results to expect from the actions they take. For example, we recently did usability testing on a product where the word "Loupe" appeared next to a magnifying glass icon in an interface that we designed. The target user set didn't know what a loupe was, so they avoided or overlooked the magnifying glass, even when asked how they would zoom in on images. As soon as we removed the word, users found and used the zoom feature without hesitation.

Nomenclature is also important to the project team as they build the product so there's no confusion about what they are discussing and how aspects of the product are meant to work and be perceived. Simple words such as "select," for example, might have specific and important meanings in the context of your product. In an image editing tool, "select" means to grab a section of pixels in an image using a lasso, marquee, or magic wand tools; it doesn't mean to "choose" an option. Significant areas and high-level workflows in the application will need agreed-upon names so, for example, when someone talks about "asset management," everyone will know what he's talking about. One way to settle nomenclature questions is to use analytics tools such as Google Keywords to see the words that people use when searching for products like yours. Another way to learn what nomenclature to use is by paying very careful attention to how users talk about the product during user interviews. Often, the way that a business refers to features and products will be very different than how their customers think about them.

You should start a centralized glossary of product-related terms during initial architecture and maintain it through the full course of the project. This will simplify collaboration by project team members and stakeholders and will also help the people doing QA and user documentation at the end of the project. You can maintain the glossary in whatever way is most convenient for you and your team. We've used Microsoft Excel and Word documents, project wikis, and other online collaboration tools to manage this.

Opposite page: Example moodboards

Technical Architecture

Though the bulk of the software engineering work will be done during the development stage, key aspects of the technical architecture need to be identified and locked down early. The issues addressed in technical architecture are foundational decisions that are generally irreversible, or they are explorations of anticipated stress points and dependencies to ensure that major foreseeable issues have been identified and mitigated.

The traditional approach to building a complex product is usually to begin with extensive technical architecture aimed at building out the "back-end" infrastructure to near completion before seriously considering how a user will interact with the product. In these cases, the interests of technical expediency usually take precedence over user needs because the engineering decisions and progress are all made before the UI and UX get serious consideration. The "right" decision in engineering is the one that delivers the quickest progress, not necessarily the one that enables the best UX. When the team finally gets around to building the UI, its design is primarily directed and constrained by what the existing technical infrastructure made possible, rather than what was in the best interests of the users.

While technical architecture still aims to discover the straightest, easiest, least risky path for the software engineers, it does so without compromising the user needs or potential UX quality for the sake of engineering expediency.

For a UX-focused product, the user's needs and the requirement for good UX must guide all decision making that happens in technical architecture. While technical architecture still aims to discover the straightest, easiest, least risky path for the software engineers, it does so without compromising the user needs or potential UX quality for the sake of engineering expediency. This orientation toward user needs has both subtle and profound implications in technical architecture.

As with UX architecture, the considerations and decisions of technical architecture should be handled by specialized professionals. Many of the big decisions will be obvious to an experienced professional, and deep professional experience is essential to charting the most perilous challenges and dependencies. This part of the chapter presents an overview of some of the considerations addressed in technical architecture, but we will assume you have the support of a professional technical architect.

Getting a Lay of the Land

One of the first tasks in technical architecture is to look around the organization and discover what already exists that might serve as a resource or shortcut in building the new product. If your company is building a new version of a product with the goal of improving its UX, much of the work building the "guts" of the application for previous versions can, in large part, be used for the new version. Even if certain materials and code aren't directly usable in the new project, they can nevertheless be instructive. They can give indications of how specific key problems can be solved, what risks and challenges prior efforts encountered, and how to locate resources to answer key questions.

Getting a sense of the political landscape affecting the product's technical constraints is also important. The IT staff that maintains the existing systems and acts as the gatekeeper to some of the resources that the engineering team will require might feel threatened by your project. New projects often signal changes in their priorities and budgets, or they might even threaten their job security. Getting an early sense of where political issues might jeopardize successful execution of the product will help you get an early start on securing political footholds and heading off some of the resistance. In addition, in cases where a product is deeply entwined with a key business process, you should identify early on the ways in which the new version will affect or force change in business processes. This will let you get a head start on managing the politics and practical effects of the change. Your organization's ability to shift its process to conform to the new demands will be a significant component of the risk associated with the project.

Making Platform and Framework Choices

The terms "platform" and "framework" are often used inconsistently and interchangeably. We consider platforms to be the foundational basis for a product, including the language used to code it. Frameworks are collections of libraries, components, and other resources built on top of a given platform to simplify the development of applications on that platform. For example, Java Foundation Classes (JFC) is a framework built on the Java platform, and Adobe Flex is a framework built on the Adobe Flash Platform. Each is intended to make development of application UIs easier.

The platform and framework choice affects the entire project because it determines who will develop the application and how they'll go about it. It also determines what resources and utilities are available to the team and what constraints they'll operate under. Ideally, you'll be able to select the platform that best suits the needs of your product, but often the choice has already been made for you by other factors. If you have access only to an internal development team, then whatever platform that team is adept in will probably be your only choice. If you're building a new version that's an integral extension of a previous version, you'll probably be compelled to use the same platform as the original.

It might be possible to segregate the development efforts, to allow one aspect of the product to be developed using one platform and another aspect to be built using a different platform. In cases where the technical guts of the product have been developed for a previous version and the new version aims to upgrade the product's UX, it's frequently easiest to build the new UI on a platform more conducive to good UI and UX design. You'll just need to work in the original platform to develop the API from the existing backend for the new UI layer.

In principle and whenever possible, your desire to build a superior UX should guide the platform and framework decision. The development platforms and frameworks that represent the shortest engineering path to a feature-complete solution often don't lend themselves to high-quality UX. Sun Microsystems' Java platform is very mature, has a tremendous number of available frameworks and libraries to suit any possible goal, and has one of the largest communities of professional development talent. However, until Sun's recent release of the nascent JavaFX platform, it was extremely difficult to create good UX using Java. On the other hand, technologies such as Adobe's Flash Platform and Flex framework, as well as Microsoft's Silverlight, aren't good for developing the backend workings of the product but are vastly better at building superior frontend UX.

Understanding Data Requirements

Generally speaking, software has three primary data considerations:

- *How application data will be stored in and retrieved from databases*
- *How asset data (images, documents, files, and so on) will be stored and retrieved*
- *How data will be trafficked between the places it's stored and the places it's needed or created*

It's frequently the case that the databases will already exist—customer databases, sources of financial market information, merchandise sales data, and so on. In these cases, the main challenge is figuring out how the product will access those databases and what the product will require that can't be handled using existing databases. Applications that deal with significant volumes of asset data (Flickr, for example, handles millions of images for its users) must have a plan for how those files will be stored and retrieved, as well as how the storage requirements will scale as the volume of asset data increases.

When dealing with external databases and repositories of asset data, the server managing that data usually isn't in the same room as the computer running the software that needs that data. In rich Internet applications, for example, the computer running the software (the "client") is in the user's home or office, but the data is in a server farm somewhere in another state, country, or continent. Also, large enterprise applications usually rest on third-party CRM systems spread across multiple locations, all working off of the same data. Technical architects need to develop a plan for how this data will get to and from the client software securely and reliably and, if large volumes of data are involved, how the bandwidth demands and costs will be managed.

Mapping Interactions with Other Systems

Software products often rely on external systems to handle certain functions, provide access to certain types of data, and shortcut certain challenges. The software that airline passenger service agents use, for example, relies on a tremendous number of external resources. Each resource is a wholly separate system of software, data, and hardware operating in other ("remote") locations and based on different platforms. Each of the following functions available to a passenger agent is managed by a separate system:

- *Searching available future flights and routes*
- *Booking reservations*
- *Managing frequent flyer information*
- *Creating tickets for reservations*
- *Managing check-in operations*
- *Creating baggage tags*
- *Managing preflight boarding and gate operations*
- *Checking flight statuses*
- *Handling lost baggage claims*

If airline passenger service agents had to connect to and be familiar with all these systems individually, their jobs would be extremely difficult. Instead, access to all of these capabilities that exist on different remote systems has been brought together in the passenger service agent's client application.

Developers of the client application need to be able to connect to and rely on these external systems without having to understand how they work or having to worry about whether they might be malfunctioning. This is a reflection of the concept of abstraction that's at the core of how object-oriented programming works. The use of external resources is meant to save the project time by letting the current development effort focus only on new and improved developments without having to reinvent any wheels. But this benefit is realized only if the external systems are easy to interact with and are entirely reliable in performing their designated roles.

One of the most critical parts of technical architecture, then, is investigating the available external resources in an effort to understand their capabilities and to assess their completeness and reliability. Following that investigation, technical architects map precisely how the client application will interact with the external resources in something called an application programmer interface (API). APIs allow the developers of the client application to interact with the external resources without knowing how those resources work. They also make it possible to make changes and improvements to the external resources independently without disrupting how they interact with the client applications. To put it simply, APIs define what requests the client application will make, exactly how it will make them, and exactly how the responses will be provided by the external resources. This makes it so the only thing the developers of the client application need to be concerned with in interacting with the external resources is making their requests conform to the API and preparing for responses in the form defined in the API.

Although connecting to external resources presents some of the greatest opportunities for cost savings, it can also represent the greatest risk to the success of the project. It makes it so the project's success is dependent not only on the project's own development effort, but also on the reliability of the external system and its fidelity to the API. Problems with external systems can cause huge losses of time in software engineering. The problems often aren't immediately apparent and engineers are forced to spend their valuable time searching for the source of unexpected behaviors, only to discover they're originating from an external system and not from their own code.

Ideally, by the time your project begins, all of the external resource development has long been finished and all APIs have been thoroughly tested so they're reliable and trustworthy. External resources are, however, frequently under development at the same time as the client application. Sometimes the resources are new, and sometimes old ones need additional special development of an API to expose some capabilities that previously weren't available. In these cases, engineers on the client application project can find themselves contending with unexpected changes to the API or interacting with APIs that represent functionality that hasn't been finished or thoroughly tested. This always causes slowdowns in the project.

Even if the engineers are prepared for the possibility that the external resource might not behave as expected, they're still forced to spend time developing coping measures that help them test their code in the absence of a reliable external resource. And as the external resource development nears completion and client application engineers begin connecting to it, the bugs in the external resource become bugs in the client application. Additionally, engineers on the external resource project might, unbeknownst to the client application engineers, make well-intentioned changes that suddenly cause a cascade of failures in systems that were working just hours prior.

External resources are very important to keeping the project focused and efficient but can also be the source of nightmarish problems, so technical architects pay special attention to these dependencies in planning the project and assessing risk. Risk arises from unknowns and uncertainty, and external resources represent their own set of unknowns and uncertainty. Issues in the external resources can be especially pernicious because the client application's project team has less visibility into and control over the external systems. Technical architects aim to reduce these risks by working to understand to what degree the external resources can be trusted and by working out thorough, thoughtful APIs that help narrow the field of risk.

Finding Shortcuts Through Third-Party and Open Source Components

As they assess the project's requirements, technical architects will identify features, required components, and other elements of the product that present a particularly high degree of risk or difficulty. Wherever possible, it's preferable to employ an existing solution to these elements rather than develop them from scratch. This not only saves engineering time, but greatly reduces the risk contained in the unknowns of developing that element from scratch. It's also helpful to use existing solutions for elements of the application that are disproportionately difficult to build in relation to their significance in the broader product; this helps the team focus on the important problems.

A good example of this type of element, which occurs in many products, is a "WYSIWYG" (what you see is what you get) HTML editor. These allow the user to create and edit HTML documents complete with tables, pictures, links, and other rich elements by manipulating the document visually rather than by editing its code. This capability is tremendously complicated to develop, but it's frequently a necessity in products that need to allow users to manipulate rich text, create emails, or build simple web pages visually. Fortunately, a number of developers and companies have built highly configurable standalone components to solve this problem so that developers can just plug it into their applications without developing it themselves.

For all of the peculiar diversity of software, there are nevertheless a great number of features and capabilities, such as WYSIWYG editors, that are commonly required. With a little research, technical architects can often identify prebuilt components from third parties that can allow them to bypass the effort and risk associated with developing the component's capability from scratch. These components might be available through a paid license (the price is almost always worth it) or might be offered under an open source licensing agreement that allows them to be used for free, with certain caveats.

Third-party components can save a great deal of time, but they can also present risks and downsides that can negate their benefits:

- *As with external resources, plugging third-party components into your product makes your product partially dependent on the quality of those components.*

- *They can be difficult to customize to fit seamlessly into your application, whether functionally or visually. Prebuilt components provide some mechanisms for customization, but they might not integrate fully with your product. Constraints inherent to the component might limit your ability to make it support good usability or UX. Or it might not integrate seamlessly, both visually and in its approach to interaction design.*

- *A component's breadth and complexity can cause it to be ungainly and inefficient. Many components are made to be applicable and useful to a broad range of implementations. This can mean the component includes a lot of stuff that you don't need in your product, and that imposes performance burdens. Also, components that try to solve a broad range of problems tend to achieve that breadth of applicability at the cost of the quality of their specific details.*

- *The licensing scheme for the product might be intolerable for your purposes. There are certain open source licensing schemes that permit free use of the code but in return require that any modifications you make to it be made publicly available. Some even go so far as to require that products built using them be offered for free and never sold commercially. Open source licensing schemes are very standardized, so it's usually easy to figure out whether a given component bears intolerable requirements. Paid licenses for third-party components should also be inspected thoroughly. They can incorporate bizarre and excessively intrusive provisions that might be incompatible with the intellectual property standards of your company or with future licensees of the product.*

Discovering Business Logic

The term "business logic" has a very specific meaning in the field of software development. Business logic comprises the algorithms, math, logic, and computations that are specific to a business and necessary to the operation of the product. For example, the business logic for an airline ticketing agent application includes the algorithms used to determine optimal flight routes from one city to another. The business logic for a product for a stock brokerage company might include the financial analysis and proprietary computations used to build the reports and charts available through the product.

Essentially, business logic is any complex math or logic that has already been solved by the business and therefore needn't be solved again by the engineering team. The engineers will be required to implement the business logic in code, but simply by following a preexisting solution. It's helpful to identify the necessary business logic in advance during technical architecture, as it provides an understanding of what problems the engineers won't need to solve.

It's also important to start identifying the business logic early because it typically isn't fully documented in a binder labeled "Business Logic" sitting on a shelf somewhere in the building. Elements of the business logic are usually scattered about in existing software code, Excel spreadsheets, or in the minds of subject matter experts. An early effort to bring it all together ensures the business logic will be available to engineers just as soon as they need it. It also helps identify where experts might need to do more work to more fully develop the available business logic for the purposes of the product.

Software Architecture in Big Design Up Front (BDUF)

In Big Design Up Front (BDUF) projects, the "big design" is essentially an extra-extended initial product architecture stage. Ideally, the initial product architecture stage should be limited to answering the big questions that cannot be changed later without significant disruption. Initial architecture in BDUF is taken far beyond that limit. Professional designers work for long periods of time to provide a highly detailed description of the solution in the form of wireframes, graphic comps, system design diagrams, and other mostly visual materials.

This approach has its advantages. Elaborating on requirements in a visual form gives a much more accurate and comprehensible picture of the problem and its solution than you get with written requirements alone. Since professional product designers will be involved, the solutions described are likely to be more accurate than thick binders of written requirements prepared by stakeholders. And for some projects, a BDUF effort is absolutely necessary to reassure stakeholders about the road ahead or to meet the requirements of a rigidly prescribed software services purchasing process. The perceived advantage is that the end result is an impressively detailed collection of materials that seem to paint a clear and certain picture of the solution.

This approach is vastly more effective than relying on a thousand pages of written requirements prepared by nonprofessionals. But it suffers from the same weaknesses as written requirements, as we discussed in Chapter 3. To recap some of the key issues:

> Business logic typically isn't fully documented in a binder labeled "Business Logic" sitting on a shelf somewhere in the building. Elements of the business logic are usually scattered about in existing software code, Excel spreadsheets, or in the minds of subject matter experts.

- *No matter how deeply you study the problem in the abstract and on paper, you cannot eliminate uncertainty and the unknown. The earlier you are in the project, the less you understand it because a great number of discoveries, revelations, unknowns, risks, and changes have yet to surface. Any design that's done up front is design that's done from a position of relative ignorance.*

- *The big design effort delays the commencement of the development process and keeps engineers on the bench and out of the process far longer than they should be.*

- *It tends to exhaust the majority of the UX design time available to the project. This deprives the rest of the development effort of ongoing support from UX professionals to respond to the inevitable adjustments and changes that result from the discovery of risks, unknowns, stakeholder direction, and other unforeseeable eventualities. This places a greater burden on software engineers to absorb the effects of the adjustments and changes. It also forces them to play the ill-fitting role of UX designers.*

- *It gives stakeholders the false impression that there is great certainty and a minimum of unknowns in the solution. This can cause them to think their participation is no longer needed and that the rest of the project simply entails fulfilling on the requirements described in this stage.*

- *It seems to specify a clear, locked-down scope, so stakeholders will expect to have certainty in scope, schedule, and cost. Certainty of scope isn't possible this early in the project, so this sets up stakeholders for disappointments and surprises as the inevitable changes occur.*

The core of the error of BDUF as it relates to software architecture is that it attempts to use software architecture to build a complete and accurate picture of the solution. But the problem itself still needs deeper exploration, and the project is ready to have only foundational, critical answers provided. Software architecture should provide those critical answers, but the rest of its purpose should be to improve upon the framework requirements. The framework requirements address the problem, not the solution, enabling correct, just-in-time decisions and solutions during the product's development. The exercise of restraint and a humble recognition of the unknown demand that nothing be asserted as solved or certain before it actually is.

Project Infrastructure Needs

The practice of software development, including everything from UX architecture and design through to QA and deployment, requires some supporting technical architecture that might not already be in place in your company. This infrastructure supports the collaboration that occurs amongst project team members, protects data against catastrophic loss, protects the code base from errors, and supports testing of the code throughout the project. Although most of the collaboration, coding, and asset development won't happen until later in the project, you should set up the infrastructure to support it early in the project, to ensure that a lack of infrastructure doesn't impede progress.

Code Source Control

No matter how big the project, and no matter how few developers are working on it, code source control infrastructure is always extremely important. You might already be familiar with the names of common source control systems: CVS, Subversion (SVN), Git, Visual SourceSafe, and others. You likely won't need to worry about choosing which is best for your project; developers usually have strong opinions about which is best or at least have more experience with one or another.

Source control systems perform many critical functions:

- *Maintaining one centralized code repository for everyone to work from so everyone is working from the complete and most current version of the code.*

- *Periodically backing up the entire repository.*

- *Keeping copies of every single version of every element of code. This is useful in cases where a new version of some element causes problems and needs to be rolled back to the previous version; it also provides a record of what changes were made by whom and for what reasons.*

- *Preventing engineers from accidentally overwriting one another's work if they're working on the same element at the same time by alerting developers to conflicting versions and allowing them to be easily merged.*

- *Supports "branching" of the code base in cases where two different versions that share a common base need to be managed and maintained.*

Even on projects with only one engineer, a source control system should be considered mandatory. Besides preventing catastrophic losses of data, it eliminates the risk that the developer will make some unknown mistake and spend substantial time trying to discover and fix it. It also serves as a good historical reference so the developer doesn't have to solve the same problems twice.

Graphic Asset Management

Through the course of the project, the UX and UI designers will generate a tremendous number of graphic assets. Some will be intermediary or exploratory materials such as mood boards and wireframes, whereas others will be files containing graphics intended for use directly in the product. Like software code, the graphic assets will be the subject of collaboration. It's useful to maintain historical versions of all of these files to permit rollbacks to previous versions, to provide a reference to earlier ideas, and to serve as redundant backups. But unlike with software code, there aren't strong solutions for managing graphic assets in a controlled repository.

Nevertheless, it's important to do some planning and put the necessary infrastructure in place to support collaboration over and protection of graphic assets. Without a plan and infrastructure, people will usually share assets through email. Besides putting a strain on email bandwidth and storage, this approach can lead to overlapping, competing, or diverging versions of the same files. Everyone needs to be working off of one central source of the most current assets to prevent duplicated work, confusion, and lost data through accidental overwriting. The assets, along with significant prior versions of the assets, should be stored in a central location that's regularly backed up so the death of a single designer's laptop or a single server hard drive can't set the project back by weeks.

There are some products that help support centralized management of files like graphic assets. We use Adobe Version Cue because it's strongly integrated into the Adobe suite of products that our designers use. As with code source control systems, your designers will likely have a preference of what system or method to use. Even without the aid of a product, most of the needs of graphic asset management can be met by doing some basic planning. A centralized, backed-up storage area should be set up. A simple mechanism for designers to consistently "check out" files to work on and to "check in" new versions of the files should be agreed upon. And a consistent file-naming scheme should be established so specific assets can easily be found and the most current version of each can easily be identified.

Testing Infrastructure and Environments

Testing software code isn't something that happens all at once at the end of a project during the QA stage. Software engineers constantly test their code piece by piece (this is called *unit testing*) to ensure that each piece appears to work properly in isolation. As the code base grows larger and these units of code become more interdependent, it becomes important to test larger sections of the code or even test the entire code base. These tests ensure that recent changes or developments haven't created adverse effects or caused previously working pieces to start behaving abnormally.

Depending on the size of your project, the infrastructure requirements for ongoing testing can be significant. In most large projects, the entire code base is compiled at least once a day and a long series of scripted tests are automatically run against it to check whether the changes made during the day caused any of the automated tests to fail. In more complicated projects, engineers and automated testing systems need to pull together and compile subsets of the code, or a range of configurations of the code, to test larger units and various test cases. This type of testing requires specialized software and development environment configurations. The engineers on the project should have a strong understanding of what they need and how to set it up. It's just up to you to anticipate and respond to their needs.

It is also typically necessary to test the code within hardware and software environments that simulate how the final product will be deployed. If the product has dependencies on external resources, the individual engineers' development machines often won't have direct or realistic access to those resources, so they must test their code within an environment that does. The engineers might also be using computers that aren't similar to the client machines that actual users will have. Engineers' computers are usually much higher performing and configured differently than users' machines. Or engineers might be developing on a Mac when the majority of the user base uses Windows-based computers. In these cases, engineers must have access to machines that have a range of capabilities and configurations that are typical of the users' machines.

Chapter 8

The Iterative Development Process

Though the iterative development process gets only one chapter in this book, it should represent the majority of your project's work, budget, and lifecycle. The business planning, user research, and initial product architecture stages give a broad-strokes view of the solution, and the development stage is where the understanding of the problem and its solution is deepened, refined, and finally implemented. Entering the development process, you should have answers to the foundational questions that are the high-level absolutes for the product, but every other question remains to be answered. The development stage is the time where the team does the greatest measure of investigation of the problem and its solution; in other words, most of the project's design work occurs during development. The development stage is also the time when all of the unknowns finally surface, to which you must quickly and flexibly respond. Through the preceding chapters, we've encouraged you to exercise restraint in the early planning and architecture of the product. In development, that restraint pays off. Having more room for all of the design work involved in development makes it easier to deliver a complete and high-quality product.

Remember that for UX-focused projects, the meaning of "development" is more expansive than the ordinary connotation. The development stage involves much more than just software engineering. It is a collaborative problem-solving effort that includes (ideally) all perspectives—business, UX design, UI design, software engineering, and users. Bit by bit, feature by feature, the problem that was described in the framework requirements and through initial product architecture is reduced into a working solution. Each aspect of that solution will be discovered through some combination of UX design, UI design, and software engineering, all within the governing constraints set by the business and users.

> *Remember that software engineering is a design practice just as much as UX and UI design are. Design, in the sense that we use it, is a creative problem-solving effort. Sometimes the solutions to those problems take a visual form: UI designers produce interface comps, UX designers produce wireframes and storyboards. Sometimes the solutions aren't visual: UX architects create contextual scenarios and software engineers produce code. But in every case the solution is arrived at through a thoughtful, creative process of problem solving.*

The notion that everyone on the team has a hand in the development process is one of the key ideas that separates UX-focused projects from traditional projects (where only software engineers work in development). The responsibility for a good UX outcome falls on all members of the team working in all professional disciplines, and their responsibility persists through the full course of the project—including, and especially, through development.

Those who place too much trust in the value of upfront planning usually think of the development stage as the time when existing designs are implemented (like the construction stage in a bridge-building project). But the work done in development is a process of tandem design, testing, and implementation. It's more a process of creativity and directed experimentation than it is a construction project. The majority of time is spent on the studying, designing, and testing that lead to the solutions. Those solutions must be discovered; they are not arrived at immediately or directly.

Software products are too enormously complex to approach as a single, monolithic concept and development effort. For progress to be made, the product must be broken into pieces that are small enough to be understood, designed, built, and tested. Software engineers do this constantly by parceling a component's functionality into approachable, reusable logical pieces and devising ways of combining those pieces to create the desired component. This assembly of smaller pieces into a large whole is one of the things that seems to suggest that building software is like a construction project. In Chapter 3, we discussed how in bridge-building projects there's a perfect design for the project to keep reorganizing around, even as unexpected issues come up during the construction project. In software, though, there is no such perfect design of the final product. That design is being developed in tandem with the actual building of the product.

This means that, unlike a construction project, it isn't possible to parcel up everything in a software project in advance. Without knowing what the solution to the puzzle looks like, you can't break it up into small pieces. So then how can the project team break up the products into approachable, logically significant pieces? By using an iterative approach to developing the product. Iterations are essentially short, focused sprints in which a narrow problem is investigated, and a possible solution is designed and implemented. The entire development process consists of iterations, starting out with small ones that address the narrow universe of what's known, and growing to much larger ones as the product is understood and implemented more fully.

In this chapter, you'll learn how an iterative approach to development makes progress easier and helps avert many of the common causes of failure in software projects. Remember, though, that there's no universal, perfect approach to methodology or process in software. For this reason, we've kept the discussion in this chapter at the level of the principles and benefits sought after through an iterative approach to development, rather than attempting to prescribe a one-size-fits-all approach for all projects.

Regarding "Process"

There's a risk that all the talk of process and flowchart-like diagrams coming up in this chapter might make you fret too much about whether you're properly adhering to prescribed procedures. Successful approaches to building software are not about rigid processes, flow charts, or strict methodologies. No project is alike, and so there's no single approach that will work for all possible projects. There are, however, a small number of principles that we'll describe in this chapter that serve as veritable beacons by which you can navigate through the rocky, dark, unexplored sea of your project. By steering the project as closely as you can toward these principles, even if you're not able to fully achieve them, you will make the project less rocky and the results more successful.

Iterations and Feedback

Much of what goes on during development is akin to the process a scientist goes through to make a discovery. The scientist develops a hypothesis, and then undertakes a series of experiments to test and explore it. At the end of each experiment, the scientist looks at its results, and based on them decides how to modify the hypothesis or the course of experimentation. This process involves a lot of trial and error. Each experiment represents a single iteration that helps the scientist incrementally develop a more accurate understanding of the truth he's investigating.

An artist creating a painting follows a similar process. He applies a few lines or a few strokes of the brush and steps back to look at the result. Responding to what he sees, he then adds or modifies lines and brush strokes to bring it closer to the goal and repeats this iteration until the painting is complete. Neither the scientist nor the artist expects to get the theory, painting, or any component of either right from the very first attempt. Neither has a perfect image or design of what the solution to their problem should be. Both are following processes of planning, experimentation, study, and trial and error that require many iterations, each representing some degree of failure, to home in on the right result. Figure 8-1 shows a very simple iterative process.

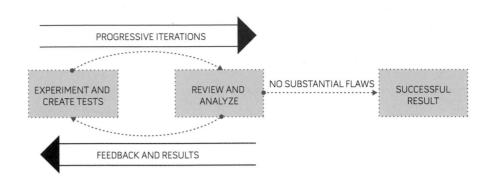

Figure 8-1. A simple iterative process

This should be a familiar process that is naturally at work in any software development project. Designers iterate on their own work to produce final designs, software engineers iterate on components to build robust results, and stakeholders propose, discuss, analyze, and revise concepts and constraints. At this point in the history of software development, it would be a surprise to discover a team that didn't use an iterative process, at least within the confines of each of the professional disciplines.

The crucial step in the scientific process is the moment the scientist takes to analyze the results of the previous experiment and make thoughtful, directed adjustments to the hypothesis or next experiment. For the artist, that crucial step is when he steps back to the canvas to take in what he's done and decides what needs to be done next. This element of building feedback—of surveying and learning from the current state—into the design process is what allows positive progress to be made. Without feedback, the scientist would be lost in an endless series of random, aimless experimentation, and the painter would toil endlessly on a painting that's always changing but never improving. Feedback in iteration is the heart of what makes an iterative process useful; it's what makes it productive and purposeful. This concept applies just as much in software development as in art or science. The goal is to make purposeful, intentional steps in an ever-improving direction.

Feedback in iteration is the heart of what makes an iterative process useful or even purposeful.

At the end of each iteration in software development, the project team should have a better understanding of the overall problem and of the solution they're attempting to craft. Each iteration represents an investigation, the findings of which are analyzed and used to determine the course of the next iteration. Each iteration exposes unknowns and advances the team's understanding of the problem and the solution. More iterations mean more opportunities for the team members to refine their knowledge. As their understanding develops and gains accuracy, they become better at designing solutions and directing the course of development.

Frequent iterations mean that those moments of feedback—of stepping back to assess what's been done and determine what needs to happen next—happen more frequently. And the shorter the iterations are, the less time it takes to arrive at a point of receiving feedback and making a course adjustment. As well, shorter iterations mean that less is invested in each round of trial and error. Frequent, small errors are much easier to learn and progress from than a few enormous, infrequent ones. The longer an iteration goes without feedback, the wider and deeper the opportunity for the effort to go significantly and irreversibly off-course becomes.

We briefly examined this concept in Chapter 3 in the section entitled "Efficiency and the unknown." A waterfall process is weak in its siloed and limited opportunities for feedback. This tends to mean a lot of work is done and most of the budget expended before anyone realizes how far off course they've gone. This frequently results in total catastrophe and requires expensive, major course corrections. The cost of this approach is further compounded if the team fails to switch from a waterfall process to something more iterative after the first delivery, such as an agile process. Though an iterative project might head off in the same wrong direction as a waterfall process, the discovery of the error and the resulting course correction occurs much earlier and benefits from much more valuable feedback. Figure 8-2 demonstrates this clearly.

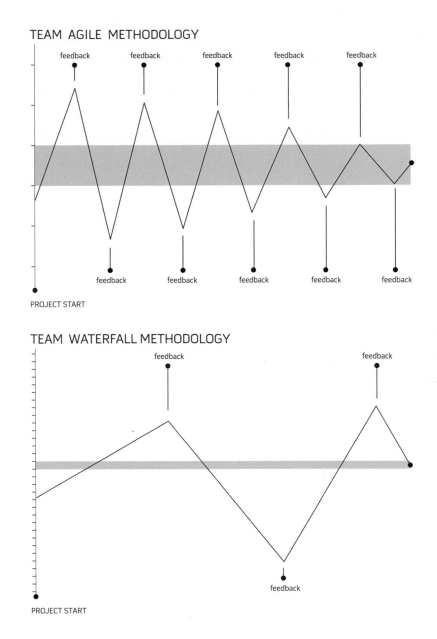

Figure 8-2. Error and course deviation in waterfall and iterative processes

The frequency and timeliness of feedback is what distinguishes healthy projects from unhealthy ones. Generally speaking, the more feedback that is built into a project, the more depth of understanding will go into it and the more knowledgeable the project team will grow through the course of the project. It's also important that the feedback comes from all facets of the project and from all the professional disciplines involved in building it; more diverse perspectives provide more comprehensive, robust feedback.

> The frequency and timeliness of feedback is what distinguishes healthy projects from unhealthy ones.

And so we've introduced the two most important principles behind an iterative approach to development for UX-focused projects:

- *Improve the efficiency of progress by building in more opportunities for feedback.*
- *Improve the quality of the feedback by ensuring that it reflects diverse perspectives.*

The means by which you apply these principles depends on the particularities of your project. But in choosing and then applying an approach to developing your product, you can judge its likelihood to succeed based on its propensity to generate more frequent, higher-quality feedback.

The Scope of Iterations

In order to build more frequent feedback into a project, iterations must be small. As Figure 8-2 showed, the waterfall approach goes through only four major iterations (each line segment). This means there are only three opportunities for feedback. By contrast, the iterative process goes through about 40–50 smaller iterations (in the simplified diagram, anyway; a real iterative process will go through far more than 50 iterations), which means there would be 39–49 opportunities for feedback. So smaller iterations lead to greater amounts of feedback, which in turn lead to a smoother ride and better results.

This begs the question of how you decide the scope of an iteration—that is, how much progress should you expect of an iteration? Iterations need to be small enough to allow for a high frequency of feedback, but not so small as to be impracticable. The various submethodologies of Agile methodology each has its own answer to this, some more complicated than others. For example, Scrum frames iterations in terms of time, requiring "sprints" of about two to four weeks. Feedback occurs through a regiment of short daily meetings, forward-looking and retrospective post-sprint meetings, periodic planning meetings, and through team structures.

Our inclination is to scope iterations based on functionality rather than time. An iteration should ideally be concerned with the smallest meaningful unit of functionality. By "meaningful," we mean a unit that, though it might be rather insignificant within the whole scope of the project, is whole unto itself, meaning that it can stand alone from a UX and software engineering perspective. To discover these meaningful smallest units, and also to determine in what order they must be developed, the hierarchy of application components must be traced down to its lowest meaningful level.

One way to approach this problem in the beginning is to ask the question, "What component or feature is the heart or essence of the product?" Think, for example, of Twitter. What single feature or component truly defines Twitter? It's not the capability for users to choose a personal style for their Twitter pages, nor is it the ability to add metatags to "tweets" (for example, #iranelection, @someuser). It isn't even the ability to follow Twitter feeds of friends. The most basic and core feature of Twitter is the ability to post 140-character messages to a web page. Without this, you don't have a product remotely like Twitter. This capability would therefore be the first focus of the project. It can be further broken down into two parts: a means for posting new tweets into the Twitter service, and the means for displaying those tweets on a web page. A system isn't much good without any data, so you'd likely start with the posting capability.

This is likely the smallest meaningful unit of functionality within the Twitter example. This capability requires two components:

- *A web page with a 140-character text input box and submit button.*
- *The capability of storing the submitted tweet in a database.*

But each component cannot stand on its own; each requires the other. A focus on just the web UI or just the backend mechanisms would make the focus meaningless from the perspective of either the software engineers or the UX team, respectively. But taken together, they comprise a function that can stand on its own and is meaningful to the user, to the UX team, and to the engineers. That gives stakeholders and users something meaningful to look at and respond to.

As the project progresses, the focus of subsequent iterations will shift from the smallest meaningful component to whatever is the next most important, smallest meaningful increment of progress that can be made. Sometimes this means that the development of a new component will be undertaken, but more often this leads to a meaningful refinement of an existing component or the bringing together of smaller units of functionality to build a larger aspect of the product.

Prioritizing the Subjects of Iterations

At the end of each iteration, you need to take stock of what exists and decide what the subject of the next iteration will be. For a UX-focused product, the decision should be based on the question: what advances the quality of the UX the most? You'll never truly know until the very end of the project how much you'll be able to accomplish and how many capabilities you'll be able to include. This is why it's crucial to prioritize solely according to what will deliver the best improvement to the product's UX. If you've done that, then when you run out of time and money, the product's UX will be as good as it possibly could have been.

The traditional approach to software is to attempt to solve almost all of the backend engineering challenges before beginning to focus on the application UI. With this approach, the software engineers must anticipate the needs of the product's UI and UX and build capabilities to service those needs. But this presumes the UI and UX needs can be anticipated in advance from the requirements, which is never true. This is a repeat of the problematic approach of waterfall and BDUF, with the same problems: much of the time and budget available to the development stage will have been expended before the unknowns related to UX/UI design can be explored. Engineers are left to make decisions without the benefit of feedback from UX/UI design. If backend engineering work gets too far ahead of the UX and UI work, you might run out of time or money without a truly complete product. There might be a depth and thoroughness to the backend, but its capabilities won't be fully carried forward to the UX or UI of the product. This means that the project will have failed to actually deliver on those capabilities, and that the engineering time applied against them will have been wasted.

The UX/UI design and engineering of the product should be moving forward closely in tandem. This ensures that every capability that is engineered is also fully executed, and that everything that is designed is also implemented by engineers. By working in tandem, each team also has the benefit of timely feedback from the other, and can adjust course at the same time in response to risks and unknowns as they're uncovered.

Finishing Iterations with Something Complete

With each iteration, the result should be something that can stand on its own. At the end of an iteration, you should have something that everyone—the software engineers, UX designers, UI designers, stakeholders, and users—can examine and provide feedback on. This is useful in making sure everyone on the team has something to contribute to an iteration, leading to more valuable collaboration and feedback. But it has another, extremely valuable effect: at the end of each iteration, you have a product.

In the Twitter example, imagine if your project funding had been pulled after the team had managed to develop only the capability to post 140-character messages to the Web. This would be a tragedy and loss of the larger hopes and goals for the product. What wouldn't be lost, however, is the value of the work that was done. The capability to post 140-character messages to the Web would still exist, despite the cancellation of the rest of the project. If the company decided to resume the project or use that capability elsewhere, the time spent building it wouldn't have been wasted.

The value of this increases as the project grows. The longer a project goes on, the more is on the table, gambled against a good outcome. Every time you finish an iteration with a functioning product, you essentially take the cash off the table and bank it in a secure outcome. Whatever might happen next in the project, the money spent so far has bought something that functions. And so with each iteration, you're reducing the degree of financial risk represented by the project.

Contrast this against the approach often taken to large development efforts. Rather than put small amounts of money on the table and bank on frequent payouts, you have to put all of your cash on the table in hopes of one big payout at the end. Without a focus on producing something complete in frequent iterations, there's a risk that everything will be in progress and nothing will be complete up to the end of the project. When the time or money runs out, it's easy to wind up with a product that is 90 percent done in most respects but not fully complete or releasable. A product that doesn't work or stand on its own can't be released, and is therefore worth nothing. To make matters worse, you usually don't realize that you're going to run out of time and money without producing anything complete until it's too late to do anything about it. Many projects run like this end up requiring budget increases, forcing stakeholders to gamble even more money so that all the money that's still on the table isn't wasted.

But if you've focused on producing something releasable with each iteration, you're in a much less risky position. As the money and time start to run out, the final scope of the product becomes more apparent. That scope will be whatever exists after the most recent, complete iteration, plus whatever can be completed and refined before the timer runs out. Even if that final scope is somewhat less than some might have hoped it would be, you still have a finished, working product to show for your efforts. If the project has been guided by strong framework requirements and a focus on UX, any shortfalls should be minor in the context of a releasable product that conforms to the business and user requirements. In this scenario, stakeholders have a choice of either releasing the product as is or spending more time and money to add to the scope. This is a much better set of options than the alternative of choosing between risking more money in hopes of completion or deciding to lose all of the money invested in the project.

Estimating Iterations

Scoping iterations according to functionality rather than in terms of time doesn't mean that time ceases to be an important consideration. As they go through successive iterations, the team should not only refine their understanding of the product's problems and solutions, they also should become more practiced at estimating the complexity of what they need to do. The accuracy with which the team can estimate the complexity and time requirement of reaching goals is a key factor in the risk associated with the project; the greater the accuracy of estimates, the greater the certainty of being able to meet objectives within the project's constraints.

And so as the team scopes iterations, they should also be making time estimates for them. They can do this by estimating how long a given iteration will take, or by estimating how much can be completed within a given fixed interval (usually four to six weeks). If the team is diligent and trustworthy, missed estimates should be less of an indication of a failure and more of a barometer of risk. If things are taking longer than professionals expect them to, that will apply pressure across the whole project timeline. If the team is part of the way through an iteration but isn't on track to meet the estimate, you have an early warning about risk associated with what they're working on. This gives you and the team a chance to respond to that risk by making adjustments to the scope of the current iteration or of future tasks and iterations. How often and how significantly estimates are inaccurate are also indications of how much unexpected friction the team is encountering, which is in turn an indication of overall risk. If you're encountering higher risk, you'll need to start preparing to reduce the ambitiousness of the project to stay within schedule and cost constraints while also trying to mitigate the causes of the friction creating the increased risk.

The routine of making estimates will, over time, help the project team to be more and more accurate in making those estimates. The more reliable their estimates become, the more accurately you can estimate what can be completed within the project's constraints. Risk in a project is greatest at the beginning; this is when the team is the least practiced at making estimates, and also when the least is known about the problem and its solution. As development progresses, risk should be reduced as the team gets better at estimating, as they come to understand the problem better, and as the unknowns surface and are dealt with.

And, finally, setting time goals offers the ordinary benefits associated with goals and deadlines. It helps focus the team, preserves momentum, and provides you with a mechanism of day-to-day accountability. Scheduled goals are also a useful constraint to prevent perfectionism from causing problems.

Basic Iterative Process

To see how feedback operates to the benefit of the project, and why giving more room to the development stage is important, let's examine in depth how iteration works. Figure 8-3 illustrates the flow of progress and feedback in a basic iterative process.

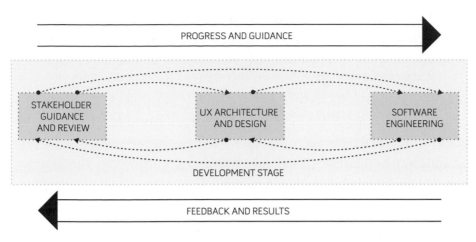

Figure 8-3. An iterative development stage

This is a "basic" process because, as we'll discuss later in this chapter, many more degrees and types of feedback can, and should, be added. This shows how the flow of progress and feedback for each iteration works in a development stage where everyone is involved. Rather than having the different disciplines start and finish their work in isolation and iterating only on their own progress and observations, each group has the opportunity to review all progress being made and provide guidance forward through the project. In any given iterative cycle, the progress and feedback activities would go roughly like this:

1. *The team decides what the next focus of progress should be.*

2. *The UX architecture/design team (which is now working inside the development stage instead of before it) learns from guidance from stakeholders and also from feedback and the results produced by the software engineering team. They produce a more refined set of designs for a given aspect of the product. This progress and any related guidance is fed forward to software engineering, and the results, lessons learned, and risks encountered through the work done during the cycle is fed back to stakeholders.*

3. *The software engineering team receives guidance from stakeholder reviews of results achieved thus far, along with designs and guidance fed forward from the UX architecture/design team. They construct the component or perform the required changes. The results of their work and any lessons learned or risks encountered are fed back to the stakeholders and the UX architecture/ design team.*

4. *The stakeholders review the results of the work being done by the UX architecture/design team and the software engineering team as well as information about unknowns and risks encountered. They provide guidance to the other teams about how to bring the product more closely in line with goals and how to adjust course in response to eventualities that affect schedule, cost, or expectations.*

In this setting, all the teams are kept up to speed on the current state of the project and any new information and unknowns that are discovered. The accuracy and quality of their work benefits from their access to the fullest and most current understanding of the state of the project. They're also receiving feedback from people who represent each of the critical perspectives in the project, which enriches their understanding and improves the quality of their work.

Figure 8-3 was just focused on the development stage, but the development stage is one part of a larger product development process. Figure 8-4 shows the development stage in the context of the larger project.

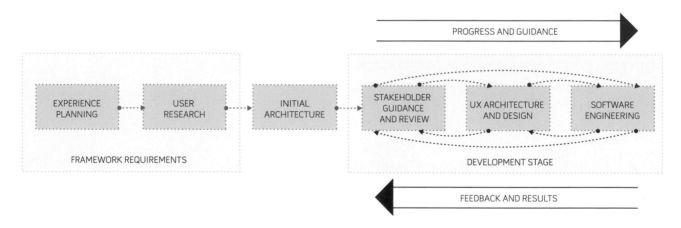

Figure 8-4. The whole project development lifecycle

The equivalent size of all the parts of the lifecycle in this diagram belies an important requirement of UX-focused projects: that the vast majority of time and resources should be spent during the development stage. Through the preceding chapters, we encouraged you to:

- *Take a realistic view of the value of upfront planning and minimize how much time is spent on it.*

- *Exercise restraint in business planning, refraining from making guesses about the solution before development begins.*

- *Acknowledge the "initial" quality of the initial product architecture stage and keep it focused on only the critical questions without delving into detailed product design.*

All this should add up to less time and money spent on the upfront stuff and much more time and money available for the development stage. This is especially important when you consider the bulk of UX, UI, and systems design has been wrested from the upfront stages and placed into the development stage. If plotted against time, or against resource allocation, the project might look more like what's shown in Figure 8-5.

TIME SPENT / RESOURCES CONSUMED

Figure 8-5. Project stages against time and resources

The more time and money available to the development stage, the more iteration that can take place—leading to more feedback and therefore greater quality and smoother progress.

You might have already noted one very unrealistic aspect of the development stage as we've described it so far: that the stakeholders could participate so intensively as to be involved in every iteration. This is rarely a possibility. We've included stakeholders in this way so far because it is the truly ideal way of doing things; having well-informed, highly engaged stakeholders who provide active feedback throughout the project will result in better outcomes. And you're unlikely to risk disappointing or blindsiding the stakeholders, because they'll have been involved in progress and decision making all along the way.

But the ordinary impossibility of having stakeholders involved to this degree is why we put such a strong emphasis on the role of the project leader in Chapter 4. Even when the stakeholders have little time to be involved, it's critical that their point of view and the high-level business goals for the project be taken into intensive consideration all throughout the project. This is where the project leader, acting as a proxy for the business needs and the goals of the stakeholders, can step in to relieve most of the burden from the stakeholders. So, a more realistic view of an agile development stage might look something like what's shown in Figure 8-6.

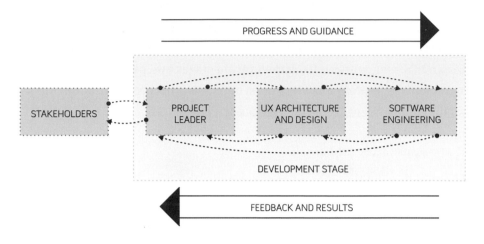

Figure 8-6. Project leader acts as a proxy for stakeholders in an iterative development stage

In this diagram, the dashed lines represent less frequent feedback and guidance. The project leader participates in the project in the stakeholders' stead, but this doesn't mean the stakeholders drop out of the process altogether. They must vest a high degree of trust in the project leader, but will naturally expect periodic updates, and the project will strongly benefit from their guidance. An additional benefit to this approach is it ensures that the stakeholders deal only with the project leader and aren't communicating with and receiving materials from project team members directly. Most stakeholders, especially those who are very detached from the project or who are unfamiliar with how software gets made—like laws and sausages—will need to have feedback and results "packaged" to a certain degree. The project leader will want to retain a high degree of control over the stakeholders' perceptions and expectations and have an opportunity to properly introduce and explain things.

Mapping Progress and Feedback Across Multiple Cycles

The diagrams so far have just shown the structure of iterations within the development stage, but the development stage is comprised of many iterations. These iterations don't take place one at a time in sequence, with one being fully completed by everyone involved before the next one commences. Instead, the progress of the project is a series of interlocking iterations. There's a natural order to how each of the professional disciplines participates in the project: the UX/UI design team proposes a particular solution in visual terms, the engineering team builds that solution, and the project leader (or stakeholders) offer feedback on it. While the software engineers are building a given iteration, the UX/UI design team isn't sitting idle, but has rather moved on to the next cycle. At the same time, the project leader is reviewing the results of the previous cycle. Thus a simplified view of everyone's activities across multiple iterative cycles looks something like what's shown in Figure 8-7.

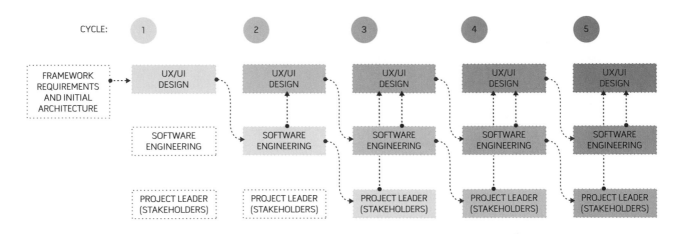

Figure 8-7. Simplified multicycle map

So, for example, while the UX/UI design team is working on cycle 3, the software engineers are implementing the component specified by UX/UI design in cycle 2, and the project leader is reviewing the implemented results of cycle 1. Each passes on feedback based on the discoveries and challenges encountered and the course changes required as the project moves forward. Figure 8-7 is, however, oversimplified for the sake of visual simplicity. In this view, the flow of progress and feedback moves very rigidly from UX/UI design to software engineering to the project leader, and never in the other direction or in any other order. Additionally, the UX/UI design team alone leads the entire project and receives all of the feedback. A highly structured process like this might in fact be necessary to keep people from being overloaded with feedback, but the goal of increasing the amount of feedback still exists. It's therefore possible to conceive of a project where feedback and progress is being shared quite vigorously, as shown in Figure 8-8.

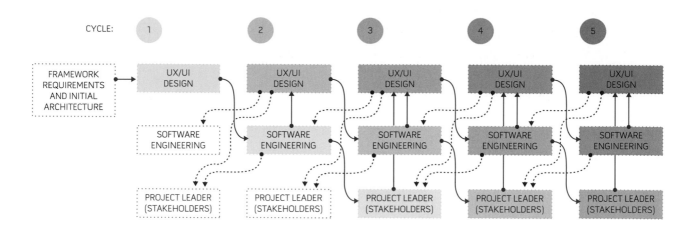

Figure 8-8. Complex multicycle map

This complicated diagram is consistent with the previous diagrams in this chapter that show the structure of iteration. Progress and guidance is fed forward from everyone to everyone, and feedback and review is open to everyone, no matter which cycle they're currently working on. This level of collaboration is likely to be difficult to achieve in practical reality, but it's good to acknowledge the ideal. Following the more simplified flow can be effective, but it means that it can take the time span of two iterations before any team has the opportunity to give guidance or receive feedback. This means their understanding of the product will always be slightly behind the understanding that's potentially available to them.

Increasing the Amount of Feedback

Increasing the amount of feedback that occurs during the project generally causes it to be more successful. The amount of feedback that occurs in a development stage is a direct function of the frequency of iterations and the amount of time allowed for iterations. The number of iterations can be increased by giving the development stage the most room possible and by tailoring iterations to the smallest meaningful unit of progress. The amount of feedback is also a direct function of the number of perspectives the feedback is coming from. With that in mind, you can pull some levers to increase the amount of feedback that occurs through the development stage.

Increase collaboration efficiency

Sharing results and providing feedback across teams and iterative cycles is a collaborative process. To the extent that this collaboration can be made more effective and efficient, the average duration of iterations will decrease, leading to more feedback; the effectiveness of the feedback in influencing correct change will also be increased. Effective collaboration also eases the strain imposed on the project team by lots of incoming feedback, allowing them to receive more of it from more sources without disrupting their forward progress. We usually use a product called Trac (*http://trac.edgewall.org*) to help facilitate collaboration on a project. Trac ties into the engineers' code base and provides centralized issue-tracking, planning, and discussion features. This provides a nexus of collaboration that helps us avoid the inefficiencies inherent to decentralized, email-based approaches and gives the project team access to information and decisions generated by other people.

Bring in more perspectives

So far we've discussed agile approaches in which the stakeholders or project leader, the UX/UI design team, and the software engineers are working in tandem and providing feedback to each other. These three points of view are critical and cannot be excluded if the project is to end with a successful UX. But there are points of view beyond these three that should, whenever possible, be included in the project's iterative cycles.

New perspectives might be found in people within your company whose views are important but might be underrepresented by the stakeholders. For example, the Herff Jones eDesign application was conceived, in part, to make it easier for sales representatives to convince schools to switch to Herff Jones for their yearbook services. The sales representatives also act as account managers and customer liaisons, so they are directly in touch with the needs and concerns of the students and schools. Involving representatives of groups like this in the development process (even if only for the major iterations) can be a tremendous help.

QA is typically treated as a phase done at the end or near the end of the development stage. But involving continuous, professional QA all throughout the development process helps lead to more solid results and reduces the risk of serious issues or unknowns coming up too late in the project. If they're involved in the whole of the development process, or at least in the key milestones, professional QA teams can not only dramatically reduce risk, but they also can add a valuable outside perspective of feedback to the process. They might notice things that aren't noticed by the other teams that are more deeply engaged in the project. They can alert the engineering team to problematic areas in the product as it progresses and help to quickly correct faulty development practices.

The most important additional perspective that can be brought in is that of the user. The business planning and user research stages should have yielded a strong framework for making good decisions on the users' behalf, but that framework and its application will be imperfect. Many traditional projects tack on a "user acceptance testing" phase at the end of a project following QA, but if user feedback is held to after the development phase is concluded, it doesn't have an opportunity to positively influence the product much. It's impractical to involve users in every small unit of iteration, but getting user feedback as frequently as possible makes a huge difference. Testing wireframes, prototypes, components, rudimentary versions of features, designs, and other major elements of the application with users on an ongoing basis ensures the direction of progress is firmly aligned with the user's needs. Strong user feedback also gives the team tremendous confidence in the correctness of their path and decisions.

Iteration in Sub-Ideal Project Approaches

To better understand how abundant, well-rounded feedback leads to easier, better results, it's helpful to examine project approaches that interfere with feedback: waterfall and BDUF. You might also find yourself forced to make do with a sub-ideal project approach mandated by your company's policy or regulatory constraints. Sub-ideal doesn't mean failure is guaranteed; it just means that the path to success will be harder to discern and will be more troubled. In any case, it's interesting to note the ways in which a sub-ideal process differs from a more ideal one, because these differences will be focal points of weakness and risk that will need to be paid attention to, factored into estimates, and actively mitigated.

Strict Waterfall Process

As we discussed at length in Chapter 3, the central fallacy of the waterfall process is its presumption that each stage of progress can be made perfect before handing off to the next stage. Stakeholders must set out perfect specifications that inform perfect design requirements, which, in turn, are meant to leave engineers with a perfect blueprint and no unanswered questions. Inevitability, though, the specifications and design requirements will be highly inaccurate. This leaves the software engineers to contend with all of the unknowns on their own without the benefit of stakeholder or UX design feedback and within a schedule and budget set based on an inaccurate view of scope. Figure 8-9 helps illustrate the other fundamental weaknesses of the waterfall process.

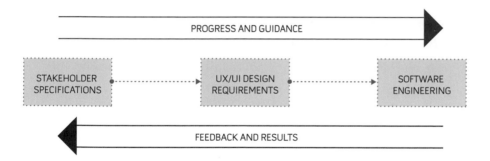

Figure 8-9. A strict waterfall process

At a high level, a waterfall process involves only three significant iterations:

- *The first delivery of the specifications by the stakeholders*
- *The delivery of the UX/UI design requirements*
- *The delivery of the product by software engineering*

Though minor iterations with feedback occur within the confines of each of the three stages before being handed off to the next stage, there is no feedback between the stages. The waterfall process cuts off each professional domain from the others, depriving them of the benefit of feedback from each other.

A waterfall process also makes it so the project has only two significant opportunities for course correction:

- *When the UX/UI designers attempt to translate the specifications into design requirements*
- *When the software engineers attempt to turn the design requirements and specifications into working software*

But these two course corrections are hobbled by the inability to consult the other professional domains and by the apparent need to adhere as closely as possible to the inaccurate early specifications and requirements. At each stage the teams are sure to find errors in the materials they're handed and be compelled to address previously unknown issues. But since the errors are enshrined in unchangeable specifications and requirements (or, in the case of client-vendor situations, in a contract), they tend to go uncorrected. And since people from the other professional disciplines are mostly unavailable when unknowns are encountered, decisions arising from those unknowns must be made without the benefit of advice from the UX and business perspectives. The software engineers end up making a lot of business and UX design decisions under pressure without advice, and without permission to exercise thoughtful creative latitude.

If you're forced to use a waterfall process, the inherent weaknesses of the approach will trouble your progress and weaken your results. Sorry! You do, however, have some limited control and opportunities to make things go a little more smoothly.

Allow discretion and latitude down the line

It will be helpful if everyone involved (especially the stakeholders) can be made to understand the inherent weaknesses of specifications, requirements, and designs formulated up front before development begins. If specifications and design requirements can be treated as well-reasoned guidance rather than sacrosanct marching orders, a degree of latitude is opened to the UX/UI designers and software engineers to make thoughtful decisions based on the guidance and the actual realities of the project as they emerge. The UX/UI design team must have the discretion to change and improve upon the specifications set out by the stakeholders, and the software engineering team must have the discretion to improve upon the design requirements and the specifications.

One simple way of providing latitude is to change how you name documentation. Rather than "requirements" or "specifications," the early stages of a waterfall process might produce "guidelines" or "recommendations." These documents, being produced so early in the project, will be based largely on assumptions, so it's also very helpful to identify those assumptions and include them in the documentation. This will give the team reading the documentation a better understanding of what's firm and what's uncertain.

Don't segregate the professional disciplines

Waterfall processes typically require business requirements and specifications to be built first, then design requirements, and then a working product. The business requirements and specifications are apparently the domain of businesspeople, design requirements the domain of designers, and development the domain of software engineers. This means there's a tendency to assign only businesspeople to the first stage, only designers to the second, and only engineers to the third. But there's nothing in the demands of a strict waterfall process that requires this segregation of professional disciplines. When building the business requirements, involve the input of designers and software engineers; when building the design requirements, assign someone with software engineering experience to the team; and when development begins, do your utmost to ensure that at least design, if not also business, is actively involved. In the end, you'll still have produced the required sequence of major deliverables, but they'll be better for having benefited from rounder professional guidance.

It might seem that if this can be achieved that one is no longer using a waterfall process, but the other major weaknesses of the waterfall process are still present. Large amounts of time, money, and resources are still being expended in wastefully extensive upfront specification and design processes, depriving the development stage of the best measure of resources. Even if all of the disciplines are participating all along the way, this deprivation of resources from development will mean the number of significant iterations will be drastically reduced. This reduces feedback and the frequency of course corrections, increasing the frequency and severity of deviations and errors.

Allow the time and budget for major changes after the first delivery

If you're using a waterfall process, you should be forewarned that the first delivery by the engineering team is probably going to be far off the mark. If the budget and schedule were based on the presumption that the specifications and design requirements were perfect blueprints for the product and the first delivery would therefore also be perfect, you're in big trouble. Anticipating early failure—in fact, not considering it failure in the first place—and reserving a large amount of time and budget for continued development after the first delivery will permit you the opportunity to fix what's broken in a more relaxed atmosphere. This is essentially a backwards way of circumventing the waterfall process by creating budgetary and schedule room for additional major iterations that benefit from the feedback arising from the first and each subsequent delivery.

The more time and money you hold back for after the first delivery, the healthier you make the development stage. Holding back money and time will effectively reduce the scale of the first delivery, making it a smaller iteration. Once that delivery drops, you'll have an opportunity to solicit feedback from stakeholders, and hopefully designers and even users as well. Based on this input, you can free up another portion of the reserve of budget and time for a second iteration, and then a third, and so on. But again, the other weaknesses of the waterfall process will still limit you, despite this sleight of hand. Any resources consumed in substantial upfront specification and design efforts will be unavailable to you for iterations in the development stage, and it might take some effort to convince stakeholders to interpret the deliveries as successive iterations instead of as a string of failed deliveries.

If you manage to make room for iterations following the first delivery, make sure you're also set up to get good feedback against the early iterations. For reasons that have never made much sense to us, a lot of companies plan to do the user testing on a product only after it's been built, when the feedback is only of academic value and can't improve the product. Bringing that user feedback as far forward in the project as possible will give it a greater opportunity to positively affect the success of the project.

Rush the first two stages

This is a trick with which you can effectively cram a more ideal process into the form of a waterfall process. It's absolutely guaranteed that specifications and design requirements built up front are going to be full of errors and omissions. This will be true whether you spend six months or six days on them. So why not spend six days on them? Specifications and design deliverables, especially those built to satisfy bureaucratic or regulatory requirements, typically get a cursory look-over to see if they're credible, and are then stuffed in a drawer or put on a shelf, never to be looked at again. Try to get your stakeholders to acknowledge the weaknesses of too much upfront planning and design and to secure their willingness to participate in a more dynamic process. Then you can spend only as much time on the first two stages as is required to satisfy the cursory review and to do the proper, restrained amount of planning. This will give you the time, money, and prerogative to have more frequent feedback within the scope of the development stage.

Iteration in a Big Design Up Front (BDUF) Process

It can be a bit difficult to distinguish between BDUF and waterfall. Both tend to require that a significant portion of the time and budget be spent on upfront planning and design. However, an important distinction between the two is that BDUF acknowledges that the professional domains shouldn't be segregated. Since the upfront design is just "big" and not "wholly comprehensive," some UX/UI design resources are made available during the development stage. It also inherently acknowledges that the design requirements arising out of the second stage will be imperfect, necessitating the availability of design resources during development to participate in their refinement. A BDUF process diagram would look something like what's shown in Figure 8-10.

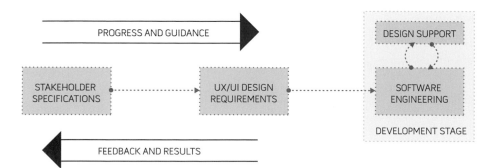

Figure 8-10. A Big Design Up Front design process

This is far from ideal, but it's a huge step in the right direction. Besides building in the critical acknowledgement of the need for ongoing design during the development stage, it also allows for a limited amount of cross-disciplinary feedback. The software engineers will be using an iterative process to keep progress moving, and now each iteration can benefit from guidance given by UX/UI designers to the previous iteration. Unforeseen issues and unknowns uncovered during the development stage (most of which will have UX/UI design implications) can be addressed with the benefit of some support by designers, rather than requiring the software engineers to hash it out on their own.

But BDUF nevertheless suffers from many of the same problems as waterfall. Although design might be less segregated from the development stage, stakeholders are still often left siloed into the first stage rather than brought in to participate in the development stage. The emphasis on big upfront design also means that resources that ought to be available to the development stage are consumed before development has a chance to begin. The degree of feedback is also unduly limited in BDUF, and like waterfall, it tends to suggest that specifications and design requirements can be treated as nearly perfect for the purposes of scheduling and budgeting. This all adds up to the concentration of a great amount of risk in the development stage, since it's still left to absorb all of the unknown and uncertainty in a setting of limited resources and unrealistic expectations.

Because the problems with BDUF are just lesser versions of those in waterfall processes, the advice for mitigating the problems is the same. The more feedback across disciplines that can be forced in, the more the weakness of upfront planning is acknowledged and the more room for iteration that can be made; the smaller the big upfront design can be made, the closer you get to a more effective process and a more successful project.

Chapter 9
Release and Post-Release

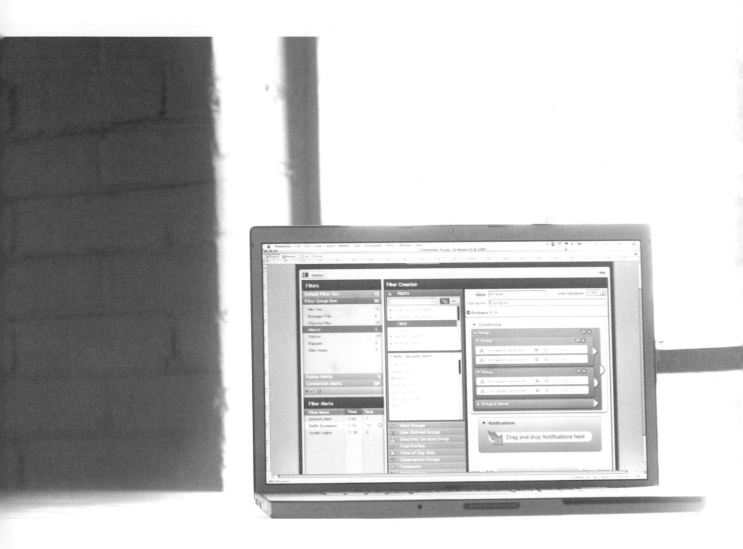

If you were able to follow an iterative development process, the experience of bringing the product to release should be more pleasant than other projects you might have worked on. Wrapping up a project should be much more like winding down after a long run, rather than making a life-or-death sprint. Releases should be anti-climactic, and anticlimax—the absence of surprises, drama, and uncertainty—is a good thing in high-stakes situations such as product development.

For projects that follow a waterfall or similarly sub-ideal process, releases are often the first opportunities for serious QA efforts, user acceptance testing (UAT), and stakeholder review. In other words, the releases—the moments that are ostensibly the unveiling of a finished product—are some of the first significant opportunities for feedback. The relative lack of feedback during development guarantees that the first release will miss the marks of success, quality, and expectations. This ensures that the unveiling of the first release is stressful and fraught with acrimony; it will be viewed as a failure by stakeholders and users. This underscores the importance of following an iterative development process. It's natural that the first major iterations of anything are going to miss the mark; that's the point of iterating—to check in and see how to change course. But if an iteration is so long that it comprises the entire development stage, no room is available for the major course corrections that will necessary. The inevitable changes have to be made under a cloud of perceived failure and the burden of scant remaining time and resources.

If you've made frequent releases in the form of iterations and feedback has been continuous from QA, users, and stakeholders, "releases" are simply special iterations and contain a minimum of uncertainty and surprises. And if you've made sure each iteration ended in a working, meaningful product, there shouldn't be a lot of last-minute loose ends to tie up. Making a release just means picking an iteration to polish up a bit, unveiling it with the proper fanfare, and putting it out for broader feedback, or ultimately for deployment.

Managing Expectations

Ideally, your stakeholders should already be fully aware of what will be released. They should have a sense of pride and ownership about it that is a product of their active participation. If you have managed them properly, they shouldn't be in for any surprises. Any cuts, changes, or compromises that were made during the course of the project should have been brought to their attention immediately as they occurred. The audience for releases of the product is generally much wider than just the team members and stakeholders who worked on the project. Other stakeholders who initially declined to participate, the stakeholders' stakeholders, higher-ups in the organization, and employees in the company generally will often see the product for the first time when the alpha release is made.

Although you might have deftly managed your stakeholders' expectations during the project, before making a release you need to set expectations properly more broadly in your company. During the whole of the planning and development stages, nonparticipating people will have been left to develop their own private preconceptions about what the product will look like. Everything you discovered during the design and development of the product will have led it down a different course than you initially represented. In addition, your stakeholders probably have done a relatively poor job of managing their own stakeholders' and bosses' expectations as the project evolved. Stakeholders who were fully supportive and were aware of why the product turned out the way it did can quickly turn adversarial if they start getting criticism from their own stakeholders and superiors. And a staff that isn't enthusiastic about the product will be less likely to adopt it as an internal tool or will be less supportive of getting it out to customers.

Releases should never be shown to people without any introduction. Just as the project leader needed to seize control of the stakeholders' expectations by, in part, managing their experience of viewing progress, releases need to be properly packaged and presented as they're shown around. Depending on the scale and importance of the product, that might take the form of company-wide meetings or presentations, one-on-ones with key higher-ups, or internal marketing efforts. Prior to demonstrating the product to anyone, you need to ensure that they've been primed to receive it well.

They should have heard and understood the product's mission and success criteria. They also need to understand the specific purpose the product was built for, notwithstanding ancillary benefits they might have hoped for. You want people to judge the product based on how it serves the needs of the company and not just on how it might help out their individual departments or roles. They should also be told how the product was built: the reason for the primary focus on UX, the deep integration of user research and (hopefully) continuous user feedback, and any notable issues, opportunities, and constraints that changed the course of the project and factored strongly into the outcome.

Video or audio of the user research you did early in the project can be helpful here. Put together a sample of what users were saying early in the project and compare them with their reactions to the new product. Customers that switch from frustration to delight make an extremely compelling argument that you've done something successful and important.

The Alpha and Beta Releases

Modes of product deployment are shifting away from physical media or extensive on-site installs to web downloads, SaaS, "cloud" applications, managed ASPs, and so on. This has caused the meaning of predeployment releases to morph. Within heavily regimented, waterfall-like processes, the alpha and beta releases might have a specific meaning and specific demands to satisfy some bureaucratic requirement. But you should understand releases in terms of their purpose and not simply as obligatory process steps.

Releases are major opportunities for an inundation of feedback. That is their only truly important purpose, at least from the perspective of building the product. Major releases should be planned and formulated around the goal of receiving feedback. The type of feedback you're seeking will guide your choice of who is included in the release audience and how complete or bug-free the product should be prior to making the release. An alpha release is typically made when the product is feature-complete but there is still a significant queue of known issues; it is released to a limited internal audience, or a carefully selected external audience. The purpose of the alpha release is usually to widen the range of perspectives and increase the volume of feedback provided on significant issues. Product teams, and even QA teams, can get so familiar with

Students working on an alpha release of the Herff Jones eDesign product

or submerged in the product that they overlook significant issues that fresh, outside observers notice immediately. Alpha releases are also often the sales and marketing teams' first real look at the product. An early glimpse of the product helps them get a head start on messaging and selling the product.

Beta releases are typically made when the product is functionally complete, and the majority of significant issues have been repaired. Beta releases go out to much wider audiences than alpha releases, often including a significant number of actual customers. The purpose of beta releases from the perspective of developing the product is to again increase the range of perspectives and the volume of feedback. Many of the minor or stranger bugs surface only when the product is being prodded from every imaginable direction. Finding these bugs requires a large group of people to truly explore all of the peculiar use cases for the product and find new and unexpected ways of operating it improperly.

Alpha and beta releases are also often treated as opportunities to market the product. Inviting people to a "sneak peek" of the predeployment releases of a product can be a useful way of building closer relationships with key customers or generating early buzz for the product. But unless the audience for your product are themselves software professionals who understand how predeployment releases work, you should consider for the sake of everyone's sanity separating marketing-oriented releases from development releases. The marketing alpha release should be more like the development beta release so customers aren't being exposed to significant defects. The marketing beta release should simply be a final or near-final deployment candidate.

Receiving Orderly Feedback

Since getting feedback is the purpose of making predeployment releases, and since time and money are dwindling at the end of the project, it's important that the feedback is received in the most orderly, useful way possible. As valuable as the feedback can be, it also can be distracting and damaging if you make the mistake of soliciting it through email or letting participants enter issues directly into the development issue queue. Email doesn't work, because of the high volume of feedback you will receive. It's very difficult to ensure important issues are triaged and addressed, and you'll get many, many emails reporting the same issues over and over again. It's also important to mediate between this feedback and the project team. The team will be blitzing to get as much done as possible before the project ends, and a flood of unfiltered, untriaged feedback is a huge distraction. People who aren't software professionals usually don't know how to report issues in an effective way, and amidst all of the stress, project teams have a tendency to get irritated with inane, redundant, or poorly formulated feedback.

So, unless you're dealing with very limited release audiences, you should provide a special infrastructure through which participants can provide feedback. Many issue tracking systems have a means of creating a separate class of users and issue tickets that are held separate from the development queue. Issue tracking systems give participants an easy, online means of providing feedback that lets them see whether they're reporting something that's already been reported by someone else. Issue tracking systems also make it easier for you to manage and track the feedback. You, a product manager, or another member of the project team can review participant issue tickets, clean them up, and triage them into the development issue queue. If it isn't possible to segregate participant feedback from the development issue pool within the development issue tracking system, set up a separate bug-tracking system to receive the feedback, and manually transport the important issues into the development system.

You can also improve the quality of the incoming feedback by providing participants instructions on how to provide useful feedback. It can be maddening to open a ticket that says something like, "When I click the OK button, nothing happens." There's no way of telling where and under what conditions the issue occurred and whether it's important. When setting up the feedback-tracking system, make sure to also create either individual logins for participants or a required field for the participants to give their names. This way, if you get a confusing or incomplete ticket, you know who to ask about it.

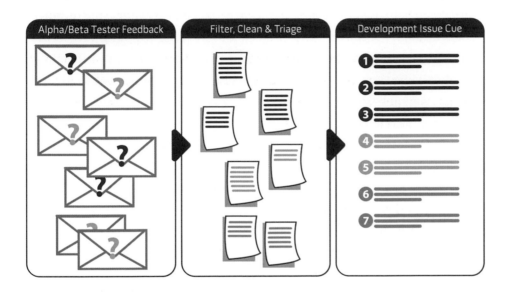

Last-Minute Housekeeping

The project team will usually start out a project enforcing best practices around organizing code and assets, documenting or automating builds, and other helpful practices. But the effects of impatience, pressure, rushing, and general entropy usually mean that at the end of the project things are a little disorganized. This needs to be cleaned up. Things need to be left in a state such that, whether two weeks or two years in the future, it's easy to find the necessary information and to build the product from the source in case changes need to be made.

Without getting into the technical nitty-gritty, code repositories can get confusing and disorganized through the course of the project. Multiple versions or "branches" of the product might exist and cross-reference each other, or the code might reference special libraries that exist on only one engineer's laptop. All of this needs to be consolidated into one definitive repository that either includes all of the required resources or comes with documentation explaining what external resources are necessary and how to access them. If the software engineers did a poor job of commenting their code throughout the project, it's usually not worth it to have them go back through and retroactively comment everything. However, they should identify critical, confusing, or complicated areas of the code and provide future developers with some guidance on how it all works.

The design team members also will have produced a considerable number of assets through the course of the project. Most of these will be intermediary materials or minor variations of the same asset. They will all be reflections of not only the final design of the product but also the progression of thinking that went into the final design. These materials should be preserved and organized. Besides being useful to future changes and improvements on the product, they can have broader uses across the company and in the marketing of the product.

User Documentation

As hard as you might have tried to make everything intuitive and easy to use, some level of user documentation is always necessary. A positive software experience requires that users can figure out how to use it easily, without frustration, and with confidence. The user documentation should be as much a reflection of your care for the user's experience as the software itself. The archetypal example of bad UX in product design is that of the VCRs of the 1980s and 1990s. That horrid UX was compounded by instructions that were incomplete and poorly translated from Japanese into English. The experience of using a new product should be a delight, not a frustration.

It's usually best to make the user documentation available as part of the application rather than as a separate binder of paper. And rather than sequestering it in the "F1" help area, the current trend in products is to make help documentation available in context. This allows users to directly access help on the specific subject of the tasks they're attempting to perform, the controls they're attempting to operate, the information they're trying to input, and so on. This type of contextual help requires infrastructure built into the application itself, so if your product will be heavily reliant on support documentation, this feature should be accounted for in requirements and designs. User documentation can take much longer to produce than you might expect, so if your product requires a significant amount of documentation or uses an inline contextual system, you might consider giving the technical writers an early start. In fact, technical writers attempting to make sense of the product for users can be a very valuable source of QA and quasi-user feedback, so building documentation in tandem with the final QA efforts can be very helpful.

And Champagne Corks Fly...

Once all of the important issues have been addressed and the clock and money have run out, it's time to end the development effort and declare the product done. This is cause for celebration. But because of the anticlimactic nature of the end of an iterative development stage, it can be easy to forget to have your "champagne moment." If things have gone smoothly and you've managed to apply the advice we've given, the moment of completing development on a project should be less like collapsing across the finish line in an Olympic race and more like watching the clock strike 5 p.m. on a Friday.

But finishing development of a product is a major accomplishment—not unlike finishing an Olympic event. For some members of the team, it might be the most significant thing they have ever accomplished. The shockingly high incidence of project failures also means that the release of any working product, no matter what issues might yet haunt it, is a significant success. Your team has overcome a challenge many, many companies have been beaten by. Placing a ceremonious end-cap on a project acknowledges the magnitude of the accomplishment and can be good for everyone's spirits.

Adoption

The end of the development stage of the product shouldn't mean the end of giving it serious attention. After the long slog of developing the product, you and your company might be tempted to launch the product and then try to put it entirely behind you. But the joy and the curse of being successful in developing a great new product—or a fantastic improvement on an existing one—is that you're going to be living with it for a long while.

Software products are meant to be useful to and used by people. A product that doesn't get used, though it might be an impressive accomplishment in itself, is a failure and was a waste of money. Unfortunately, the *Field of Dreams* adage—"If you build it, they will come"—is not at all true of software. Adoption is something that must be aggressively sought after and built. A company's commitment to the success of a product can't stop at the point of completing its development; its adoption needs to be the focus of a major effort.

In the case of products built for customers and clients, this should be pretty obvious, since generating adoption is roughly the same thing as generating sales. The exception to this is when the product you've developed is a new version of an existing product. If salespeople and account managers are going to make the effort to transition their current customers and clients onto the new version and learn how to support it, they have to believe in the new version and be excited about selling its benefits. This means that you need to be prepared to do a significant amount of internal marketing of the product. This supports adoption on the part of your sales and account management staff that will carry over to adoption by customers. Just announcing the completion of the new version in a memo, email, or short presentation isn't close to sufficient. You should apply the same vigor to getting your staff excited as is applied to getting customers excited.

The same is true of products that were built for internal use. Such products are conceived to make some task or function easier for the company and the staff, to simplify some complex process, or to contribute some other serious benefit to the company and its staff. Unfortunately, though, many companies that produce internal products don't realize it's necessary to market the product to their own employees, falsely assuming that it will be adopted as a simple matter of course. Change, even to something superior, requires a bit of discomfort and effort on the part of the employees, and might temporarily make their work more difficult before making it easier. Internal politics can also create complications, as when departments that were left out of the development process contrive resistance, or when false preconceptions are left unchecked. All of these can add up to an inertial resistance that must be overcome. The techniques that are applied to marketing a product to customers should be applied to marketing it to employees. You need employees to be excited about the product before they use it so they're willing to commit the investment of time and energy it will take to adopt it. Also remember that their enthusiasm will wane and adoption will drop off if the product isn't properly supported internally.

Post-Release

If your project has been successful, you and your company will be thrust very quickly into repeating that success. You might start working on a new version of the product or move on to improve some other aspect of your company's offerings or internal systems. The project you've just finished provided valuable lessons about the product itself, how to deliver better UX, and how to build software generally. This will set up you and your company to succeed more easily in the next project. These lessons must be captured so they can be a catalyst for a future success.

Review

Many companies call the post-deployment review a "post mortem," but it really should be something much more complete and far less morose than that expression suggests. In a sense, your team's development of the product was one big iteration in what will hopefully be careers full of new, better iterations on building a software product. The end of any iteration is an opportunity to look back at what happened and decide what to do next and how to adjust tack. It's also an opportunity to judge the success of your efforts according to the original expectations and guidance that were set for you, and to take lessons from the unknowns that emerged and the ways you found your early assumptions challenged.

Checking against the original business goals

The project mission, success criteria, and business requirements constrained and guided the development of the product as part of the framework requirements, and they now offer you a clear, fair measure for your success. Make a point of getting your team, stakeholders, and your stakeholders' stakeholders together for a meeting and reacquaint them with the product's original goals. Explore together how effectively the project responded to those goals. It might take time for the project to be tested and adopted before you can be certain about meeting the success criteria. But it should be easy to judge whether the project met its mission and fulfilled on the high-level business requirements, and whether it's well poised to meet the success criteria. Any time the conversation about success starts to deviate into realms where it's being judged subjectively based on a stakeholder's or executive's errant expectations, the original business expectations are a useful tether to keep measures of your accountability fair. It's fine to examine how the product might have failed to live up to additional expectations that didn't come to light during the business planning process, but you shouldn't be held accountable for those issues. For that sort of issue, the conversation should be about why the expectations didn't come up in business planning and how to avoid that happening in the future.

The achievement of the success criteria is likely to require time and investment beyond the development of the product through aggressive marketing or internal adoption initiatives. Part of reviewing the project against the success criteria will be an opportunity to get your stakeholders focused on what additional steps need to be taken to fully realize the product's goals. They've already invested a significant amount of money in building the product and shouldn't inadvertently waste that investment by failing to follow through on final details such as marketing and infrastructure.

Reviewing the success against the original business goals is also an opportunity to learn how your organization can become better at setting those business goals in the first place and responding to fundamental changes that occur throughout the project. The emergence of unknowns, risks, and opportunities probably forced you to alter the business goals to some degree. The discoveries, events, and decision-making processes that led to those changes should be examined to understand whether the process for making the change was sound and whether it produced the right results. If it worked well, it should be remembered for future projects. If it didn't, the group should settle on a better means of handling such important changes for the future. Ways in which the project differed from the expectations of people inside and outside of the project team should also be explored to see if there are ways of improving how the business planning stage is conducted or how expectations are managed in future efforts. And the project team should be consulted to find out how effectively the business requirements guided their progress and whether they felt sufficiently informed by those requirements.

This is also a good opportunity to haul out the lists of user attributes, feature ideas, business requirements, and other thoughts that that were deferred or abandoned during the business planning process. These lists make it clear that those details and ideas were intentionally excluded as a result of planning efforts conducted with stakeholders. Going back to the raw materials of the early thinking about the project also often serves as a stark and interesting reminder of just how poorly everyone understood the project in its early stages. With the benefit of hindsight, many of the ideas will seem crazy or very off-base. If intelligent restraint was exercised during business planning, this should serve as a reinforcement of the value of restraint during the business planning process. It should also underscore the importance of the humility of unknowing at early stages of the project.

The list of ideas that didn't make it into the final product, along with the list of things that, in the final evaluation, should have been included, can form a good starting point for future product planning. New business planning efforts can be accelerated using old ideas that have been tempered in the forge of an actual project. The ideas will be better understood and their validity will be supported based on actual data and experience rather than assumptions and guesswork.

Checking against original user goals

Ideally you should already have done extensive UAT and should be quite aware of how actual users are responding to the product. Like the business perspective, user needs formed a critical piece of the framework requirements that constrained and guided the project. Since the discoveries from the user research phase of the project were so fundamental in determining where the project wound up, the success of the project should be judged against the initial understanding of user needs.

This is especially true if your company took any shortcuts or bypassed the user research phase. That decision to rely on either an absence of data and guidance or on make-do assumptions would have directly affected the framework requirements, and thus the whole rest of the project. Your product may satisfy the needs you assumed users had, or it might be useful to users you assumed were important, but if those assumptions were wrong, you may have disappointed actual users. That failure is the fault of shortsighted early decisions to shortcut user research, not of poor performance on the part of the project leader or the team. The ways in which assumptions manifested in the actual product to the disappointment of the actual users should be examined deeply to better understand the actual users and to help drive home an appreciation for the value of user research.

The results of the user research phase were intended to provide the project team with the empathetic framework for figuring out what actual users would need and prefer, and the success of that framework and of its application should be examined. UAT should have led to important new insights about users and refinements to your understanding of their needs. You might find that user research overlooked a set of users who formed a unique nexus of needs. Or you might find that your team's use of the research led to some errors that hint at ways you can improve the research and the team's thinking about users.

We recommend a fresh user research phase for every project, even if it's just a new version of an existing one. User needs change over time and in response to changes in the product, and research guided by prior real experience leads to stronger results. The research from the project you've just finished and the new data arising from use of the product by actual users will be enormously valuable to the next iteration of user research. Any available knowledge should be recorded in some way to ensure that it isn't lost in the weeks or months between the end of this project and the beginning of the next one. And if you have to go through a new development effort without the benefit of a user research phase, everything you learned about users in building this product can give you at least some real data to work from.

Measurement and Tracking

At the end of the project, you should have plenty of qualitative input flowing in from users, customer support, salespeople, and other sources. That input should tell you what's good, bad, or needs improvement. And if you have the right means of observation, actual usage of your product can yield enormously valuable feedback.

In web development, there's a clear and universal understanding of the value of tracking analytics for the site. Web analytics allow companies to see how often their web pages are visited, where users are dropping out of business-critical functions, where people are spending most of their time, and so on. It's just as important to look at real usage and performance of a software product. And a software product can provide more informative data about its use than a website can.

Everything in a software product can be tracked, right down to movements of the mouse and every keystroke. The challenge in learning from usage of a live application is less about collecting the usage data (though some engineering is required to accomplish this) and more about determining what aspects of the available usage data you need to pay attention to. You can collect a tremendous amount of data, but only some of it will have something meaningful to say about how your product is performing. Qualitative feedback can be useful in making decisions about what usage to observe and what data to gather. If you're receiving diffuse reports of difficulty operating some particular feature, you can add mechanisms to track how that feature is being used and under what circumstances. This gives greater specificity to the problem and helps make the case for additional time and money to fix the issue. Tracking can also be done by analyzing the data that accumulates through ongoing use of the product, to try to detect the trends and implications hidden within it.

The fuzziness of some qualitative feedback can, in some cases, cause serious problems for you and the product, owing to the assumptions people will continue to make. They either overgeneralize certain negative feedback ("no one uses this feature") or dismiss the feedback as the outlier experiences of unimportant users. Diving deeper into the negative feedback by studying a question with a range of sample users will tell you what's really important and what isn't.

Conducting usability studies on the product after it's released can also be valuable, provided your company is prepared to act on the findings and recommendations of the study. Jared Spool of User Interface Engineering tells an interesting and now-famous story titled *The $300 Million Button*:

> *http://www.uie.com/articles/three_hund_million_button*

As the name of the story suggests, Spool helped a major online retailer increase its revenue by $300M by simply examining a key aspect of their UX. This demonstrates that even the smallest change in response to actual user feedback can drive major results for the business. Though the route this particular company took to the $300M improvement was by way of user research, the story also suggests that had the company done an in-depth look at their own duplicate registration and password reset data (which are quantitative measures), they might have discovered the same issue.

Tracking the application can be helpful beyond just addressing critical and $300M issues. Knowing how users are and aren't using the application is useful as you enter the early stages of building the next version of the product or building another product. Real data and follow-up qualitative research is useful in refining your understanding of the users' needs, prioritizing business requirements, and understanding where to concentrate resources and efforts.

Measuring and tracking the application is also important in judging its success in the context of the business. Many success criteria set in the early planning for the project will take months to prove out. You must pay attention to the performance of the product to know whether you met the success criteria or to identify the circumstances that might have led to your failure to meet them. Investments in UX also tend to have valuable effects throughout an organization that go beyond the ones anticipated in setting the success criteria. For example, the Herff Jones eDesign product exceeded revenue and market share growth targets dramatically, but it also caused a 600 percent growth in the number of yearbooks produced online. Because the new eDesign online process is strongly integrated with Herff Jones's customer support and production processes, greater adoption of the new product led to reduced cost in support and production. Plus, the improved UX is bound to confer benefits to the Herff Jones brand, reduce costs to account management and customer retention, and provide a powerful new selling tool for the outside sales staff. All of the effects of the product on the company should be discovered and measured so that the full return of the investment can be understood and appreciated.

All of this, in turn, will be useful as it again comes time to generate support from stakeholders for additional investments in the product you've just finished or for new investments in another one. Measuring and proving the return that was realized from the investment in UX eases the burden of selling people on the value of UX the second time around. If there are questions as to why more money needs to be spent on the product, real quantitative and qualitative data can help you sell the need to invest in certain improvements and enhancements. The measurement and review process is a precursor to returning to Chapter 2 and starting the process of generating support and budget for the next critical initiative. Your new, proven success will give you a boost of trust, data, and support for UX that might have been lacking the first time around.

Afterword

In a way, the advice we've given in this book doesn't end with the last chapter on the last day of your project. As we discussed in Chapter 9, the learning and success of one project feeds into the next project. If you're finishing the work that's covered in Chapter 9, you'll likely find yourself back in Chapter 2, trying to build support for a new initiative. Once you've been through a UX-focused development effort following our advice, you'll be a pro yourself, better able to understand how our experience and advice aligns with your experience and situation.

The UX field is a cutting-edge area of the fast-moving domain of software development. As such, the field is changing on a daily basis, and we're learning things and developing new approaches to difficult problems every day. We encountered many exciting ideas while researching this book that either came too late or were far too complicated to make it into this book. And since the book covers such a wide range of professional disciplines and fields, we were forced to address some topics at only a high level. As a result, we've created a page on our website to provide new information and access to extended resources to you. And if you're reading a printed or Kindle version of this book, the page also has a list of the links found in this book.

http://effectiveui.com/book-resources/

We'll also be posting updates on Twitter. Please follow us: **@uitweet**.

EffectiveUI
Senior Class of '09

Anderson, Eric
Anderson, Jonathan
Aron, Chris
Arries, Tiffany
Baca, David

Bagur, Michelle
Balzer, Jeremy
Barnum, Dave
Beeks, Lara
Bell, Ryan

Blagovirnyy, Roman
Blanco, John
Bonet, Brent
Bose, Sumi
Bowers, Jason

Branam, Jonathan
Breidenbach, Eddie
Casey, Greg
Cheng, Jim
Christmann, Lance

Christmann, Sean
Conboy, Kevin
Congleton, Aaron
Cordes, Shivanii
Crutchfield, Nathan J.

Fellin, Jason
Flavin, Rebecca
Franco, Anthony
Fritschen, Christine
Gagliardi, Amanda

Garcia Wolfe, Faye
Gorton, Elaine
Graston, Jeremy
Guiberson, Ken
Hansen, Patrick

Hefner, Allison
Henry, Jacob
Horning, Catherine
Jamison, Bobby
Jamison, Joshua

Johnson, Jim
Jordan, Lucas L.
Kirkland, Lori
Koloski, Beth
Lindley, Peyton

Martelli, Nick
McIntosh, Andy
McLean, Drew
McRee, John
Molla, Brook

Oliver, Erika
Olmsted, Michelle
Ossola, Melody
Owen, Greg
Owen, Phil

Owen, RJ
Parker, Elias
Phillips, Carrie
Phillips, Heath
Pinter, Zachary

Reid, Jon
Rellos, Mahe
Robinson, George
Salamon, Michael
Salenieks, Karina

Saltzman, Dan
Sanchez, Juan
Schmidt, Doug
Singleton, Valerie
Smith, Mark

Smith, Tony
Strobert, Mike
Sykes, Joy
Teal, Ellen
Umbaugh, Brad

Varnell, Tracey
Walt, Tony
Washburn, Shelley
Weborg, Daisy
Wilcox, Bret

Wilcox, Eileen
Will, Caroline
Williams, Chuck
Willis, Tiffinie
Wilson, Robb

Not Pictured
Blythe, Jason
Ortiz, Juan
Skrenes, Kevin
Stussman, Kevin
Wood, Tim

Index

About the Authors

Jonathan Anderson helped found EffectiveUI before becoming managing editor of *UX Magazine*, an online resource for user experience professionals and enthusiasts. In this role, Jonathan develops and oversees original content creation and sourcing that explores the maturing field of UX and details industry trends and emerging technologies.

John McRee is a lead experience architect for EffectiveUI who has been designing highly intuitive and engaging user interfaces for more than a decade. Specializing in design process management, user research, information architecture, and interaction design, John has designed software for a diverse group of clients, including many Fortune 500 companies.

Robb Wilson is co-owner of *UX Magazine* and a technology research consultant for many Fortune 500 companies, including Qwest and National Geographic. An active member in the UX community, Robb's work affords him the unique opportunity to meld business strategy with creative processes and emerging technologies. He has worked as a creative executive at Time Warner and is an industry thought leader, providing innovative insight on emerging technologies and trends. Robb has founded four successful technology companies.

EffectiveUI (*www.effectiveui.com*) is an award-winning, user-centered design and development agency that creates and implements custom web, mobile, and desktop applications. By fully engaging customers with innovative technologies and user experience strategies, EffectiveUI delivers more exciting, meaningful, and personalized interactions with software products. Since 2005, the company has created applications for today's most respected brands and industry innovators. It has earned an Adobe Gold Partner distinction and membership in Microsoft's Global Agency Partners.

EffectiveUI leverages Adobe Flash, Flash Lite, Flex 3, AIR, and Microsoft Silverlight technologies to create powerful, results-based business and consumer applications for major Fortune 1000 companies, including eBay, GE Health, NBC Universal, United Airlines, Viacom, National Geographic, Discovery Channel, T. Rowe Price, and Adobe.

Colophon

The animal on the cover of *Effective UI* is a rainbow lorikeet (*Trichoglossus haematodus*), a small, brightly colored species of parrot found primarily in northern and eastern Australia. It inhabits all types of forests (rainforests, open forests, and mangrove forests) as well as heaths, parks, and orchards.

Named for its multicolored plumage, this striking bird features almost every color of the rainbow: it sports a dark blue or violet head and stomach; an emerald green back, tail, and vent; a deep orange breast and beak; and accents of yellow and red. Its adult height is about 12 inches and it weighs approximately 5 ounces. Its physical characteristics also include a short curved beak and small feet with two toes aiming frontward and two aiming backward. Unlike many other species of birds, males and females are difficult to distinguish, though females may be a bit smaller.

The rainbow lorikeet's diet consists of flowers, pollen, nectar, seeds, insects, and some fruit. It employs the sharp point of its beak to rip at fruits and flowers, and then uses its paintbrush-like tongue to lick the juice or nectar. The tip of the tongue is covered with hairy projections called papillae that enable the birds to more easily catch pollen and extract nectar. They are often observed hanging upside down as they feed, grasping tree branches with their powerful claws.

Rainbow lorikeets can be very noisy (they have a shrill call while flying and chatter while eating), active, and gregarious. These traits—as well as their vibrant coloring—make them popular pets. However, they require a diligent owner who is willing to accommodate their special dietary needs, clean up their cage daily (lorikeets are notoriously untidy eaters), and provide continued obedience training. The owner must also be tolerant of the birds' "chattiness"; the lorikeet has an amazing talent for mimicry and has been known to imitate household appliances such as the telephone and microwave.

The cover image is from the Dover Pictorial Archive. The cover font is Adobe ITC Garamond; the text font is Droid Serif; and the heading font is Pill Gothic.